TAKING ON THE
TRUST

The Reporter's Handbook: An Investigator's Guide to Documents and Techniques

Telling the Untold Story: How Investigative Reporters Are Changing the Craft of Biography

Armand Hammer: The Untold Story

Trade Secrets of Washington Journalists

Terrace Hill: The Story of a House and the People Who Touched It (with Scherrie Goettsch)

TAKING ON THE
TRUST

||||||||||||||||||||||||||||||||||||||||||||||||||||||||||||||||||||||||||

THE EPIC BATTLE OF IDA TARBELL
AND JOHN D. ROCKEFELLER

||||||||||||||||||||||||||||||||||||||||||||||||||||||||||||||||||||||

STEVE WEINBERG

W. W. Norton & Company

New York • London

For information about permission to reproduce selections from this book, write to Permissions,
W. W. Norton & Company, Inc., 500 Fifth Avenue, New York, NY 10110

For information about special discounts for bulk purchases, please contact W. W. Norton Special
Sales at specialsales@wwnorton.com or 800-233-4830

Manufacturing by RR Donnelley, Harrisonburg
Book design by Chris Welch
Production manager: Andrew Marasia

Library of Congress Cataloging-in-Publication Data

Weinberg, Steve.
    Taking on the trust : the epic battle of Ida Tarbell and John D. Rockefeller / Steve Weinberg.
— 1st ed.
        p. cm
    Includes bibliographical references and index.
    ISBN 978-0-393-04935-0 (hardcover)
    1. Tarbell, Ida M. (Ida Minerva), 1857–1944. 2. Rockefeller, John D. (John Davison), 1839–1937.
I. Title.
    PN4874.T23W45 2008
    070.92—dc22
    [B]   2007044699

W. W. Norton & Company, Inc., 500 Fifth Avenue, New York, NY 10110
www.wwnorton.com

W. W. Norton & Company Ltd., Castle House, 75/76 Wells Street, London W1T 3QT

1 2 3 4 5 6 7 8 9 0

FOR SCHERRIE

CONTENTS

PREFACE

The tome does not look especially impressive today. It rests on an out-of-the-way shelf, one of millions of volumes in a cavernous university research library. Its green cover is faded now, after decades of steady wear, occasional abuse, and, ultimately, lack of use. It is still mentioned in early-twentieth-century-America history courses on campuses. But few have read it from beginning to end, all 815 pages of dense type.

This is a shame. The book is arguably the greatest work of investigative journalism ever written. *The History of the Standard Oil Company*, published in 1904, is its unprepossessing title.

More than a century has passed since the painstaking research and writing that went into the book. Today, the years 1900 through 1905 feel like a bygone era. Yet during that tumultuous period, the book created a social maelstrom that built and destroyed reputations, altered public policy, and changed the face of the nation. This was the era of the great robber barons. Powerful men colluded to create even more powerful monopolies. By the dawn of Theodore Roosevelt's presidency, however, there arose a cadre of devoted journalists and publishers intent on uncovering the perfidy of the economic juggernauts.

The confrontation embedded in this remarkable time, characterized by *The History of the Standard Oil Company*, pitted the unparalleled documentary skills of America's most recognizable investigative journalist against the financial resources of the most rapacious, most powerful businessman in the nation. This investigative journalist, Ida Minerva Tarbell, worked as a staff writer for *McClure's Magazine*. A woman of formidable intelligence and character, she labored at a time when men dominated the realm of journalism. The tycoon, John Davison Rockefeller, born into a broken family, had built an empire on black gold and had become the wealthiest individual of the Gilded Age. With impressive business savvy and upright character, Rockefeller served as the guiding force within Standard Oil Company, the nation's most sprawling corporate "trust," a term out of fashion today except as part of the word "antitrust."

Tarbell's book, which began as a magazine series, brought her fame and established a new form of journalism known as muckraking. She became a model for countless journalists, and despite the passage of more than a century, her work remains an example of how a lone journalist can uncover wrongdoing. Moreover, through her exposé, Tarbell forever tarnished the peerless reputation of John D. Rockefeller. Charles R. Morris expresses the consensus among historians when he writes that Tarbell's analysis "has dominated the perception of the man and his rise ever since." Ideas about Rockefeller changed because Tarbell researched and wrote a great book. Allan Nevins, a Columbia University history professor, wrote a friendly biography of Rockefeller, but he nonetheless praised Tarbell's exposé. Rockefeller, who refrained from discussing Tarbell publicly, told an employee privately that much of what his own son knew about Standard Oil "is his memory of what he has read in her book, with only here and there a statement of fact by me."

Reading Tarbell's exposé of the Standard Oil Company is a remarkable experience; in many ways it seems that it could have been composed only yesterday, not more than a century ago. The strangleholds that Sam Walton's Wal-Mart and Bill Gates's Microsoft demonstrate in their business realms are reminiscent of the sway held by Rockefeller's Standard Oil.

Tarbell's book played a significant role in my own career. In addition to practicing the craft of investigative journalism since 1969, I have studied it carefully—in large part because I served as a spokesman of sorts for that branch of journalism while serving as executive director of Investigative Reporters and Editors (IRE). Based at the University of Missouri Journalism School, IRE serves thousands of members around the United States and increasingly around the world. The techniques Tarbell used to gather information about a secretive corporation and its evasive, powerful chief executive taught me that a talented, persistent journalist can penetrate any façade through close readings of government documents, lawsuits, and interviews with knowledgeable sources inside and outside the executive offices. Tarbell's methods have allowed me to train investigative journalists around the world while directing IRE and ever since.

This book is a hybrid of biography and dramatic narrative. That dramatic narrative cannot be told effectively without studying Rockefeller's life as well as Tarbell's. Previous authors have chronicled the long lives of Tarbell (1857–1944) and Rockefeller (1839–1937). But none has devoted an entire book to their epic collision course.

Tarbell's life has been written about much less frequently and in much less detail than Rockefeller's. Only two books examine her life with some depth—her factually accurate but selective autobiography, *All in the Day's Work,* and Kathleen Brady's *Ida Tarbell: Portrait of a Muckraker.* Brady told her readers, citing Tarbell's journalist colleague Ray Stannard Baker, "that anyone who attempted to write Ida Tarbell's life would have the problem of writing about goodness." She commented, "This proved to be true, but the real challenge was trying to explain an enigma." She quoted Tarbell's own words: "I have often found it difficult to explain myself to myself, and I do not often try." As Brady noted, "She was seldom more forthcoming to anyone else, and those who knew her best have long been dead."

More recently, a few scholars have called attention to Tarbell's writings. In 1994, Ellen F. Fitzpatrick edited the collection *Muckraking: Three Landmark Articles,* focusing on exposés by Tarbell, Lincoln Steffens, and Ray Stannard Baker published by *McClure's Magazine.* In 1996, Robert C. Kochersberger, Jr., edited a book that reprinted a wide range of Tarbell's published pieces, *More Than a Muckraker: Ida Tarbell's Lifetime in Journalism.*

First in the class of numerous Rockefeller chronicles is Ron Chernow's *Titan*, published in 1998. Chernow's chapter on the Tarbell-Rockefeller confrontation is titled "Avenging Angel," a reference to the investigative journalist. Some of the biographies published before Chernow's contain useful facts, insights, and conclusions, but they include worrisome biases. For example, Allan Nevins at times seems like little more than an apologist for Rockefeller in his 1953 book *Study in Power: John D. Rockefeller, Industrialist and Philanthropist.* The Nevins Papers at Columbia University, not so incidentally, contain considerable important raw material on Rockefeller the private individual, Rockefeller the corporate chieftain, and Tarbell too.

All the Rockefeller biographies address the impact of Tarbell's exposé. One of the earliest, published by John T. Flynn in 1932, called Tarbell's book "a mixture of historical narrative and indictment. No critic could complain that she had not examined the facts, for the evidences of minute and painstaking investigation were stamped upon every part of the work." Flynn judged Tarbell's epic to be "the ablest document of its kind ever produced by an American writer."

David Freeman Hawke, whose Rockefeller biography appeared in 1980, commented that "only three times in the American past have writers produced works that transcended their literary qualities and became in themselves powerful enough to shape history. The first was Thomas Paine's *Common Sense*; the second, Harriet Beecher Stowe's *Uncle Tom's Cabin*; third, Ida M. Tarbell's *History of the Standard Oil Company.*"

Rockefeller's 1909 memoir, *Random Reminiscences of Men and Events*, is brief, quirky, and notable for significant omissions; still, it provides a partially opened window into his mind and his character.

One welcome challenge of this book has been to demonstrate Tarbell's importance to her era, as well as to show the relevance of her life for today's readers, without exaggeration. Rockefeller's outsized role during his life and the relevance of that life for today's readers are far more obvious and would be difficult to exaggerate, given the impact of his wealth and business practices. Daniel Yergin, the author of *The Prize: The Epic Quest for Oil, Money, and Power,* one of the most knowledgeable books ever published for a general audience about the oil industry, wrote that "Rockefeller was the single most important figure in shaping the oil industry. The same might arguably be said for his place in the history of America's industrial development and the rise of the modern corporation." Yergin noted that Rockefeller ranks as "the most hated and reviled American businessman—in part because he was so ruthless and in part because he was so successful."

Rockefeller's personal story, as opposed to what he accomplished in the Standard Oil offices, is more difficult to tell than Tarbell's. She wrote thousands of letters, hundreds of magazine and newspaper articles, and many books other than her Standard Oil exposé, and she spoke publicly around the nation for decades. Almost all of that is preserved, allowing a biographer to know what she was thinking at the time she thought it. How she might look to posterity apparently did not enter her mind as she shared her thoughts and feelings. In contrast, Rockefeller rarely wrote about his thoughts and feelings, rarely revealed himself in public. He left behind only a memoir that he wrote during his late sixties, a book meant to justify and defend himself after Tarbell's research had diminished his reputation. The memoir is neither broad nor deep nor candid. A decade later, Rockefeller sat for extensive interviews with a hired journalist named William O. Inglis of the *New York Evening World.* Much of what he discussed during their sessions together is self-serving. Some of the material Inglis preserved is clearly based on Rockefeller's faulty memories and his defensiveness as he passed age eighty.

Evaluating the source material left behind is just part of a biographer's responsibility. Another is to keep the research findings in perspective. Biographers frequently exaggerate the significance of their subjects' lives. A subtle type of biographical exaggeration is reductionism. No single factor—not greed, not pride, not idealism—can explain the thoughts and actions of any human being. Biographers who construct their narratives around one factor are guilty of reductionism and should be read with skepticism.

That said, the most important of many factors that drove Tarbell year after year into the 1940s, her octogenarian decade, can be stated simply: a passion to discover and disseminate the truth about political, economic, and social issues. She believed that research could lead to an approximation of Truth, indeed with a capital "T." Before her exposé of Rockefeller, she researched the lives of Napoleon Bonaparte and Abraham Lincoln. The books that arose from this research convinced her that Truth about the actions and motivations of powerful human beings could be discovered. That Truth, she became convinced, could be conveyed in such a way as to precipitate meaningful social change.

Tarbell's research into the life of John D. Rockefeller convinced her that good and evil could be embodied simultaneously in one individual. Reducing Rockefeller to a symbol of good or evil would be a biographical sin in itself. Although Tarbell was at times ruthless when chronicling Rockefeller's life, she did not make that mistake; she did not distort his accomplishments into a sensationalistic paradigm of good or evil. In fact, she titled the final chapter of her exposé "The Legitimate Greatness of the Standard Oil Company."

Rockefeller presented a substantial challenge to Tarbell. Unlike Bonaparte and Lincoln, he was alive and at the zenith of his power. He had no intention of letting a journalist—and a mere woman at that—question the way he had amassed and used his fortune. Tarbell's biggest obstacle, however, was neither her gender nor Rockefeller's opposition, but rather the craft of journalism as practiced at the turn of the twentieth century. She investigated Standard Oil and Rockefeller by using documents—hundreds of thousands of pages scattered throughout the nation—and then amplified her findings through interviews with the corporation's executives and competitors, government regulators, and academic experts past and present. In other words, she proposed to practice what today is considered investigative reporting, which did not exist in 1900. Indeed, she invented a new form of journalism. *Taking On the Trust*, a capsule dual biography of unlikely antagonists, pays homage to the journalistic tradition that Tarbell helped create.

Tarbell's masterpiece, *The History of the Standard Oil Company*, influenced the U.S. Supreme Court—where the justices mandated the breakup of multinational trusts—as well as the court of public opinion, where Rockefeller's reputation disintegrated. So far during the twenty-first century, no journalist's exposé has led to the breakup of Wal-Mart or Microsoft or led to Sam Walton or Bill Gates losing his sterling reputation as a private-sector demigod. Plenty of journalists, however, have delved into these modern-day trusts and their controlling founders, thinking that perhaps the published results will serve as the successor to *The History of the Standard Oil Company.*

Journalists who write today enjoy considerable advantages over Tarbell. They work within an established tradition of investigative reporting, often backed by a news corporation with a substantial budget. Tarbell lacked a tradition to guide her, and publisher Samuel Sidney McClure had barely achieved financial solvency with his magazine and book company spinoff when she began her work.

But believing in Truth as a means to change the world for the better, Tarbell invented journalistic techniques to accomplish her goals. The saga of how she reached that point and of how John D. Rockefeller and the Standard Oil Company ended up in her path is about to begin.

Taking On the

TRUST

‖‖‖

CHAPTER ONE

Ida Tarbell

A Childhood Portrait in Oil

I da Minerva Tarbell grew up as a child of the oil fields. Born to an oil pioneer, she reached maturity a short trip from the first American oil well, in Titusville, Pennsylvania. Though other journalists might have possessed the courage to take on the world's largest corporation, certainly none had been so profoundly affected in their youth by John D. Rockefeller's business practices.

Tarbell was conceived in Pennsylvania as civil war threatened to break the nation apart. Her father was a lanky, blue-eyed, spade-bearded man named Franklin Sumner Tarbell, who sometimes wore a brown wig to cover early baldness. He tended to move briskly, but with a paradoxical calmness of mind that stemmed from a deeply religious nature. His righteous wrath, loosed on its target without warning, could be intimidating. But most of the time, Franklin Tarbell's impressive intellect and quick sense of humor made him popular with adults and children. He loved fishing (but not hunting) and hungered to explore unknown lands, and he later was fascinated by Henry Stanley's African explorations.

In 1857, when his wife, Esther, was pregnant with Ida, Franklin set out for Iowa to seek land so they could build a new life in a part of the country that was more economically stable than northwestern Pennsylvania.

At that time, Iowa had been a state for a mere eleven years, and Franklin figured that he could do better working the rich black soil out west than if the family remained on their bleak Pennsylvania farm. A farmer's income, combined with earnings from Franklin's vocations as teacher and welder, would provide adequately for the family, he hoped.

The Tarbell family was not alone in their desire to leave an eastern homestead for opportunity farther west; the Rockefeller family had moved from upstate New York to Ohio in 1853, when John D. was fourteen years old. For some migrants, economic hardship served as a catalyst. Others expressed sympathy for the abolition movement and felt a moral or political obligation to leave any state that still endorsed slavery. But for many migrants, including Franklin Tarbell, the restlessness seemed to defy common sense, and the Tarbells' planned migration to Iowa puzzled many of their neighbors. The journey would be arduous. Though conditions were hard, the Pennsylvanians were not on the edge of starvation.

Common sense cannot always be squared with the desire for the brightest possible future, however, and the future did not look particularly bright in rural northwestern Pennsylvania at the beginning of the 1850s, when Franklin Tarbell met Esther Ann McCullough. Planning their lives carefully, the couple married on April 17, 1856, after a six-year engagement. They were both twenty-six years old. Within a year, Esther became pregnant with Ida. She and Franklin wanted greater possibilities for their unborn child than those available in Hatch Hollow, Pennsylvania. The name of the settlement, in fact, suggested provinciality, and indeed the tiny crossroads consisted of just one school, a Methodist church, a sawmill, and a creamery.

Born in Norwich, New York, Esther had moved to northwestern Pennsylvania as a child, along with an older brother, a younger brother, and two younger sisters, at the insistence of her father, Walter Raleigh McCullough, who sought new farming and commercial opportunities as his family expanded. A New Hampshire native, Walter had married Sarah Scoville Seabury, a native New Yorker. Another sister arrived after the move.

As a child, Esther relished hearing about her heritage from her mother: "Remember that your father is a McCullough of an ancient and honored Scotch clan, his mother a Raleigh of Sir Walter's family, that I am a Seabury, my great-uncle the first Episcopal bishop in the United States, my mother a Welles, her father on [George] Washington's staff." Esther would eventually repeat that same litany to her own daughter, Ida, who included it in her autobiography.

That proud heritage included good education for the women of the family, not just the men. In fact, Esther had attended boarding school at a Methodist female seminary in Poughkeepsie, New York, as well as a private academy near the McCulloughs' Pennsylvania home. By age eighteen, she had learned her lessons well enough to become certified as a teacher of arithmetic, geography, reading, writing, and grammar for the Amity Township schools, quite an accomplishment in an era in which female illiteracy rates exceeded 50 percent.

As a schoolteacher, Esther received about one fourth the amount paid to her male counterparts. Such low-paying jobs often became the lot of unmarried women. Some of Esther's friends and acquaintances looked to marriage as an escape from the low-wage treadmill. Esther found other merits in matrimony, but she agreed with many women—and the enlightened men in their camp—that females in the workforce ought to receive the same pay as males doing the same jobs.

Unlike some of her contemporaries, Esther cared not only about equal pay but also about property ownership and voting issues. She read about the intellectual feminist pioneers Elizabeth Cady Stanton and Lucretia Mott, and about the discussions held in 1848 at the Woman's Rights Convention in Seneca Falls, New York. She did her best to track the follow-up efforts of the early women's rights advocates, who later joined with Susan B. Anthony through such organizations as the Woman's National Loyal League.

As the women's rights agenda grew, women activists joined with abolitionists to push for an end to American slavery. That alliance became a mixed blessing, as explained by historian Ellen Carol DuBois in her book *Feminism and Suffrage: The Emergence of an Independent Women's Movement in America, 1848–1869.* Those relatively few women who opted for political engagement tended to focus on the abolition of black slavery rather than on their own second-class status.

Esther Tarbell developed an acute awareness that she would receive no pay for her labors as a parent and a homemaker. She also understood that depending on where she and Franklin settled, state law might define her as an economic dependent, with no rights to her husband's earnings or tangible property. But she wanted children; she was ready to move to Iowa to raise them if Franklin could find a promising opportunity there.

Esther and Franklin understood each other so well that difficult decisions had become easy for them to discuss as partners. They knew that a move to Iowa would be physically taxing and emotionally draining. Transcontinental train travel was not yet practical in 1857. A wagon trip would be difficult, and maybe a risk to the pregnancy. Separating from parents, siblings, and friends would be wrenching. But Esther felt confident that Franklin would bear the journey well and would find a way for her to join him later.

Born in Oxford, New York, just ten miles from Esther's birthplace, Franklin Tarbell was the middle of three boys. His mother died when he was eight years old. His father then remarried; that marriage produced two stepbrothers and a stepsister.

Franklin grew up to become self-reliant and self-assured. After his family settled in Pennsylvania, he trained to become a teacher, earning money by piloting flatboats filled with merchandise to delivery points along the Allegheny, Ohio, and Mississippi Rivers. The journeys supplied him with a great deal of travel experience as well as endless tales to share with his family. His river piloting, often in perilous weather, during which he survived on less-than-appetizing meals in the prerefrigeration era, steeled him for the hardships of long-distance travel.

Thus the couple decided that Esther would stay behind while Franklin made his way to Iowa, where he eventually found a desirable plot of land in the extreme southwest corner, just north of the Missouri border. The federal government, hoping to attract settlers not only to Iowa but also to other unsettled territory west of the Mississippi River, offered to sell land cheaply (at $1.25 an acre) or even give it away (sometimes as bounties for war veterans willing to kill Native Americans). As a result, an estimated 36 million acres became available in Iowa during the 1840s and 1850s.

By the time Franklin Tarbell arrived in 1857, the state's population had surpassed 600,000, at least six times more than when Iowa had become part of the union eleven years earlier. Like Tarbell, many of the settlers came from Pennsylvania. Large numbers also came from Ohio, Indiana, and Illinois. Significant but smaller numbers traveled to Iowa from Virginia, North Carolina, Tennessee, Kentucky, and Missouri.

The Iowa of the late 1850s could be harsh, even life-threatening. One flashpoint involved precarious relations between the newly arrived Caucasians and the Native Americans, who were being displaced from their longtime homes by government deception and vigilante violence. In 1854, a trader named Henry Lott had murdered a Sioux Indian family. A brother of the dead family's patriarch vowed revenge. The year that Franklin Tarbell arrived in Iowa, the Sioux carried out their revenge. Warriors attacked a compound of settlers during a harsh winter, and thirty-four settlers died in what became known as the Spirit Lake Massacre.

Day-to-day living proved difficult apart from warfare. Settlers found it hard to keep warm during the winter months. Their hastily built one-room cabins, made with logs piled seven high, provided a cramped living area at best, typically 18 feet by 16 feet; that architecture fared poorly in shutting out the cold. Sod houses, an alternative to log cabins, rarely proved more effective. Surviving diaries and letters sent to friends back east tell how family members sometimes had to huddle together during the coldest nights to prevent frostbite or death.

Anxious to construct a comfortable house for his wife and their unborn child, Franklin Tarbell took a job in a sawmill to pay for building materials. He built the house with his own hands. His letters back to Hatch Hollow conveyed enthusiasm. He told of the unbroken skyline, the vast prairie, the flowers and birds (different from those back east), the excitement of people in the passing wagons bound for points even farther west. Despite the imminence of the Civil War, the settlers of Iowa seemed peace-loving and hardworking. Everything looked rosy.

With the advent of prepaid postage stamps during the 1850s, mail service had become sophisticated enough so that settlers like Franklin Tarbell could usually communicate, however slowly, with those back home. Franklin wrote to Esther that she should prepare for an August departure; he believed they would be able to negotiate the journey—hundreds of miles long—by horse-drawn wagons without causing a miscarriage or premature birth. If all had gone as planned, Ida Tarbell would have been born a daughter of the plains.

As it turned out, Ida was not born in Iowa. Before Franklin could return to Pennsylvania to retrieve his wife, the economy changed for the worse. During the summer and autumn of 1857, a variety of circumstances beyond the control of any single family, including poor harvests and commercial overexpansion, led to bank closings up and down the East Coast. Consumer and commercial panics ensued. With no national bank, no federal regulation, and inadequate cash reserves, banks began to default on individual accounts. The Tarbells were one of the families who could not gain access to their savings.

Ironically, pioneers like Franklin Tarbell, abetted by land speculators, contributed to such financial collapses. The mass movement of settlers to the west created a demand for acreage that exhausted the initial supply. A secondary land market arose, triggered by speculators who aimed to profit by purchasing relatively cheap parcels, then selling at inflated prices. Newly arrived farmers complicated the situation by purchasing more land than they planned to use, hedging against the decline in values that seemed inevitable once they started exhausting the soil with their harvests of corn, soybeans, and wheat, among other crops. Fooled by the rising land prices, many landowners edged over into speculation, mortgaging their farms, rangelands, and plantations. When land prices declined and the mortgages came due, the inevitable defaults allowed railroad executives, bankers, and various bottom-feeders to swoop in and take control of land at bargain prices. Cash became scarce, and settlers began to hoard their meager savings, causing a ripple effect among manufacturers, wholesalers, and retailers, who laid off workers, aggravating the crisis.

If the Tarbells had settled in Iowa before the nation's economic meltdown, they probably would have weathered the bank panic—that state had no established banks in 1857, so they necessarily would have kept their money elsewhere. Instead, Franklin found himself stuck in Iowa, and Esther, a thousand miles away, could not retrieve their savings.

When Esther gave birth to Ida, on November 5, 1857, the anguished Franklin had still not returned home. Esther's parents attended to her needs as best they could. Fortunately, Ida was a healthy baby, and Esther settled into routines at her parents' Cape Cod–style log house with oak plank flooring. Pear and maple trees dotted the acreage. A working dairy farm supplemented by poultry provided the main means of support.

While Esther and Ida waited for Franklin to work his way back to them, larger events unfolded, events that would affect the family in unseen ways. The year 1857 stands out in nineteenth-century American history as one of growing rancor. National policy debates and daily events revealed a significant intolerance of immigrant Catholics. The nation's crowded, disease-infested urban areas became deeply divided as a result. In his book *America in 1857: A Nation on the Brink*, historian Kenneth M. Stampp comments on how the Protestant sects that had previously dominated religious life lashed out at the increasingly visible Catholic minority. "To some of the more hysterical [Protestant] nativists, every Catholic immigrant was an agent of the Pope," Stampp notes. The rowdier of the nativists caused election-day riots in Baltimore and Louisville as they protested the voting rights of the newcomers.

Racial intolerance, aimed not only at slaves in southern states but also at freed blacks in northern states, threatened to sunder the nation. An Illinois lawyer named Abraham Lincoln had begun his political career, his vehicle the newly formed Republican Party, a northern coalition that opposed the expansion of legal slavery into territories planning to enter the union as full-fledged states.

The year before, in 1856, the Republican Party had organized its first attempt at the White House, nominating explorer John C. Fremont for president. The more established Democrats prevailed with Pennsylvania's James Buchanan, who carried the vote in all but one of the southern slave-holding states. Buchanan, like many of his contemporaries, wondered why anybody would push for the abolition of slavery. He believed that slaves would fail if freed—that they were better off staying with masters who treated them humanely by providing food and shelter. Of course, many slaves viewed their treatment as anything but humane, anything but fair. The Supreme Court weighed in with its 1857 ruling against a Missouri slave named Dred Scott. Scott's desire for freedom, the wishes of his "owners," the customs of Missouri, and the laws of Congress amounted to nothing significant, the Court ruled; no slave could be considered a citizen, and therefore no slave possessed standing to sue for emancipation.

Though the debate over slavery had grown acrimonious and the violence, especially on the frontier, had worsened, for a brief interval after Buchanan's 1857 inauguration it appeared that the union might be saved—that a compromise could be reached on the spread of slavery to new states such as Kansas. But Kansas became a bloody battleground, and those hopes were dashed.

In many ways, the settlement of the Kansas territory differed little from the settlement of Missouri or Iowa. But in at least one important way, Kansas was unique—a substantial portion of its settlers arrived not just for economic reasons but to register a vote for or against slavery. Anti-slavery groups paid settlers to move to Kansas from the east. Pro-slavery groups managed to capture a majority of the Kansas legislature, using illegal tactics such as ballot-box stuffing and pressuring those who counted ballots to register false results. Law-abiding residents of the territory feared violence every day, especially along the border with Missouri.

Of all the partisans on each side, John Brown is almost certainly the best known today. In 1856, after pro-slavery troops entered the city of Lawrence, where they destroyed an anti-slavery newspaper office, the abolitionist Brown planned revenge. He organized a group that included four of his sons and attacked a pro-slavery settlement, where they murdered five men. Federal troops eventually lowered the level of violence, but by then "Bloody Kansas" had become a symbol that inflamed the march to civil war. Brown and his followers moved their campaign east, where they targeted a federal arsenal as part of a renewed protest against slavery. Convicted of violent crimes, Brown died by hanging in 1859. The symbolism of that death could not be denied. As the threat of southern secession moved toward reality, Lincoln's Republican candidacy grew more important.

Beyond the roots of the Civil War, the seeds of the vital tariff debates that would preoccupy policymakers for the next fifty years began to germinate during the 1850s. Tariff questions divided the citizens, their representatives in Congress, and the political parties. Tariffs on imported commodities such as cotton, wool, tobacco, rice, and iron meant more to the average citizen during the nineteenth century than they do today, because those levies generated larger revenues for the federal treasury than any other source.

Accomplishments such as exposing the realities of tariffs and oil to a mass audience were no more than a distant dream in the year of Ida Tarbell's birth, however. Hatch Hollow was isolated, and it appeared that the Pennsylvania homestead would be little Ida's residence for many years, maybe always, with perhaps minimal schooling in Wattsburg, a few miles away. Wattsburg, a remote outpost founded on the banks of French Creek in 1796, had gradually grown to a population of several hundred. A primitive road connected the settlement with the larger town of North East, which in turn was on the way to Erie, a real city twenty miles distant. A wooden plank road opened in 1853, and its builders charged a toll of twenty-five cents for each team of horses that passed through. Farms fed the settlers and eventually became successful enough to export products. Dairy farmers did especially well; Wattsburg earned a reputation throughout the region for its high-quality butter. A few Presbyterian, Methodist, and Baptist churches served spiritual needs.

With Esther occupied by motherhood and thus unable to teach, Ida's maternal grandparents largely supported her until Franklin returned to Hatch Hollow, when Ida was about eighteen months old, in the spring of 1859. Franklin had financed his return with frequent stops in country schoolhouses. Though they delayed his homecoming, the short-term teaching jobs enabled him to earn enough money to feed himself and to replace tattered clothing and worn-out shoes.

Despite his long journey and the dampening effect of the economic recession, Franklin still planned to move the family to the Iowa homestead. He and Esther began packing household items to withstand the bumpy overland route, and he piloted a flatboat to earn money for the trip. Then something happened that would forever alter the lives of Franklin and Esther, their daughter, and the distant John D. Rockefeller too.

In August 1859, as Franklin Tarbell visited acquaintances along the start of the route to Iowa, he learned that a journeyman prospector named Edwin L. Drake had been drilling for oil near Titusville, which was about forty miles southeast by stagecoach from the Tarbell homestead. Known as a remote lumber town, Titusville featured concentrations of pine and hemlock on its hills. For decades timber men had cleared the trees from the rugged hills on a rotation basis. Then they floated the logs to Pittsburgh on the currents of the Allegheny River.

Many of Titusville's settlers had prospered elsewhere, especially in New England and New York State, before moving to Pennsylvania. Still, nobody besides Drake and the investors backing him foresaw the gushers of thick black oil ready to break through the land's surface if tapped just right. In fact, practically no one thought that oil extracted from below the earth's surface would possess significant value. Before Drake started drilling, indigenous Indians, random settlers, and a few adventurous geologists knew that oil sometimes seeped from rocks, streams, and shallow springs in northwestern Pennsylvania. While sitting in a film on top of the water, the oil would give off a flame if ignited. Those who believed that the slick substance could heal skin sores or damaged internal organs used pans to skim it from the water's surface, or dipped wool blankets into the water to absorb the oil, then wrung it out drop by drop. A map of Pennsylvania printed in 1755 in London includes the word "Petroleum" scrawled across the body of water that eventually became known as Oil Creek.

In time, belief in the practical uses of the substance spread widely enough for a commercial product called Seneca Oil, advertised as a cure for coughs, colds, and rheumatism, to appear in East Coast shops. Then Samuel M. Kier, an entrepreneur from the Pittsburgh suburb of Tartentum, advertised Kier's Petroleum, or Rock-Oil, as grease that could be burned to provide light.

Still, oil exploration might have bypassed the Tarbell family's region if Ebenezer Brewer had failed to grasp the potential. Part owner of a lumber business just south of Titusville, Brewer insisted that the oil bubbling to the surface of the springs on the timberland be skimmed and sold to increase the company's profits. Curious about the naturally occurring substance, Brewer sent a sample to his son, Francis B. Brewer, a Vermont physician with a scientific background. Experimenting with the substance on himself and his patients to treat a variety of problems from colds to arthritis, Brewer became convinced that the oil on the land owned by his father's lumber company could make the family wealthy. Through a chain of professional connections, he met two New York City lawyers who helped him organize the Pennsylvania Rock Oil Company and invest in expertise to extract the oil around Titusville.

Getting the oil would not be simple. Underground extraction was in its infancy. Explorers had noticed that oil could sometimes be found not just on the surface of streams and springs but belowground as well. Entrepreneurs drilling for saltwater as part of the salt manufacturing process often encountered a noxious dark-green substance akin to the rock oil found on the surface. To those entrepreneurs, the oil was a nuisance. They would place the mixture in cisterns until the oil rose to the top, then discard the oil wherever they could.

Hired by the New York and New Haven lawyers representing the Titusville interests, Edwin Drake first visited Titusville sometime in the year of Ida's birth, traveling by train to Erie, then riding a stagecoach the final fifty miles over two days. He received payment from money raised by Titusville residents selling speculative stock. Having worked previously as a railroad conductor, Drake was at best an intense amateur when it came to drilling for oil. He had accepted the job partly because his physician suggested that a move to a rural area from urban Connecticut might improve his fragile health. Drake's chief attraction for those hiring him, other than his availability, seemed to be the railroad pass he held for free transportation.

It is impossible to know whether somebody other than Drake would have found oil more quickly or failed to find any. What is certain is that Drake's intuition told him to penetrate farther below the earth's surface than had been attempted before. But he lacked practical knowledge of what tools to obtain or how to use them. He would have to rely on trial and error, a time-consuming, expensive approach.

For two years Drake thought through his plan and sought reliable workers around Titusville to help with the physical labor. He waited months for heavy equipment to arrive at the remote site over primitive roads and treacherous waterways, and he repeatedly rode one hundred miles to Pittsburgh and back, looking for a driller to hire. Because he earned a reputation around Titusville as a dreamer at best and a lunatic at worst, finding workers proved quite difficult. In early 1859, William A. Smith, a blacksmith, reported for duty. Smith had never drilled for oil, but he had bored into the earth seeking salt deposits.

Finally, during the spring of 1859, Drake and his crew broke through the resistant earth. Month after month of drilling yielded nothing, however, and the enterprise became known as "Drake's folly." When his distant financial backers said they would terminate funding, Drake replied plaintively, "You all feel different from what I do. You all have your legitimate business which has not been interrupted by the operation, which I staked everything I had upon the project and now find myself out of business and out of money."

Then, on August 27, 1859, at about seventy feet below the surface, Drake's drilling equipment struck oil. The substance that became known as "black gold" gushed from the depths with more force than skeptical onlookers could believe. On September 13, slightly more than two weeks after Drake's well began gushing, the *New York Tribune* published a report from a correspondent known as Medicus, who had finally succeeded in reaching remote Titusville. "The excitement attendant on the discovery of this vast source of oil was fully equal to what I ever saw in California when a large lump of gold was accidentally turned out," Medicus wrote. The excitement contained strands of regional pride, nationalism (perhaps the United States would dominate the world's supply of a natural resource), and a belief in divine intervention (God had blessed a chosen citizenry with new riches).

Almost certainly the first person to grasp the moneymaking potential of the Drake Well fully was Jonathan Watson. The Brewer, Watson lumber company had leased the land with the successful well to Drake and his investors. Calculating that the lowland areas along the local creeks held the most potential for oil strikes, Watson, on horseback, visited forty-three Titusville-area landowners. He did not ask them to sell their land outright. Instead, he offered to lease portions of their land. Within three weeks he became the number-one leaseholder along Oil Creek and its tributaries. He was gambling with the land, and emerged a winner. Others lost in the greed-driven American lottery called land ownership, as they drilled for oil indiscriminately because of the low startup costs. In the long run, before "the environment" became something to worry about, an entire geographic region ended up spoiled; those who failed to find oil usually left their messes—uncapped wells, drilling equipment, lean-tos for protection from the elements—to pollute below the earth's surface, above the earth's surface, and on the earth's surface. As the 1860s began, however, the quest for individual riches trumped every other consideration.

The timing for commercial purposes turned out to be superb. Boating enterprises along the American coasts had not been producing enough whale oil to illuminate homes, shops, and factories. Catching, killing, hauling, and processing whales was unpredictable, physically draining work. A whale might yield 500 gallons of oil if processed efficiently, but as consumer demand grew, the number of whales diminished, owing to the more than 700 vessels competing on the ocean. Furthermore, when whale oil became available, its per-gallon price prevented most households from affording it.

Oil derived from the turpentine resin of pine trees looked like a promising illuminant. Marketed as camphene, it sold well in some areas, but transportation to places without a rich stock of coniferous trees proved troublesome. A lard oil developed by the pork industry seemed promising as well. Lard derivatives, however, could yield smokiness and odors that some consumers found unpleasant.

In the 1850s, kerosene began to replace whale oil, turpentine, and lard oil. At first entrepreneurs extracted it from coal tar and shale oil. It could hold back the darkness, and plenty of customers liked the idea of extended light adequate for work or play into the night. Still, the price of kerosene—a word coined as a marketing term by a Canadian entrepreneur—exceeded many household budgets, as whale oil had. Kerosene extracted from coal tar and shale oil could clog the highest-quality lamps, and it sometimes posed a safety hazard when used in a confined space.

Kerosene extracted from petroleum looked like a promising alternative. Its predecessor products had opened markets for a better illuminant just as the Drake Well began meeting the supply. Northwestern Pennsylvania would benefit from the propitious timing beyond anyone's imagination. A few decades earlier, the market for illuminants had seemed largely confined to family farms that included residences. As the industrial age picked up steam, however, better lighting extended the workday into nighttime, meaning that factories could offer additional jobs and increase revenue. Many factories used metals in their machinery, and metals needed lubricants to function efficiently. So oil products from the Drake Well and its progeny carried the potential to provide both illumination and lubrication.

Prospectors in search of quick riches yielded by kerosene and other oil derivatives arrived in northwestern Pennsylvania day after day, overwhelming the few hotels and general stores. By mid-October 1859, Thomas Chase, the editor of a newspaper in Coudersport, could write after spending his honeymoon in Titusville, "The tract of land on which the large spring has been opened by Mr. Drake was once purchased by the father of the writer of this article for a cow, and previous to that had been sold at treasurer's sale for taxes. Now we believe $100,000 would not buy one acre of it. Men until now barely able to get a poor living off poor land are made rich beyond their wildest dreaming."

Despite the inadequate transportation to the town, hundreds of thousands of people lived within a few days' travel of the remote site, not only within Pennsylvania but also across the nearby borders of Ohio and New York State. Comparatively speaking, the oil region was more accessible than the California gold region had been a decade earlier. Many, probably most, of the newcomers swarming to the Titusville area hoped to stay briefly and leave the rough-and-tumble place as soon as they had made their fortunes.

Others, a small minority, hoped to build a long-term, stable industry. They settled in the area with the hope of civilizing it. They saw the need for trained engineers and geologists, improved drills, efficient motors, safer ways to handle the potentially explosive oil gushing up from below the earth's surface. "It was they," Ida Tarbell would write later, with her usual precision and insight, "who laid the foundation of oil geology. At the start there was no body of facts on which to base a scientific approach to their problem. All they could do was to study and report, record the various layers of rock and sand through which the drill made its way." Tarbell explained how the oil pioneers examined the contents of every sand pump and calculated the thickness of each stratum in the earth: "Soon every producer went around with a little vial of oil sand in his pocket, and the more informed and serious ones carried charts on which were recorded the different kinds of material that had led to their oil sand. That is, each well became a geological study."

The Drake Well was such an extraordinary discovery for its time that Ida Tarbell considered it a "sacred spot" from the moment she learned of it as a child. Indeed, she tended to romanticize the Drake Well discovery and what followed from it: "Here we have demonstrations of the enterprise and resourcefulness of American men in adapting what they knew to unheard-of industrial problems, of their patience and imagination in adding by invention, by trial and error, a body of entirely new mechanical and commercial devices and processes."

Despite Tarbell's emotional attachment to the oil region of her childhood, she did not compromise accuracy when writing about it. Scholars who came after her have verified over and over the accuracy of her accounts. In the year 2000, for example, Brian Black, a member of the Pennsylvania State University history faculty, acknowledged his debt to Tarbell's research in his book *Petrolia: The Landscape of America's First Oil Boom*. "The writing and spirit of Ida Tarbell rose like a beacon guiding me beyond the romance and riches to the human and natural story available in the oil country of Pennsylvania," Black said.

Paul H. Giddens, a history professor who became a Tarbell acolyte after meeting her at Allegheny College, documented with precision her never-ending fascination with the culture of oil in books such as *The Birth of the Oil Industry*. Giddens grasped that Tarbell could never escape the influence of oil, a "strong thread weaving itself into the patterns of her life ever since childhood." Her emotional and intellectual investments in the oil culture of her youth made it impossible for her to ignore the colossus who would soon dominate the oil industry, and through that dominate all of American life. Tarbell's experiences growing up in the oil region of Pennsylvania would make her confrontation with John D. Rockefeller all the more shot through with drama later.

Franklin Tarbell found the rush to Titusville surprising in its intensity but not totally unexpected, given his understanding of greed in human nature. A more learned man than most of his peers, he had recognized the economic potential of new energy sources for years before the Drake Well came in. He perceived instantly that oil would someday light homes, factories, stores, and whole towns better than any natural resource tried until then. As Franklin watched speculators lease or purchase every parcel they could obtain along Oil Creek and the Allegheny River, he considered the opportunities for himself and his family. As the excitement mounted, he and Esther made what would prove to be a fateful decision—to put the trek to Iowa on hold, despite having already purchased land there.

During the autumn of 1857, Franklin Tarbell made his way to the Drake Well. As he neared the end of the day-long journey from Hatch Hollow, he found himself gripped by the heady atmosphere. Viewing at first hand the frantic attempts to capture the oil surfacing from below, Franklin grasped his future: he would produce storage receptacles for the oil.

Not expecting so many gallons to gush, Drake had made no provision for storing large quantities of oil. The first item he could commandeer was, comically, a washtub. Some empty whiskey barrels turned up. A local carpenter built vats from pine boards obtained at the local sawmill. But the supply of storage containers fell far short of demand. As word spread about the Drake Well, nearby barrel makers stepped up production as much as they could. To store the filled barrels until they could be shipped to large markets, the oilmen devised a wooden tank caulked with oakum and held together with iron hoops. Leakage occurred regularly because of haphazard manufacturing methods.

Perhaps 1,000 filled barrels could be crammed into a tank, but the demand was on a higher order of magnitude; drillers needed at least 10,000 barrels urgently. Before Franklin Tarbell became involved, disorganized manufacturing meant the barrels did not always stack neatly. A range of nonstandard sizes, from 38-gallon capacity to 50 gallons, made distribution chaotic. Eventually, Franklin Tarbell helped gain acceptance for the 42-gallon standard that New England craftsmen had pioneered for whale oil.

Even casual observers grasped the need for storage. A first-time visitor to the oil region commented after just cursory observation, "Barrels, barrels are the great want now, and much is lost daily by the scarcity of this article . . . The barrels are sold at two dollars apiece, and there is already a demand for a thousand a day."

Until the Titusville oil discovery, barrel making in the United States had never transcended tiny, localized volume. Raw materials had to be located near water for transport by barge for the business to be economical. Small manufacturers supplied barrels for whiskey, molasses, and turpentine, but before 1859 they had no reason to believe they would find a profitable market for oil barrels. The growth of the railroads made expansion of the industry possible. Suddenly raw materials from great distances could reach barrel manufacturers with increased efficiency.

The oil drillers listened to Franklin Tarbell's storage proposal; some already knew of his carpentry and welding skills. Being sufficiently impressed with Franklin's blueprint, and sufficiently desperate, a number of drillers agreed to furnish money.

Franklin's prototype turned out to be a success. Within months he was buying thousands of feet of lumber, employing scores of men, working them and himself day and night. The business grew and grew; the seeming endlessness of the oil coming out of the ground assured that his fledgling operation would have a bright future. Unexpectedly and quickly, the Tarbell family had linked its own fate to the oil industry.

‖‖

CHAPTER TWO

John D. Rockefeller

A Young Adult Portrait in Oil

F ranklin and Esther Tarbell made a logical choice when they decided to stay in Pennsylvania. After all, the entire region seemed to be swimming in oil. But when John D. Rockefeller invested himself and his assets in the sticky, viscous substance, some who knew him questioned his judgment.

Born in 1839 on a farm of about fifty acres in rural Richford, New York, Rockefeller came from circumstances similar to those of Franklin and Esther Tarbell. Although only eighteen years older than his future antagonist Ida Tarbell, Rockefeller grew up in a profoundly different time. When he was born, Martin Van Buren served as president of a nation with only twenty-five states, none west of Michigan. (By the year of Ida's birth, Iowa, Wisconsin, Florida, and Texas had been added to the Union.) In 1839, tensions over slavery existed, but secession was unimaginable, as was a civil war.

Unlike Ida Tarbell, Rockefeller did not grow up in a stable family. Yet in one of those inexplicable ironies of nature and nurture, his irresponsible father produced in young John a grave demeanor and a seriousness of purpose that in many ways paralleled Ida's seriousness of purpose later on. John D. Rockefeller and Ida Tarbell, it turned out, would share other traits—a sly wit, religious belief fostered by an upbringing in an organized church, puritanical values, extreme self-sufficiency, outsized persistence, regard for work as a lifelong calling rather than a mere job, and an abiding belief that one person could change the world. Both Rockefeller and Tarbell experienced an early exposure to death, as they watched infant siblings suffer before passing away. Living that close to death at a young age yielded indelible memories: both Rockefeller and Tarbell lived decades beyond the average life expectancies of their era, but neither would ever shake his or her dread of the grave.

Rockefeller's father, William Avery Rockefeller, was born in 1810 and became a con man at an early age. In western New York towns, he pretended to be a deaf-mute peddler selling novelties or a physician selling purportedly miraculous medicinal cures. Calling on a farm family near Moravia in 1836, William met Eliza Davison, a straitlaced, pious, pretty woman of twenty-three. Her well-to-do widowed father opposed the incipient romance. But Eliza rejected his counsel and married William the next year, apparently without knowing him well. Her father's concerns proved warranted. Those who knew William believed he married more for money than for love, and his later behavior proved them correct.

During the 1920s, author William H. Allen traveled to the New York State towns where John D. Rockefeller grew up and interviewed Rockefeller descendants and descendants of the family's neighbors. In 1930, he published what he had heard in *Rockefeller: Giant, Dwarf, Symbol*. Apparently the first full-length biography of John D., Allen's book is more than 600 pages long and is packed with details. Allen portrays William Rockefeller as charming in a con-man way but otherwise despicable; all of the interviewees emphasized his immorality and lawlessness.

William Rockefeller moved his bride to the rundown town of Richford, about thirty miles from Moravia, where his parents lived. Using money from Eliza's dowry, he built a small, plain house about a half-mile from the home where he had grown up. In that house, he fathered children both with Eliza and with his mistress, Nancy Brown, who lived under the same roof, ostensibly as a housekeeper. Eliza gave birth first to

Lucy in 1838, then a year later to John D. The mistress gave birth to two daughters, John D.'s half-sisters—Clorinda in 1838, Cornelia in 1839.

It is impossible to know today how relatives, neighbors, and merchants reacted to this scandalous arrangement. But they must have remarked that during this time William disappeared for days on end, leaving both women to fend for themselves. Given her husband's unreliability, Eliza practiced frugality. Local stores sporadically extended credit to her for food, but the uncertainty left her prone to scrimping. Because of these hardships, she taught her precocious son a homily he would remember his entire life: "Willful waste makes woeful want." John D., meanwhile, digested the seemingly wrenching experiences and turned them into something positive as an adult. One of his oft-repeated opinions became "Sons of wealthy parents have not the ghost of a chance compared with boys who came from the country with the determination to do something in this world."

After four years of wretched existence in Richford, Eliza insisted to William that they move closer to her family, especially her father. So Eliza, now with three children—Lucy, John D., and baby William—found themselves in a more spacious home beside Lake Owasco. At the time, Moravia's population numbered about seven hundred. Eliza soon thereafter gave birth to her fourth child, Mary Ann, and then to twins Franklin and Francis, although Francis died before reaching age two.

From infancy the children exhibited distinctly different temperaments. William and Franklin looked like their father and acted in the same hearty, loud manner. John D. and his sisters tended to look like their mother and exercised both self-control and self-abnegation. As in many families, the different qualities led to unpredictable results. John D. and William usually got along beautifully, despite their differences; John D. and Franklin, generally known as Frank, clashed regularly. Both the cooperation and the clashes yielded profound consequences for the family's fortunes as John D. became rich and famous.

Like the Tarbells, the Rockefellers, especially Eliza, placed great importance on education and faith. A one-room schoolhouse and a nearby Baptist church served as the centers of young John D.'s life when he was not working on the nearly one-hundred-acre homestead. He emulated his mother's beliefs. He admired her religious faith; for the rest of his long life he respected all women who demonstrated religious devotion, household thrift, and appropriate disciplining of their children.

Eliza played the role of stern matriarch. In his memoir, Rockefeller recalled a whipping his mother administered because of an alleged transgression at school. "I felt called upon to explain after the whipping had begun that I was innocent of the charge," he said. Her reply stayed with him: "Never mind. We have started in on this whipping, and it will do for the next time." Another time, John D. and one of his brothers violated the household rules by ice-skating on a pond at night. They heard cries for help from a neighbor who had fallen through the ice. John D. said that the boys saved the man's life by fishing him from the frigid water. As he phrased the situation in his memoir, "I felt that there were mitigating circumstances connected with this particular disobedience which might be taken into account in the final judgment." But this feeling, he disclosed, "proved to be erroneous." He experienced his mother's discipline anyway. It seems quite likely that such childhood incidents cemented his lifelong closeness to his mother. Like her, he observed, and needed, daily regimens, which she provided and his father did not.

Although he did not share his father's less savory traits, John D. did inherit from William a deep love of money and calculated risk-taking in business ventures. He wrote nothing and said nothing publicly about his father's abandonment of the family and his swindling nature. Instead, perhaps worried about appearances, he wrote, "To my father I owe a great debt in that he trained me to practical ways. He was engaged in different enterprises . . . and he taught me the principles and methods of business. From early boyhood I kept a little book which I remember I called Ledger A . . . containing my receipts and expenditures as well as an account of the small sums that I was taught to give away regularly."

During John D.'s childhood, William Rockefeller, predictably, did not blend well into his wife's hometown. Questionable financial transactions, extramarital affairs, and an allegation of rape leveled against him compromised his ability to establish himself as a worthy citizen.

Anne Vanderbeak, hired by Eliza to help clean the family home, alleged that William sexually assaulted her on May 1, 1848. As with many claims of rape, then and now, the truth is difficult to ascertain. The indictment against William did not appear until more than a year later, which raises questions about why Vanderbeak took so long to report the assault and why the prosecutor took so long to act. The prosecutor never ordered that William be arrested, and no trial ever occurred. Among the plausible explanations are that Vanderbeak did not appear credible upon further questioning and that she decided against testifying in open court. Yet another plausible explanation is that William feared a conviction, so accepted a deal with the prosecutor to leave the county.

In any case, the allegation made it untenable for William to remain in Moravia. Not even the professional con man could talk his way into the good graces of Eliza's neighbors. First he disappeared for a while. When hostility against him did not abate, he took the family to Owego, close to the New York–Pennsylvania border. The house, in a rural setting outside the town boundaries, did not include enough acreage for farming but had plenty for a bountiful garden. John D. once again ended up in a good school and near a convenient, welcoming church. When going into town, he enjoyed the cosmopolitan nature of Owego—at least compared to Richford and Moravia—as well as the physical beauty of the nearby Susquehanna River.

The family's next move, however, was not viewed in a positive light by anybody but the patriarch. In 1853, William insisted that Eliza, John D., and his siblings relocate to Strongsville, Ohio, a suburb of Cleveland. He apparently chose Strongsville not to find a decent house for his large family, but because he could pay cheap rent to his sister Sara Ann and her husband, William Humiston, by sharing an already overcrowded dwelling. He disappeared from the scene again, traveling from town to town while styling himself as a doctor with cures for cancer and other illnesses.

The arrangement with William's sister and brother-in-law inevitably disintegrated, and William moved Eliza and the children to a farmhouse on the outskirts of the suburb. Less than a year later, he insisted that John D. and his brother William live in Cleveland proper, where they could attend what later became known as Central High School. He drove his two sons over the bumpy, frequently muddy thirteen-mile route in a carriage pulled by strong horses.

William boarded his sons in the home of a local woman named Mrs. Woodin, who needed money to support herself and a teenage daughter. A devout Baptist, Mrs. Woodin sensed correctly the boys had been raised well in that same strict religious faith by their mother. Like other residents of her modest neighborhood, she could not afford the newfangled gas lamps. Most homes relied on candles. Whale oil provided brighter light but cost more. John D. and William Rockefeller apparently provided their own lighting; John D.'s meticulous account book lists frequent purchases of "burning fluid."

John D. and his brother remained at Central High School for a couple of years. Established on the then unusual principle of education for both girls and boys, "even the poorest, if possessed of talent and application," Central High School won a reputation for excellent teaching and driven students. The reserved John D. started acquaintanceships in school that lasted into old age. Levi Schofield, who became an architect, served as his golf partner after the men graduated into the world of wealth. Marcus Alonzo Hanna married into a Cleveland iron ore and coal fortune; later he became a U.S. senator representing the Republican Party and a maker of presidents in national politics.

The Spelman sisters, Lucy and Laura Celestia, stood out among the classmates. Their father, Harvey B. Spelman, an ardent abolitionist who briefly served as a state legislator to exercise his beliefs, had grown up in Massachusetts and migrated to the Akron, Ohio, area with his family. There he met Lucy Henry, a schoolteacher also transplanted from New England. They married and produced Lucy in 1837 and Laura in 1839, the same year as John D.'s birth. The Spelman family moved to Cleveland in 1851, apparently so that Harvey could expand the general store business he had started in other Ohio cities. Their home served as a stop for fugitive slaves on the Underground Railroad. The opportunity to participate in the growth of Cleveland's promising public school system appears to have induced the Spelmans as well.

The Spelman girls thrived at Central High School. Lucy, who would become John D.'s sister-in-law, thought of him during high school as "studious" and "never boisterous." She did not recall him as dour. "He was soberly mirthful," she said. "His eyes lighted up and dimples showed in his cheeks when he heard anything amusing." Lucy's sister, Laura Celestia (Cettie), noticed John D.'s mannerisms too. Nine years after she graduated from Central High School, she became his wife.

John D. Rockefeller carried affection for the school for the remainder of his life. For the fiftieth anniversary of its founding, in 1896, he and his wife played host to surviving teachers and students. For the seventy-fifth anniversary, in 1921, Rockefeller sent a message from New York City, expressing his pride in the school and its alumni, "so many of whom have made their mark and rendered valuable service to the world."

While schooling remained a constant in John D.'s life for a couple of years, not much else remained the same. The shifting of homes continued. The boys left the boarding house when the family moved to a rental residence in downtown Cleveland, then to a home in the suburb of Parma, which William apparently purchased with earnings from his medical scams, gambling winnings, and investments, including those in the lumber industry. The Parma house, situated on about ten acres near Stony Creek, had probably caught William's attention as he rode to and from Strongsville, because the Medina-Wooster Pike passed nearby. The pike served as the most direct route into Cleveland at that time.

John D.'s father allowed his eldest son to return to Central High School. Because the Parma house was too far from the school for practical commuting, John D. rejoined Mrs. Woodin as a boarder—in a different neighborhood. Like so many other Cleveland residents with limited incomes, she had to move whenever rising real estate prices made staying put unaffordable.

The undisciplined growth of Cleveland during the 1850s and 1860s is intertwined inextricably with the emergence of John D. Rockefeller as one of the most influential individuals in American history. Grace Goulder, a Cleveland researcher who documented Rockefeller's local roots for the Western Reserve Historical Society, noted that "he arrived in the city as a boy, and for more than sixty years called it home." By the time Goulder wrote, in 1972, many physical traces of Rockefeller had disappeared, including the first house he built for his mother and siblings, the house he built for his wife and children, the estate called Forest Hill, and the original Standard Oil refinery. But the legends never died.

The city that would become John D. Rockefeller's haven and the headquarters for Standard Oil had been founded at the mouth of the Cuyahoga River, on Lake Erie's southern shore, by Moses Cleaveland, a political compatriot of George Washington's. Growth occurred slowly until New York State opened the Erie Canal in 1825, thus creating a water route between Lake Erie and the Atlantic Ocean. Cleveland's citizens took advantage of the situation by linking into that route through a series of canals financed by the state of Ohio. During the early 1850s, as railroads ran tracks into Cleveland, the city became ideally positioned as a transshipment point for coal, farm produce, copper, iron ore, and lumber.

"To two young strangers from the Strongsville farm, the Cleveland of 1853 was a city of wonderment," Goulder noted. The Lake Erie waterfront played host to commercial vessels powered by the wind. The Ohio Canal featured mules on the towpath pulling barges piled high with freight. The newly built railroad terminal points bustled with men unloading coal that had been mined in West Virginia and Pennsylvania.

In 1855, the St. Mary's Falls Canal, also known as the Soo Canal, accelerated the city's growth. The population doubled during the 1850s, from about 20,000 to about 40,000. Banks arose to help finance the trading offices and warehouses of the wholesale merchants; Cleveland's Bank Street seemed akin to New York City's Wall Street.

John D. Rockefeller would soon tap into that municipal growth. But first he had to grapple with becoming the man of the family. Shaken by his father's neglect and worried about providing for his mother and siblings, he decided to become a full-time wage earner at age sixteen, before graduating from high school. Cettie Spelman graduated on July 16, 1855, with nine classmates. She read an original speech titled "I Can Paddle My Own Canoe." Her sister presented "The Mind, an Aeolian Harp." John D.'s name does not appear on the list of ten. He later recalled

wistfully that "I bade farewell to the dear old school to take up the burden of life's duties." Why he did not put off entering the workforce for an
additional month, so he could receive a diploma, is something of a mystery. "Although the plan had been to send me to college, it seemed best at
sixteen that I should leave high school and go into a commercial college
in Cleveland for a few months," he said.

The newspaper advertisement that might have attracted him mentioned newly hired teachers who offered "young men opportunities for
self-improvement." John D. paid a $40 fee to E. C. Folsom's Commercial
College to learn bookkeeping and other business-related skills during
three months of the classroom regimen. The curriculum even included
penmanship, at which he excelled. He graduated easily, although he had
not mastered all of the basics. He spelled poorly, for instance ("pare"
instead of "pair," "woll" instead of "wool").

At age sixteen, John D. seemed to have limited formal education. He
knew little about literature or music or dance or painting. He knew little
about historical theory or philosophy. Basic mathematics, bookkeeping,
and fundamentalist religious practice constituted most of his knowledge.
He would have preferred to attend a four-year college to expand his intellectual reach. But he did not hunger for a college education enough to
work his considerable will until he found a way.

With the Folsom's diploma in hand, John D. joined his siblings at the
family home in suburban Parma. He longed to remain with the family. He stayed about a month and listened to his mother's prayer that
he would attend college, perhaps to study for the Baptist ministry. His
father, however, refused to relent on the matter of college tuition. As
a result, he returned to the city. Mrs. Woodin had relocated again, and
for a third time, in a third location, John D. became part of her family
as a boarder. He and she attended the neighborhood Erie Street Baptist
Church together, sometimes accompanied by Mrs. Woodin's daughter
and her beau.

The First Baptist Church congregation, located in a wealthy part of
Cleveland, had organized the Erie Street mission in 1850, with a goal
of alleviating the perceived "religious destitution" of that less fortunate

neighborhood. Rockefeller felt so at home with the minister, J. Hyatt Smith, and various members of the modestly appointed congregation that he received his formal baptism there. Though still in some ways an awkward teenager, he began teaching the Bible class for interested members of the congregation.

During his secular high school weekdays, Rockefeller established relationships that would last until death. During his spiritual church weekends, he established lifelong relationships too. Henry Chisholm, older than Rockefeller and a recent immigrant from Scotland, numbered among the first. When some of those religious friends became successful in commerce later—Chisholm, for example, organized what would become known as the American Steel and Wire Company—Rockefeller benefited doubly from the fellowship of church.

When at church, Rockefeller threw himself into absorbing the sermons, Sunday school teaching, missionary outreach, and miscellaneous custodial chores, with vigor as intense as he exhibited at his first job. He took special pride, while still a teenager, in almost single-handedly persuading the working-class members of the congregation to scrimp so that they could afford to donate even fifty cents per week to retiring the church's onerous and soon-to-become-delinquent $2,000 mortgage. The money accumulated within a month or so; the Erie Street church remained open rather than falling victim to foreclosure. Rockefeller himself contributed to his church generously in relation to his earnings. He kept track of every expenditure, down to each nickel: five cents for shoelaces, ten cents for a religious newspaper, another ten cents to buy a gift for the deacon, yet another ten cents to help a poor boys' center in New York City, eighteen cents for a toothbrush, one dollar to pay for the pew where he preferred to sit during the sermon.

Church became a welcome break from an even more regular but less pleasant routine: John D. spent the remainder of the hot, humid Cleveland summer visiting business establishment after business establishment, searching for a job that would allow him to use his vocational education productively. Jobs taken by exceedingly young men later became part of nineteenth-century business lore. Andrew Carnegie, four years

Rockefeller's senior and raised in dire poverty, found a job as a telegraph messenger in Pittsburgh at age fourteen. Carnegie progressed from there to employment at the Pennsylvania Railroad and eventually dominated the steel industry and practiced philanthropy on a grand scale. No future tycoon's job search, however, became memorialized in quite the same way as Rockefeller's.

Despite the city's explosive growth during the 1850s and the companion expansion of the employment base, Rockefeller had no unique talents to offer potential employers. Armed only with a list of potential employers taken from a Cleveland city directory, he knocked on doors. After six weeks of determined, draining treks throughout the metropolis, the sixteen-year-old finally found a job as a bookkeeper at the firm of Hewitt and Tuttle, produce shippers and commission merchants. The partners needed help with their accounting. For the remainder of his life, Rockefeller considered September 26, 1855, a momentous day. Each year, September 26 carried at least as much meaning for him as family birthdays and national holidays, as it marked his entry into the world of business.

During his three-month apprenticeship at Hewitt and Tuttle, Rockefeller kept the firm's ledgers. The labor yielded his first paycheck, $50 total. He felt ecstatic. Earning money for honest labor approximated religious deliverance, he reminisced later in life. The job continued, and at the end of 1855 he received a raise, increasing his income to $25 a month.

The senior partner, Isaac L. Hewitt, had already earned a reputation as a successful businessman willing to act as an entrepreneur. Five years earlier he had organized one of the first ventures to extract iron ore from remote Michigan tracts, then haul it to Cleveland for local use and for export. Henry B. Tuttle worked for the Cleveland Iron Mining Company, then strengthened his business bond with Hewitt by becoming the junior partner in the wholesale produce company.

John D. seemed immune to workplace drudgery and apparently never tired of mundane tasks or thought himself greedy—after all, in his mind, God blessed honest labor and might reward those who accomplished it well. He began providing for himself (rent at the rooming house, the service of a washerwoman) plus partially underwriting the care of his mother and his siblings. Indeed, it seemed that Rockefeller had the patience of a much older man. Cleveland historian Grace Goulder found and studied images of the Rockefellers more than one hundred years after the family posed for photographers. About one family picture, she remarked that John D. "sits very straight in his chair, a hand on each knee, no hint of a smile or boyish merriment on his sensitive face." He and his four siblings look well dressed, "but in a style seemingly more suitable for middle age than for youth."

John D.'s older sister, Lucy, married in November 1856; her husband, Pierson D. Briggs, began to provide for her. About then, William, a dutiful younger brother, prepared to graduate from high school. Mary Ann, a cautious sort, and Franklin, rebellious by nature, remained at home with the watchful Eliza. The housing dilemma—where Eliza and the children should live for their convenience while serving the purposes of the peripatetic patriarch—bound John D. to his father. Then the binding loosened in an unexpected manner and one of those Cleveland housing shifts yielded a liberation of sorts.

William Rockefeller sold the house in suburban Parma, insisting that his wife and children move to a rental house on Cedar Street in Cleveland proper. With the family in Cleveland and William there or absent as he pleased, it seemed to everybody that permanence should become a goal. William purchased a residential lot on Cheshire Street (later known as East Nineteenth Street) and told his son to supervise construction of a family home while staying within a budget; the money could be found in a local bank account.

This home-building assignment might have carried an element of teaching self-reliance. John D. obtained cost estimates from eight contractors, certainly a procedure worth learning. When completed, the house looked attractive and felt comfortable. More likely, however, William Avery Rockefeller wanted to separate himself permanently from the family with a more-or-less clear conscience. When Eliza's father died in 1858, he left her money that helped substantially with the household budgeting. She participated in church worship and church socials. Otherwise, she found adequate contentment in her own family.

With impeccably self-interested timing, William again abandoned his wife and children to pursue business as a traveling confidence man—sometimes using the alias Dr. William Levingston—and to carry on with a woman named Margaret Allen, who was young enough to be his daughter (apparently he was forty-two and she was seventeen when they met). The day that he secretly married his mistress in 1855, he became not only an adulterer but also a bigamist. Eliza probably never knew. If she did know, she remained his lawful wife nonetheless. After the secret marriage, William moved around often, with Margaret Allen in tow: to Ontario, Canada; Philadelphia; Havre de Grace, Maryland; Freeport, Illinois; and Park River, North Dakota.

John D. could never completely grasp the extent of his father's shameful legacy and might not have known about the bigamy until many years later. But he worked hard to win temporary respite from that reality. Many days he arrived at Hewitt and Tuttle by 6:30 A.M., ate lunch at his desk, left for dinner, but then returned until perhaps 10 P.M. He realized his own kind of pleasure from that long workday. Those extended hours at the office became the rhythm of his life, a calming sense of structure during his final years as a teenager. Because of his religious beliefs, he avoided the sorts of social activity attractive to so many teenagers: theater, dances, card games, drinking. He did allow himself to attend the occasional church picnic or other church social, but Friday night prayer and Sunday worship often served as the only time away from his bookkeeping job.

At the office, Rockefeller found it fascinating to scrutinize the bills received, pay them after appropriate adjustments, balance the ledgers, and perform all the other numbers-based functions of his employment. He realized that businesses that paid haphazard attention to numbers operated at a disadvantage; they could never know with absolute certainty how much they could afford to spend, how they could reduce costs, or how stretched they might become when undertaking expansions. Rockefeller told the story of observing a business owner in an adjacent office who glanced at a plumber's bill that seemed a yard long and then told the bookkeeper to grant payment. "As I was studying the same plumber's bills in great detail, checking every item, if only for a few cents, and finding it to be greatly to the firm's interest to do so, this casual way of conducting affairs did not appeal to me," he recalled.

Rockefeller looked up from the ledgers frequently enough to receive a broad business education while employed at Hewitt and Tuttle. "My work was done in the office of the firm itself," he wrote. "I was almost always present when they talked of their affairs, laid out their plans and decided upon a course of action." Because Hewitt and Tuttle had branched out into many commercial activities, Rockefeller's education could be considered a liberal one indeed. The partners owned residential property, warehouses, office buildings, and retail outlets. Rockefeller scrutinized their operations when he collected rents. Property in transit complemented the real estate. The firm shipped by rail, lake, river, and canal. Rockefeller learned the financial particulars of each transportation mode.

Developing people skills accompanied the bookkeeping skills. "Passing bills, collecting rents, adjusting claims and work of this kind brought me in association with a great variety of people," he said. "I had to learn how to get on with all these different classes, and still keep the relations between them and the house pleasant." Those who took notice of Rockefeller later, after he achieved unimaginable wealth and power, confirmed his early self-evaluation. They noted that despite his reserved personality in social settings and his steely negotiating skills in business settings, he indeed tended to get along well with employees from all socioeconomic classes and competitors from all sorts of commercial realms.

Ambitious to become an entrepreneur, Rockefeller began buying and selling commodities, including pork and flour, for his own account at the firm. When Tuttle, the junior partner, left the company, Rockefeller received additional job responsibilities from Hewitt. But instead of elevating Rockefeller's pay to the $2,000 a year that Tuttle had received, Hewitt raised the bookkeeper's salary from $500 to $700.

Surprised and distressed by Hewitt's miserliness, Rockefeller expressed interest when Maurice B. Clark, a twenty-eight-year-old Englishman, approached him about a partnership in a new produce trading company. The men had attended Folsom's business school together four years earlier. By 1859, Clark worked down the street from Hewitt and Tuttle at a competing produce house and lived in the same neighborhood as the Rockefeller family. Rockefeller was intrigued by Clark's overture and scraped together the $2,000 he needed to become a partner. (Rockefeller's contribution is the equivalent of about $46,000 in the early years of the twenty-first century, using the Consumer Price Index.) This sum apparently included a $1,000 loan from William Avery Rockefeller, which John D. agreed to repay at an annualized interest rate of 10 percent.

"It was a great thing to be my own employer," Rockefeller recalled. "Mentally I swelled with pride—a partner in a firm with four thousand dollars capital!" The firm called itself, simply enough, Clark and Rockefeller. A Cleveland newspaper editor called them "experienced, responsible and prompt businessmen" in print. The office on River Street (later known as West Eleventh Street), a noisy trade area running north and south along the Cuyahoga River, offered access to the docks from the rear. John D.'s brother William worked nearby, as a bookkeeper at the firm of Hughes and Davis.

The partners contracted to buy meat, grain, and other edibles. Then they arranged to ship the goods, usually perishable, to purchasers. They found themselves heavily dependent on weather conditions; an unexpected freeze could cause produce shortages or transportation delays.

When the firm needed money to expand, Rockefeller held his first meeting with a banker, Truman P. Handy. The leading banker in Cleveland at the end of the 1850s, Handy had arrived in the city in 1832 from Buffalo, New York. His banking skills enabled his enterprise to survive numerous financial panics during an era of money-lending and borrowing unregulated by government. A public school reform advocate, Handy knew Rockefeller from Central High. A devout Presbyterian, he also knew Rockefeller from their joint activities in the Young Men's Christian Association and in the Sunday School Union. According to Rockefeller, Handy quickly granted the request for a $2,000 business loan, asking only, "Give me your warehouse receipts; they are good enough [collateral] for me."

Rockefeller recalled, "I felt that I was now a man of importance in the community." He returned to Handy for loans many times, and each time he reflected about the wondrous nature of trust in the commercial world.

As Rockefeller matured, he felt confident enough to question the decisions of the older, more experienced Clark. At one juncture Clark wanted to agree to a request from their largest customer for the firm to "allow him to draw an advance on current shipments before the produce or a bill of lading were actually in hand." Rockefeller worried that granting the customer's request might harm the firm's finances. Over Clark's objections, he visited the customer, hoping to "convince him that what he proposed would result in a bad precedent." When that approach failed, Rockefeller insisted to Clark that no accommodation be made. Clark agreed, and they held to their decision. The customer continued sending business to the firm even though he lacked a special deal. From the experience, Rockefeller derived the lesson that it is always best to take a "firm stand" when it comes to "sound business principles."

George W. Gardner, a previous business associate of Clark's, joined the partnership in April 1859. Five years older than Rockefeller and from a well-to-do Cleveland family, Gardner brought capital to the firm, and also a name better known in the business district than Rockefeller's. The partners rechristened the firm Clark and Gardner. Outwardly, Rockefeller professed calm. The change made commercial sense. Inwardly, he was apparently angry, especially because his abstemious ways led him to judge Gardner as a wastrel, in part because of Gardner's penchant for sailing his yacht during business hours.

Though the firm no longer bore his name, Rockefeller took pride in the business and jealously guarded its interests. As the 1860s began, he was twenty years old, a fledgling tycoon. The 1859 fiscal year yielded sales of about $500,000 and a profit of about $4400. Rockefeller's share easily topped the salary he had earned at Hewitt and Tuttle.

While thinking about the conflict between the northern and southern states, Rockefeller calculated how the firm—his firm—could ride it out and perhaps even profit. Oil was not on the horizon at first. The Drake Well stood hundreds of miles away in rural, inaccessible northwestern Pennsylvania, far removed from the bustle of downtown Cleveland. But the more Rockefeller learned about the potential of oil, the more the distance narrowed.

‖‖‖

CHAPTER THREE

Civil War

Dodging   Bullets   as   the   Oil   Flows

The entry of the Tarbell family into the new realm of oil turned on a coincidence of geography. The entry of the Rockefeller family into the new realm of oil turned on a calculation of commerce. Franklin Tarbell quickly saw a weak point in the economy developing practically at his doorway. Rockefeller saw another valuable commodity that might be traded profitably, despite his brief initial skepticism. Both of these developments took place against the backdrop of the Civil War. By the time the war ended in 1865, the groundwork for the collision course between Ida Tarbell and John D. Rockefeller had been laid, as she and he found their lives bound to a new source of energy that would alter the daily existence of billions.

Rockefeller had barely reached the age of majority in 1861, when the war began. He felt secure in his business venture. Fiscal year 1860 yielded a profit of $17,000, quadruple that of the previous year. Gardner, ill-suited according to Rockefeller's values, had left the partnership. He went on to find his own way, serving as Cleveland's board of trade president in 1868 and as the city's mayor from 1885 to 1887, with a second term from 1889 to 1891.

Still gaining knowledge about shipping fruits, vegetables, and other foodstuffs, Rockefeller did not at first find a compelling reason to track the oil flowing from below a remote Pennsylvania patch of earth. In fact, most Clevelanders knew nothing about the Drake Well until almost three months after the oil began flowing. Why Cleveland newspapers published nothing for such a long stretch is a mystery, but research by Grace Goulder located no reference to the oil until November 18, 1859. J. G. Hussey, a Rockefeller-Clark competitor along the Cleveland waterfront, quite likely made the first journey from the city to northwest Pennsylvania to view the well. When Hussey returned to Cleveland, however, he apparently kept his plans to invest in oil to himself.

Neither newspaper accounts nor Hussey's journey turned Rockefeller's attention to oil. Nor, apparently, did the opening of the city's first oil refinery, operated by Charles A. Dean, in 1860. Rather, conversations during the early years of the Civil War with Samuel Andrews, a chemical engineer, altered Rockefeller's outlook. Andrews knew Rockefeller's business partner Clark from England, and he had become acquainted with Rockefeller himself because they attended the same Baptist church. From working in a lard-oil refinery, Andrews had learned to produce candles and coal oil used to illuminate homes and businesses. In 1860, when his employer received a 10-barrel shipment of crude oil from the Titusville area, Andrews had already calculated how to add sulfuric acid to it to help refine the substance into something practical. He became certain that the cleansed oil would sell well as an illuminant and thus decided to transform himself into a purveyor.

Andrews called on potential financial backers, including the young Rockefeller, who saw enough potential in Andrews's plan to invest $2,000 of his savings in the refining venture. When Rockefeller took risks—even at an age normally ruled by impetuousness—he worked out the numbers. Despite Andrews's unmatched experience in refining oil, Rockefeller knew failure was a possibility. Still, the potential gains seemed worth the investment. Clark, trusting his youthful partner's instincts, also invested $2,000, and brought his brothers Richard and James into the venture.

Mary Ann Rockefeller, John D.'s sister, recalled nonstop conversations among her brother, Andrews, and Clark about oil. Many of those conversations occurred in the dining room of the house occupied by Eliza Rockefeller and whichever children happened to live there at the time. Clark and Andrews would show up as John D. ate his breakfast. "They all talked oil, oil, oil until I was sick of the word," Mary Ann said. Then the three men would head for the commercial district, "still talking about oil."

While Rockefeller talked quietly with Andrews and Clark in Cleveland, other ambitious young men could not resist the excitement of the oil wells. In 1861, before achieving fabulous wealth as a manufacturer of steel, Andrew Carnegie decided to invest in drilling near the Drake Well after viewing the situation firsthand. Making the hard journey from Pittsburgh to the mouth of Oil Creek, he found the boom economy frenetic beyond his initial imagining. He chose to focus on the optimism of the wealth seekers rather than the seamy side. In his autobiography, Carnegie recalled, "What surprised me was the good humor which prevailed everywhere. It was a vast picnic, full of amusing incidents. Everybody was in high glee; fortunes were supposedly within reach; everything was booming."

It is unclear when Rockefeller made his first journey to the northwest Pennsylvania oil fields. Whenever it happened, he traveled unobtrusively. One photograph, from 1864, purportedly shows him standing by the Oil Creek Valley well owned by W. C. Chapin, but the image is too indistinct to verify whether one of the men pictured is indeed Rockefeller. In any case, his observation did not lead him to act rashly; Rockefeller kept the temptation to become a driller at bay.

He also resisted the temptation to demonstrate his manhood by joining the Union Army. From Cleveland, the Civil War looked like a business opportunity, and Rockefeller made no excuses about not offering his body for combat. He could not escape the questions, however—questions posed by others, questions forming in his own mind. He was in his early twenties, physically fit, unmarried, an opponent of slavery, hoping for a Union victory by an army that needed men to fill the ranks. How could he justify remaining in Cleveland, expanding his business interests, building up his bank accounts?

The scant evidence available about his state of mind suggests that he easily justified following the legal but morally ambiguous route of paying a substitute to fight on his behalf. His mother, the house he had constructed for her, his unreliable father, his siblings, his business partner and their customers, the woman he was courting with marriage in mind—he could not leave all that.

Rockefeller paid $300 for his substitute in battle. He also supplemented payments made to additional recruits. He provided funding for his brother Frank, who lied about his age to enlist as a soldier. John D. preferred for Frank to stay away from the battlegrounds, but the impetuous younger brother made it clear through his words and his actions that he would fight against the Confederacy. John D. decided that protecting Frank by outfitting him well constituted the best insurance policy. Later, Frank seemed to resent the fact that he had endured the dangers of combat while his older brother accumulated wealth far from bullets and bayonets.

Assured of remaining in Cleveland, far from the ugly reality of battlefield casualties, Rockefeller continued searching for promising business opportunities. During July 1863, the Atlantic and Great Western Railroad completed its route into Cleveland; its tracks ran through the newly wealthy Pennsylvania oil region. The Cleveland business community responded with a lavish dinner to celebrate the arrival of the first train. Rockefeller could envision the railroad line supplying large quantities of crude oil to a Cleveland refinery. Then that same railroad could carry the refined oil, with all its consumer uses, to Civil War and eastern seaboard markets as well as international ports.

After Rockefeller realized that he had underestimated the potential of oil to create personal wealth, he reached a characteristically prescient conclusion. Rather than seeking the quick, glamorous riches of the driller, he would focus on the refining business, the unglamorous middleman function, far from the messy wells but near so many wholesale and retail markets for products that started with crude oil, such as kerosene.

Refineries cost little to open. Rockefeller did not enter that business before anybody else, but when he did, he began with some intelligent decisions. For the site of the first refinery financed by the Rockefeller-Andrews-Clark firm, he chose three acres on a high point in a still bucolic spot just two miles from downtown Cleveland. The high point stood beside Kingsbury Run, a waterway feeding the Cuyahoga River, which in turn fed Lake Erie. Rockefeller understood the importance of developing a new waterway connection to enhance the Atlantic and Great Western railway connection. Kingsbury Run proved a shrewd choice. With the Civil War cutting off numerous north-south shipping routes, especially the Ohio and Mississippi Rivers, Cincinnati and St. Louis were fading in importance as transportation hubs. As a result, east-west routes became more vital, and more profitable, than ever before.

Still, to those lacking Rockefeller's vision, Cleveland looked like an unwise choice of a place to base a potential refinery empire. The Allegheny River connections between the oil fields and Pittsburgh seemed more navigable than those between the oil fields and Cleveland. In addition, Pittsburgh enjoyed direct rail service to the busy port at Philadelphia, which Cleveland, nearly three hundred miles farther from the coast, did not. Yet Rockefeller grasped intuitively that he could find ways to make Cleveland more successful as a refining center than Pittsburgh.

As refineries sprang up around Cleveland, a local newspaper published articles explaining the process. When crude oil arrived from Pennsylvania, the transporter delivered it to a refiner's wooden troughs. A straining process moved the somewhat purified substance into wooden tanks, which connected to still houses, where it was boiled. The vapors separated by the boiling received differing treatments. The lightest vapor became gasoline. Heavier vapors became naphtha (similar to gasoline but with a higher boiling point), benzene (the parent substance of a large class of chemical compounds used to make insecticides, detergents, and plastics) and kerosene, the most marketable at that time because of the demand for office and home illuminants.

Rockefeller insisted that the Kingsbury Run refinery run efficiently and cleanly. He wanted no part of wasted petroleum, no part of discharges like those emanating from his competitors' cheaply constructed, haphazardly operated refineries, which polluted the Cuyahoga River and Lake Erie. Rockefeller became a hands-on entrepreneur, visiting the refinery regularly to monitor waste. By observing closely, he realized that buying barrels from George H. Hopper on Cleveland's west side made no economic sense. So he bought Hopper's business, retaining the experienced barrel maker as an employee. Pushed by Rockefeller, Hopper then developed a sealant for the white oak staves that reduced the amount of oil products that oozed through the bottom and sides of the barrels.

Clark and Rockefeller's commission business still mattered. The commercial notices would announce that 1300 barrels of salt were arriving at the warehouse, or 500 bushels of clover seed. But increasingly the oil refinery captured Rockefeller's attention. Throughout the Civil War, Rockefeller fine-tuned the refinery business, trying to work smoothly with Andrews and the three Clark brothers. Inevitably, disagreements occurred, sometimes pitting the workaholic, perfectionist Rockefeller against what seemed to him the overly casual habits of the Clarks. Rockefeller and James Clark at times seemed to detest each other. Proud of his accomplishments, supremely self-confident despite a humble exterior, Rockefeller sometimes felt humiliated by James, who could be arrogant. Rockefeller complained to him about sloppy business accounting, unwise oil purchases, and use of profanity at the office. Although he continued to like and respect Maurice Clark, Rockefeller came to think of the sibling triumvirate as the enemy, not as partners interested in business equality. Gradually, he reached the decision to buy out the Clarks while retaining Andrews as a partner, if possible.

Decades later, Rockefeller provided his dramatic account of the negotiations: "I had made up my mind that I wanted to go into the oil trade, not as a special partner, but actively on a larger scale, and with Mr. Andrews wished to buy that business . . . I was full of hope, and I had already arranged to get financial accommodation to an amount that I supposed would easily pay for the plant and good will."

On February 1, 1865, the five men gathered at the Rockefeller family home on Cheshire Street. According to Rockefeller, the Clark brothers assumed that Andrews, a fellow Englishman, would side with them as they consolidated their authority. They did not want to break up a profit-able partnership, but they did want to rein in Rockefeller. As part of their plan, they ran a bluff, saying one by one that they voted to terminate the partnership and sell the assets. Choosing to interpret the vote liter-ally and knowing that Andrews would quietly remain with him, Rock-efeller secretly visited a local newspaper office. The next day, this notice appeared: "The firm of Andrews, Clark and Company is this day dis-solved by mutual consent. All persons indebted to the firm are requested to make immediate settlement at the office of Clark and Rockefeller." The five names appeared at the end of the notice.

Forced into an auction, the Clarks bid against the Rockefeller-Andrews pairing. The bidding reached $72,500 before Rockefeller prevailed. He was not sure that the refinery actually carried such a high value. The newspaper mentioned that Rockefeller and Andrews had purchased "the entire assets of Andrews, Clark and Company in the Excelsior Oil Works." Furthermore, the Clark and Rockefeller partnership dissolved its produce business.

Rockefeller and Andrews named their refinery asset the Standard Works, a name that suggested uniform product quality and solidity. Thinking about expansion, they bought land facing Pittsburgh Street on the bluff across from the existing refinery. At the start of 1866, that exist-ing refinery employed thirty-seven men to meet heavy demand for its products.

Placing confidence in a member of his own family, Rockefeller hired his brother William away from a produce-commission business. Like John D., William had earned a reputation as a meticulous bookkeeper and had worked his way into a partnership; the firm was known as Hughes, Davis, and Rockefeller until his departure. More extroverted than John D. and less bound by religious strictures, William tended to charm those he met. Sales made more sense than bookkeeping for someone with his personality. Recognizing that reality, John D. dispatched him to New York City to open the firm Rockefeller and Company. International mar-kets influenced the oil refinery business. If the Rockefellers could not guarantee strong customer demand in Europe—especially Germany and France—their refinery might stop thriving. From New York, William could keep tabs on the vagaries of European demand and supply more accurately than was possible from Cleveland.

Quietly, Rockefeller set up a listening post in Oil City, which was becoming one of the more stable of the former boomtowns in Pennsylvania. Using the Oil City Oil Exchange as a cover—after all, just about everybody in the burgeoning industry seemed to hang out there—Standard Oil representatives directed by Rockefeller could keep track of shipments coming from the wells and moving toward Cleveland to be refined.

Soon it became obvious that the Rockefellers needed to move beyond the Cleveland banks for funding sources, so they could expand their refinery business according to an ambitious plan. Cleveland bankers tended to trust them, but refining qualified as a risky investment—partly because of its newness, partly because the supply of crude oil from Pennsylvania might dry up, partly because the omnipresent danger of fire and explosion meant loans might literally blow up. "It is always, I presume, a question in every business just how fast it is wise to go, and we went pretty rapidly in those days, building and expanding in all directions," Rockefeller recalled in his 1909 memoir. Keeping track of opportunities and pitfalls became a challenge. "We were being confronted with fresh emergencies constantly," he said. "A new oil field would be discovered, tanks for storage had to be built almost overnight, and this was going on when old fields were being exhausted." As a result, Rockefeller remembered, he would find himself "under the double strain of losing the facilities in one place where we were fully equipped, and having to build up a plant for storing and transporting in a new field where we were totally unprepared."

Henry M. Flagler entered Rockefeller's life because of the quest for business expansion loans. Perhaps no other business relationship would matter as much in Rockefeller's rise. Born in upstate New York to Elizabeth and Isaac Flagler, a Presbyterian minister, Henry was nine years older than John D. Rockefeller. He left school at age fourteen and made his way to Republic, Ohio, where he worked in a general store owned by the Harkness family, kin of Elizabeth Flagler's deceased first husband. During the 1850s, as Flagler learned the grain business, he and Rockefeller became acquainted long-distance; Flagler was shipping wheat and corn through the Cleveland transit point, and Rockefeller's commission house was rerouting the commodities. Entrepreneurial by nature, Flagler earned and lost money in the salt industry, horseshoe manufacturing, and barrel making. When he moved to Cleveland during the 1860s to seek new ventures, his path crossed naturally with Rockefeller's in the business district.

Rockefeller truly liked and respected Flagler, but during the early stage of the friendship, he also used Flagler as an entrée to Stephen V. Harkness, one of Cleveland's wealthiest individuals. The Harkness fortune derived partly from distilling and selling alcoholic beverages, a commodity that offended Rockefeller. Still, Harkness, twenty-one years older than Rockefeller and practiced at the long view in business, saw the possibilities in oil refining. He possessed ready capital. He lent Rockefeller substantial sums at a crucial time, so Rockefeller swallowed his distaste for the origin of the money. Harkness became a silent partner in a new Cleveland firm: Rockefeller, Andrews, and Flagler.

Rockefeller and Flagler learned to trust each other implicitly as day after day they discussed business transactions that could show a profit, never tiring of the topic. Flagler became fond of saying about Rockefeller, "A friendship founded on business is better than a business founded on friendship." Rockefeller liked to talk about how he and Flagler both resided on Euclid Avenue. The proximity made it convenient to walk downtown together, walk back home for lunch, then repeat the round trip after lunch. "On these walks, when we were away from the office interruptions, we did our thinking, talking and planning together," Rockefeller said, noting that Flagler devised the contract language. "He has always had the faculty of being able to clearly express the intent and purpose of a contract so well and accurately that there could be no misunderstanding, and his contracts were fair to both sides."

Rockefeller credited Flagler not only with drawing up sound contracts but also with insisting on well-built refineries despite the perceived vagaries of the oil business. The refineries they operated "should be different from the flimsy shacks which it was then the custom to build," Rockefeller said. "Everyone was so afraid that the oil would disappear and that the money expended in buildings would be a loss that the meanest and cheapest buildings were erected for use as refineries." Flagler wanted none of that thinking to infect the enterprise. As Rockefeller noted, "While he had to admit that it was possible the oil supply might fail . . . he always believed that if we went into the oil business at all, we should do the work as well as we knew how, that we should have the very best facilities."

Almost immediately upon joining Rockefeller's refinery operation, Flagler employed his overall knowledge of railroad transportation, his specific railroad connections, and the understandable xenophobia of the Cleveland linkage to make a proposal to J. E. Devereux. The Lake Shore Railroad was part of the expanding New York Central Railroad system; Devereux, a proud citizen of Cleveland, had become a Lake Shore executive after serving as a general for the Union cause in the Civil War. He owned a mansion on Cleveland's finest street; he wanted the city to thrive commercially in its competition with Pittsburgh, Philadelphia, and other cities.

Flagler promised that the refinery operation would guarantee sixty carloads of oil products daily in exchange for a per-barrel shipping rate reduced from $2.40 to $1.65. A knowledgeable railroad man, Devereux understood the efficiencies Flagler's suggestion would bring to the Lake Shore line. He agreed to the arrangement, immediately placing rival refiners at a price disadvantage. The debate began about whether the Rockefeller faction was unfairly employing muscle or legitimately seeking business advantage based on volume, and about whether railroads should serve as public utilities or profit maximizers.

Only when Ida Tarbell entered the debate with words on paper more than thirty years later did the general public become engaged, with unexpected results. But despite the somewhat closed nature of the debate before Tarbell's exposé, railroad rebates played a gigantic role in the development of American commerce. Questions about their legitimacy can be discerned from legislative hearings such as those held in the Pennsylvania Senate in 1868, published with the suggestive title *Testimony Relative to Alleged Extortionate Charges Upon Freight and Passengers by the Railroad Corporations of the Commonwealth.*

The actions of Flagler figured into the hearings, as did those of Rockefeller, who wished to remain as anonymous as possible while creating an industrial empire. Given his accomplishments before, during, and after his Standard Oil years with Rockefeller, Flagler has spawned biographies too, including one written by Edward N. Akin titled *Flagler: Rockefeller Partner and Florida Baron.* Akin's research convinced him that during the early years of Standard Oil, Flagler was more than a second-in-command. Rather, he served "as the chief architect and enforcer of practices such as rebates and drawbacks," practices eventually documented and excoriated by Tarbell.

Meeting capable men like Flagler in Cleveland turned out to number among the bonuses of living there. Because of an immoral and peripatetic father, Rockefeller had settled in Cleveland for reasons other than the oil connection that led to his wealth, power, and fame. He obviously found his own ways to succeed in the burgeoning city, even though it had been thrust into his life unwanted. Ida Tarbell, in contrast, found her proximity to the source of oil determined by her parents' studied plan to ride the boom spawned by the Drake Well.

Franklin Tarbell's new oil-related business venture was taking off. Finding that he was seeing his family less and less, he decided to move them closer to the Drake Well from Ida's Hatch Hollow birthplace, about forty miles away. By the time of the move, the family had expanded; Walter William, named for each of his grandfathers and eventually known as Will, was born on July 1, 1860. The journey of the infant Will, nearly four-year-old Ida, Esther, and Franklin to the boomtown of Rouseville, where they would live in a new house connected to the barrel shop, occurred in October 1860. A horse-drawn lumber wagon took three days to cover the forty miles. Ida later recalled how the wagon sped down the Perry Street hill in Titusville before traversing the last bumpy stretch to Rouseville. The hill overlooking the town bore the name Mount Pisgah, perhaps because the valley below seemed like a contemporary promised land.

Until the discovery of oil, Rouseville had been as quiet and isolated as Hatch Hollow. That changed almost overnight in early 1860, when Henry R. Rouse and his drilling team opened the first well on the site, shortly after the Drake Well discovery. Rouse, a lawyer and teacher, was among the most astute of the early settlers in understanding the potential of the oil under the farmland. He also understood the immorality that tended to accompany the boom, so when he leased land to others, he stipulated that the sale or consumption of intoxicating liquor would mean forfeiture, thus mandating temperance in an area where the quality of life was often diminished by alcohol-fueled violence.

Rouse's development of his oil field ended in tragedy. On April 17, 1861, just as the Civil War was beginning, Rouse was killed by an oil well explosion that took eighteen other lives and seriously hurt thirteen more individuals. He was not normally careless around oil; it was his success rather than his carelessness that doomed him. Believing that wells needed to be dug deeper than the norm of 150 feet, he found the equipment and manpower to descend to 300 feet. The drill found a natural gas deposit along with the crude oil. The pressure generated by the gas powered the oil to spout about 60 feet into the air at the unheard-of rate of 3,000 barrels each day. Rouse understood the necessity of extra care around such quantities of oil, but somebody on his drilling crew apparently did not. A spark—perhaps from a lamp, perhaps from a match—ignited a fire, which was followed by an explosion more powerful than anything experienced previously in the oil region. A survivor named George H. Dimick, a Rouse employee, recalled that "an acre of ground with two wells and their tankage, a barn and a large number of barrels of oil were in flames." Those who had been working at the wells or observing the flow of oil from them became "enveloped in a sheet of flame which extended far above their heads, and which was fed by the oil thrown upon their clothing by the explosion."

Rouse survived for about five hours, despite burns all over his body. During those hours, he dictated a will that left much of his million-dollar estate to the surviving settlers to build badly needed roads into and out of the boomtown.

After the explosion, Franklin Tarbell hurried to the site and did what he could to help the injured and bereaved. He returned home physically exhausted and emotionally spent. He and Esther prayed in their parlor, then tried to settle in for a night of rest. But before sound sleep arrived, they heard sounds outside their door. A man burned beyond recognition croaked out his name. When the Tarbells realized he was an acquaintance, they hastily brought him in. Esther nursed the gruesomely burned man for weeks, until he could leave under his own power. Decades later, Ida could still recall the smell of linseed oil, which rubbed off the man's burned skin onto the sheets and pillows, and could visualize the stains, which would not come out in the laundry.

To the Tarbells and other settled residents of what had just become known as the oil region, Rouseville seemed diminished without its founding father. To the get-rich-quick newcomers, however, gruesome deaths related to the manic drilling altered nothing. The boom continued despite the danger. Sometimes a combustion seemed spontaneous, and perhaps sometimes it was. Cyrus D. Phipps and Walter Whann, two young men from oil region towns, were tightening the hoops on a storage tank adjacent to one of the more productive wells. "We had all but finished when, without a moment's warning, the tank, containing thousands of barrels of the fluid, burst, hurling Whann onto the floor of a derrick several yards distant," Phipps recalled. He himself flew "in an opposite direction, directly in the path of the fluid." He lodged in a pile of wreckage, dazed, bleeding, his clothes torn from his body. After an apparently brief recovery period, Phipps returned to work in the storage area next to the well site.

As news of such explosions spread to urban areas, city dwellers rallied against the storage of oil within their municipalities, much as city dwellers worried about the transport and storage of nuclear waste a century later. They wanted the benefits of oil and its derivative products but hoped to let the producers and other rural residents assume the primary risks.

Within six months, despite the danger, hundreds of wells lined the sixteen miles along the Allegheny River between Titusville and Oil City. Before the Drake Well came in, Oil City had been a speck of a town named Cornplanter. The name change said worlds about the shift away from an agricultural economy to something industrial and exciting but uncertain. The name change was the easy part. The harder part was transporting the oil to ports for shipment to Great Britain and other destinations.

The early drillers originally took their oil to Oil Creek by horse-drawn wagon; from there, the barrels could be loaded onto flatboats to float down the Allegheny River 132 miles to Pittsburgh. Alternately, the drillers could drive wagons to the railroad depot at Corry, 16 miles away. Neither method proved easy. Horse-drawn wagons tipped over or became stuck in the mud on the rutted paths. The teamsters who drove the wagons commanded high wages, then tended to spend those wages on alcohol. Impatient and unruly drivers abandoned the paths for farm-ers' fields; the farmers threatened such miscreants with shotguns. The teamsters in turn might be carrying guns, or at least heavy whips known as "black snakes."

Flatboat barges did not move efficiently on Oil Creek, which ran low in the summer and froze during the winter. Even at its fullest, the 100-foot-wide Oil Creek rarely exceeded 3 feet in depth. Looking to squeeze out income from the unexpected boom, local residents such as George W. Brown filled tiny niches in the water transportation chain. Brown recalled boating two miles upstream on Oil Creek with full barrels of oil that needed to be reloaded for a downstream trip. Two horses on shore, hitched to a tow line, pulled the boat. Brown received $1 per barrel hauled. Some days, shippers would coordinate an opening of the dams on the creek, which raised water levels enough to float the barges but caused new problems. The creek became congested with so many barges moving at once; inexperienced or inebriated pilots crashed into rocks, the shore, or other barges, causing injuries and spilling oil. As the spilled oil flowed downstream, children would skim it using wooden barrels or other vessels and then try to sell it in town.

Like John D. Rockefeller, Franklin and Esther Tarbell believed that railroad expansion, improved waterway transportation from locks and dams, plus the construction of pipelines—some moving oil with the assistance of pumps, some built to take advantage of gravity—would improve the profitability of the oil region. None of that would prove easy. Building a railroad, a lock-and-dam system, a pipeline, took know-how and financing previously absent from northwestern Pennsylvania. But both Rockefeller and the Tarbells adopted an upbeat attitude that they combined with a seemingly naive yet ultimately justified faith in the ingenuity of the human brain to harness all sorts of technologies.

Even the Civil War did not stop oil region development as the railroad builders, lock-and-dam crews, and pipeline designers forged ahead. Fortunately for them, the war did not interfere with construction. The crews did not end up dodging bullets. Living where they did, the Tarbells faced little danger of direct attack. Civil War battles occurred for the most part on three fronts—in the West, defined then as Kentucky, Tennessee, and Mississippi; between the Union capital of Washington, D.C., and the Confederate capital of Richmond, Virginia; and along the Confederacy's thousands of miles of coastline.

Because of his family responsibilities, Franklin Tarbell, like Rockefeller, could legally avoid military service, and did so by paying for a replacement. Pennsylvania eventually supplied about 366,000 troops under various calls from the governor, the state legislature, the U.S. Congress, and President Lincoln. Early in the war, Esther joined other women who saw their mission as encouraging younger men without children to enlist. As the war dragged on, she helped provide food for Union soldiers passing through on the way to battle and raise money for military equipment through bazaars and raffles. As prices rose and consumer goods became scarce, Esther labored to feed and clothe her own family on the money provided by Franklin's unpredictable income. Even in the profitable years during the Civil War, with demand for barrels far outpacing supply, inflation triggered partly by the Union government's printing of greenback dollars (money not backed by gold or other precious assets) ate away at Franklin's earnings.

Just as the oil industry permeated Ida Tarbell's childhood, so did the

Civil War—but mostly as an abstraction. Ida did not experience violence directly. Instead, parlor games such as "Visit to Camp," popular with families such as the Tarbells, gave players a vicarious taste of army life. Characters included a whiskered colonel, a foppish captain, a surgeon, and a military musician. Flags and eagles adorned decks of playing cards. Trivia competitions tested knowledge of battles. Variety stores sold jigsaw puzzles of war scenes. Families in uniform and holding military props posed for photographs with battleground backdrops. Children's magazines and books focused on war literature. Fairs and Sunday school fundraisers yielded money to send to military units. In the households of families close to the Tarbells, anxiety reigned about whether men would return from armed campaigns.

When the Civil War ended, thousands of soldiers made their way to the oil region, lured by rumors of lucrative employment and get-rich-quick opportunities. War profits had made numerous oil-field entrepreneurs wealthy, and merchants such as Cleveland's Rockefeller had grown flush with cash. Some of the companies that had sprung up in the shadow of the Drake Well bestowed corporate stock on the veterans in gratitude for their sacrifices. Many of the veterans had lived elsewhere before the war but felt no desire to return to their family farms. They arrived in the unfamiliar oil region wearing tattered military uniforms, with all their possessions in a knapsack except for the rifle slung over a shoulder.

This human drama—the logistically complicated process of disbanding more than 1.2 million Union and Confederate veterans, transporting them back to their hometowns, paying them, providing pensions, and helping locate civilian jobs—made such an indelible impression on Ida Tarbell that thirty-six years later she researched the phenomenon for McClure's Magazine. Writing in 1901 about her recollection of post–Civil War Pennsylvania, she noted that "officers in particular were in great demand as business partners and as promoters of new enterprises, their names being considered equal to a good lump of capital." Quite a few returning veterans risked their mustering-out pay by investing it aggressively. "They sought the oil regions of Pennsylvania, the silver mines of Colorado, the gold mines of Idaho, the cornfields of Kansas, the scenes of any one of the tremendous developments of national resources which had taken place in the four years they had been fighting, hoping there to 'make a strike' which would give them wealth," Tarbell said.

In her article, Tarbell told about how many hometown boys returned from the battlefields as disciplined men. She cheered the welcome the veterans received from those who had labored to keep the local economy humming. The welcome felt deserved to her: "That the [veterans] disappeared [into society] so promptly and quietly was due primarily to the manliness of the men themselves, their sturdy independence, their unconsciousness of their own deserts, their healthy desire for work." Many of the returning veterans contributed relative stability to the oil boomtowns. To be sure, some suffered from what was later called post-traumatic stress disorder. Still, many of the veterans brought a seriousness of purpose to their oil-field labors. They wanted to make up for lost time, and many needed wages to replace prewar civilian income. As a result, they tended to guard against boomtown lawlessness rather than contribute to it.

Established boomtown residents profited from the arrival of the veterans, as they had profited from previous influxes of oil prospectors and those who flocked around them. A longtime farmer named Hamilton McClintock turned his family residence into a lodging house by placing up to five beds in each room, with mattresses spread over the floor in the loft. Quite a few farmers hastily put up lodging halls on their land. After the Civil War ended, building materials became more plentiful and better, enabling hotels, restaurants, banks, churches, and schools to achieve a modicum of permanence.

The oil region's promoters, led by Charles Vernon Culver, decided to reach out to potential investors. After striking oil in the early 1860s, Culver parlayed his newfound wealth into a regional financial empire consisting of thirteen banks. In 1864 he won a seat in the U.S. House of Representatives; his supporters at home hoped he would use the position to promote federal aid to the region, including government assistance for the export of oil products.

Culver fervently hoped to make his hometown, Franklin, the center of

Petrolia, a clever promotional name meant to establish a myth as well as describe a reality (Oildorado and Oildom served as alternate promotional designations). But unfortunately for Culver's plan, the Franklin wells did not gush as many gallons as wells in other towns did. Furthermore, many of Franklin's leading citizens feared uncontrolled growth. As a result, Culver shifted his focus a short way down the Allegheny River, buying 1200 acres which he designated as the new town of Reno. He planned to build a dominant oil-refining complex there, served by a modern railroad to haul in the crude oil, then haul out the refined products.

The *New York Times*, praising the oil region for its significant flow of money into the federal treasury as a result of petroleum exports during the Civil War, reprinted the text of an 1865 invitation sent by Culver to newspaper editors across the nation, inviting them to join a larger audience of influential individuals: "For the purpose of affording the capitalists of the country an opportunity of inspecting personally the Pennsylvania Oil Regions, an excursion through them has been arranged, in which you are invited to participate." Culver said that two hundred guests, especially prominent businessmen, would arrive from "the principal cities in the Northern States. Everything will be arranged to make the trip as comfortable and pleasant as possible, and to afford a full and thorough view of the wonderful phenomena of the oil regions. Your expenses during the entire trip and return will be paid by the projectors of the excursion." Culver hoped the visiting journalists would see the potential for permanence in the oil region, with a spotlight on Reno. He wished they would convey the message that investors could make a great deal of money from the natural resources while transforming the towns into pleasant places for family life.

The tour of journalists and capitalists yielded plenty of positive publicity for Culver. But all the positive coverage in the world could not sustain his scheme when Pithole, the leading boomtown providing the oil for Reno's refineries, started to dry up. The repercussions occurred quickly. On March 28, 1866, a *New York Times* report noted, "We learn definitely of the failure of Messrs. Culver, Penn & Co., bankers of this city. Their embarrassment, we understand, arose from railroad and other heavy undertakings. It is hoped that these embarrassments will be only temporary." They turned out to be permanent. The next month, the *Titusville Herald* published a poem that included the verse "Reno! Reno! No words can tell/What fame you have begotten/By gulling everybody well/That you were sound, when rotten." Culver faced banking fraud charges and ended up jailed while awaiting trial.

Culver's failure at Reno fed suspicions among visiting journalists that the oil boom would wither sooner rather than later. An often-cited 1865 account by visiting journalist J.H.A. Bone provides a poignant example. Rockefeller—implicitly, through his business decisions—expressed faith in the long-term profitable nature of the oil business, but multitudes of casual readers lacked that faith, based partly on accounts such as Bone's.

Bone reached Titusville by passenger train to Meadville, freight train caboose to Corry, then another passenger train to Titusville, in a car so poorly maintained and so packed with prospectors that he feared he might suffocate. Still, during the twenty-eight mile ride, he kept his wits about him well enough to marvel at the density of oil derricks along the railroad right of way and the creek. From the train window, the derricks seemed like a thick metal forest. As the train pulled into the station, the passengers swarmed into the hotel, despite the NO VACANCY sign. More experienced oil region visitors veered immediately to the hotel dining room, where they would wait hours to eat second-class food at first-class prices. The less experienced tried their luck elsewhere. Most went hungry.

Having consumed a mediocre meal, Bone wanted to continue to Oil City, but the train did not run there and no wagons could be had for rent. He started to walk, then realized the futility as he sank knee-deep into the mud churned up by heavy traffic on the unpaved streets. Eventually Bone located a flatboat for the twelve-mile jaunt. The boat lacked seats and shelter against the awful weather. On arriving at Oil City, Bone found no vacancy at the inn; his exhaustion was so complete that he consented to pay for the dubious privilege of sharing a bed with a stranger. Somewhat refreshed the next morning, he prepared himself for the cold and the mud before exploring Oil City on foot. He saw oil being transported along the ice-clogged stream, the four-horse teams belly-deep in the water as they hauled a flatboat loaded with eighty to one hundred barrels. He saw wagons driven by teamsters, many of them Civil War veterans, stuck in the mud to the tops of the wheels.

Veterans of the oil region like Franklin and Esther Tarbell had learned to take the crowding and the messes described by Bone more or less in stride. They and many of their neighbors had found financial stability despite the cutthroat competition, and the financial stability had laid the foundations for a strong community.

The eight-year-old Ida, a daily witness to the world that Bone sought to depict, had less reason to express enthusiasm than her parents. An acrid, greasy haze pervaded the town from the drilling of oil and the transporting of it through the muck. She refused to make peace with the new family home, despite its bedroom with trundle sleepers for the children, living room with an alcove curtained for privacy, and modern kitchen. Ida disliked being forced to leave the familiar log home in Erie County, with its farm animals, pets, fireplace, woods, and summer wildflowers. Her rebellion did not, as she put it later, "come from natural depravity; on the contrary, it was a natural and righteous protest against having the life and home I had known, and which I loved, taken away without explanation and a new scene, a new set of rules which I did not like, suddenly imposed."

Living in an oil boomtown held little joy for curious children; just about everything interesting seemed to be off-limits because of the potential danger. Oil storage pits near the Tarbell home worried Esther incessantly. As Ida recalled, "Mother always had to have a watchful eye on me, possessed as I was to explore the place. It meant crossing the stream on a footbridge and it might mean drowning in oil."

One incident involving Ida and her baby brother left an indelible memory. In an experimental mood, Ida wanted to test flotation. The brook running beside the family home flowed rapidly and sometimes swelled near flood stage. Ida noticed that some items floated on the surface while others sank. "It set me to wondering what would happen to my little brother, then in dresses, if dropped in. I had to find out. There was a footbridge near the house, and one day when I supposed I was unobserved

I led him onto it and dropped him in." Fortunately for Ida, Will's skirts spread out and held him up until his screams led a nearby laborer to rush over and save him from drowning. "I suppose I was spanked," Ida said. "Of that I remember nothing, only the peace of satisfied curiosity in the certainty that my brother belonged to the category of things which floated."

That same curiosity caused Ida, in contrast to most other girls, to learn the oil business from her father. As she grew older, she learned abstract concepts about the industry, including the all-important market fluctuations. She learned that when a new well came in, prices paid to producers would drop for a while, as low as $1 per barrel, compared to a previous bid of $20. Speculators would ride the ups and downs, withholding oil they had purchased when payments to producers fell, hoping to release the commodity at just the right time in the supply-demand cycle. The fluctuations meant that oil region companies, perhaps consisting of family or longtime friends, experienced unanticipated wealth followed by seeming pauperism—at least until the next upturn.

By educating herself about oil, Ida realized that she found science, including earth science, fascinating. She noticed early that the extraction of oil did no favors for the earth. The drastic altering of the land by derricks and the attendant heavy equipment led to fires and floods. As she wrote later, "No industry of man in its early days has ever been more destructive of beauty, order, decency, than the production of petroleum." When oil appeared, she said, "every tree, every shrub, every bit of grass in the vicinity was coated with black grease and left to die. Tar and oil stained everything. If the well was dry, a rickety derrick, piles of debris, oily holes were left, for nobody ever cleaned up in those days."

William Wright, who published an 1865 guidebook, The Oil Regions of Pennsylvania, served as one of the few before Tarbell who sounded alarms about the dangers of flooding and other adverse environmental impacts. "The influx of capital has been so unprecedented that some of its people may have imagined they can snap their fingers at the natural laws. But these will, in the end, assuredly vindicate themselves," he wrote.

With Franklin Tarbell making money from barrels amid the degrada-

CIVIL WAR: DODGING BULLETS AS THE OIL FLOWS   59

tion, the family, after three years in their first Rouseville home, moved to a new house on a nearby hillside. The new location was too steep to allow drilling, and it was far enough away from the ugly apparatuses and general stench that Ida began to feel at peace. Dotted with trees, shrubs, and flowers, the hillside became her playground. On another hill across the valley from the Tarbell home, Rouseville residents hoping to turn their boomtown into an attractive, permanent city constructed a Methodist church. Esther and Franklin considered themselves Presbyterians but shifted denominations after deciding that church attendance in a different Protestant faith trumped no attendance at all. Esther and Franklin saw to it that Ida attended church services regularly; she also participated in a Sunday school class taught by Esther.

Joining a newly constructed church held its excitement for Ida, but that was nothing compared to the birth of a sister. Sarah Asenath Tarbell, named for each of her grandmothers, was born at the hillside home in 1863. Ida had doted on Will from the day of his birth, but she took special pride in caring for Sarah, six years her junior. The connection between siblings remained strong throughout their lives. Even as an adult, Ida repeatedly placed her brother's and sister's needs—as well as her parents' needs—before her own. Ida, Will, and Sarah loved each other as siblings, friends, and sounding boards, both personally and professionally.

Soon after Sarah's birth, the Tarbells hired help to assist with the growing family. Most memorable to Ida was a "cheerful, efficient, kindly" young woman named Maggie Schall, from a nearby town. Maggie served as more than a household maid, becoming a confidant to the young Ida.

Two years later, the family expanded again with the birth of Franklin Sumner Tarbell, Jr. But before reaching age three, Franklin Jr. died of scarlet fever. Given the prevalence of infant mortality in the mid-nineteenth century, children under age five died by the tens of thousands from causes that would be preventable today. At the time, life expectancy averaged forty-five years, more than thirty years less than today. While Franklin Jr.'s death was not statistically a surprise, statistics, understandably, failed to console the Tarbell family. Little Franklin's incessant screams from the pain haunted Ida the rest of her life. She debated whether even to mention his death in her autobiography. She finally did, using these words: "Little Frankie, as we always called him—blue-eyed like my father, the sunniest of us all. For weeks one season he lay in the parlor fighting for life—scarlet fever, a disease more dreaded by mothers in those days than even smallpox." Every day, Tarbell said, "I stood helpless, agonized, outside the door behind which little Frankie lay screaming and fighting the doctor. I remember even today how long the white marks lasted on the knuckles of my hands after the agony behind the closed door had died down and my clenched fists relaxed."

Schooling provided a refuge for Ida. During her childhood, it was customary to spend eight years in primary school, then leave the classroom forever. Many students left sooner, after four years. Perhaps half of all school-age children received no classroom instruction at all. John D. Rockefeller's experience as a high school dropout demonstrated the difficulty of completing the curriculum no matter how strong the desire. It also demonstrated that education was not a prerequisite to financial success.

When Ida Tarbell entered the system eighteen years later, high school still was not an option in many places. Private academy backers often opposed general taxation for public high schools, fearing that lowered enrollment would endanger their investments. Only citizens with discretionary income were able to pay for a private post-elementary academy. In many towns, students who wanted to continue beyond eighth grade frequently had to leave their families to attend a distant private school.

Though a curious child, Ida could not assume that she would receive a formal education; it appeared that she would receive no education other than home schooling. Rouseville lacked a classroom building, and educational opportunities in the oil region were even rarer for girls than for boys. Fortunately, her parents possessed the intelligence to instruct her well and the means to carry out a home schooling plan that included books, a rare commodity in Rouseville, as well as periodicals such as the *New York Tribune*, *Harper's Weekly*, and *Harper's Monthly*, with stories by Charles Dickens, William Thackeray, and Mary Ann Evans (better known by her pen name, George Eliot). Ida's education included piano lessons, based on *The Hymn and Tune Book*. By age four, the girl could read and spell correctly. She would repeat her lessons to her dolls as if she were a teacher in her own classroom. Sensing that their daughter might be a prodigy, Esther and Franklin arranged for schooling outside the home, and Ida later recalled classes with a "remarkable woman" in the home of a family named Rice, along with a few other children from the town.

Meanwhile, Ida received plenty of instruction from day-to-day living. Tramps frequently showed up at the Tarbell house. Esther and the children were not afraid of them—they were hungry but not violent, and usually willing to work for a meal. It impressed Ida that the tramps rarely left hungry; Esther kept coffee hot all day, and at the least had bread or doughnuts available. Esther and Franklin placed a white cross in a prominent place on the house, a sign of available food and other hospitality for the needy.

Ida also learned from experiences with M. E. Hess, her father's business partner. Hess maintained a home in Petroleum Center, about ten miles from Rouseville. As Ida approached her teenage years, she sometimes rode alongside Hess on a horse named Shoo Fly so she could visit his daughter in Petroleum Center. "As we rode, he would stop every now and then to name the stars, trace the constellations, repeat the legends. My first consciousness of space, its beauty, its something more than beauty, came then," she later recalled.

Ida rarely received an invitation to make a similar ride with her own father. Franklin often carried money related to his business, and he worried about encountering thieves. Crime could not easily be controlled in such an atmosphere, and numerous entrepreneurs doubted whether the risks seemed reasonable. Few of the new towns maintained a paid police force. Volunteers deputized to make arrests by a local constable in the older towns or by the sheriff in the unincorporated areas of the county had to figure out how to transport the defendants to a jail; jails were few and far between.

Throughout the 1860s, Franklin commuted between Rouseville and Pithole on his horse Flora, pistol at hand when he carried cash. Esther worried about his safety; so did Ida. Mother and daughter rarely slept soundly until Franklin had returned home unharmed.

The cash hauls, though nerve-racking, signified that Franklin Tarbell's modestly successful oil tank business was expanding. The growth of his business during the late 1860s looked paltry compared to John D. Rockefeller's commercial expansion in Cleveland, but the Tarbell family's material comfort increased nonetheless. As Franklin Tarbell acquired orders from drillers at the new location of Pithole, even more profitable business seemed quite likely.

Franklin had to hire more laborers to manufacture and transport barrels and tanks, and secondhand information about the vast world outside the oil region came to Ida from the *Police Gazette*, a publication popular with these men. The workers slept in a bunkhouse built by Franklin on the hillside; Ida could sneak in after the men left for their daily work. A typical headline read, "Butchery of the Dearing Family in Philadelphia." The *Police Gazette* fed the prejudices of its largely unsophisticated readership, but it also published stories that implicitly suggested that its hardworking readers ought to throw off the shackles of economic subjugation. The tabloid routinely portrayed striking workers favorably. The advertisements probably educated Ida too, as they hawked aphrodisiacs and contraceptives and sex-laden illustrated novels. Ida commented in retrospect, "I looked unashamed and entirely unknowing on its rough and brutal pictures. If they were obscene we certainly never knew it. There was a wanton gaiety about the women, a violent rakishness about the men—wicked, we supposed, but not the less interesting for that."

The prosperity enjoyed by the Tarbell family in Rouseville did not last, however. The town's fortunes began to decline during the last half of the 1860s as lucrative oil wells in other parts of Pennsylvania and in other states started producing. After ten years of barrel production, Franklin Tarbell could see that a downturn was coming. Iron tanks—receptacles holdings thousands of barrels, while his held only hundreds—made by better-financed competitors began to cut into his business. Ever flexible, Franklin gradually switched his focus to leasing and buying wells, thus producing oil for others to store and transport.

That shift placed the Tarbell family in direct competition, on a small scale, with John D. Rockefeller. As the Civil War ended, oil refining surpassed produce as the source of Rockefeller's fortune. Whereas many oil drillers, assuming that a major bust was coming, pumped oil immoderately to sell as quickly as possible, Rockefeller decided that oil would flow for a long time. He predicted correctly that by entering the oil business at the refining stage he could achieve considerable stability, given copious supply, low startup costs, and his own efficiencies. He also sought to gain control over other refiners, who he felt had damaged the entire enterprise by operating inefficiently.

The post–Civil War economy aided Rockefeller's plan. Investors and business operators were newly optimistic after the end of the hostilities. Westward migration all the way to California, Oregon, and Washington State created new markets for oil and its byproducts. Population growth along the East Coast created new markets too, as did a retooling of the southern plantation economy and exploitation of the rich land in the Midwest. As factories producing all sorts of goods opened, the increasingly complicated machinery needed lubricants.

Rockefeller's growing dominance of the oil industry did not mandate that his life would intersect with Ida Tarbell's. Yet when it happened, it seemed somehow preordained.

‖‖‖

Moving Up

John D. Rockefeller never wished to live in the biggest mansion of all. On the other hand, he believed that a combination of hard work, prescient business calculations, and regular church worship would reap just rewards from God, which would allow him and his family to live well.

Rockefeller's attention to mansions began in 1864. In September, culminating a nine-year off-and-on courtship that had started at Central High School, he married Cettie Spelman. At times Cettie must have seemed beyond his reach. After high school, she and her older sister, Lucy, received further instruction at Oread Collegiate Institute in Worcester, Massachusetts. The curriculum emphasized classic literature, civil rights for all people during the dawn of Emancipation, and Christian living. Reared in the Congregational Church rather than Rockefeller's Baptist Church, Cettie observed the Sabbath, a ban on dancing, a boycott of live theater, opposition to alcohol consumption, and the other uncompromising tenets of her religion just as sternly as Rockefeller observed his. Returning to Cleveland after earning her Oread diploma, she won a teaching position at Hudson Street School. She had entertained the thought of marriage to Rockefeller for years, and he had outlasted other suitors. Yet she was understandably ambivalent, knowing that school rules meant she would lose her teaching job when she wed.

An ardent suitor, Rockefeller proposed in March 1864, with a diamond ring in hand. Cettie said yes. In May, John D. attended the wedding of his brother William. His own wedding took place at the Huron Street home of the bride's parents, with Congregational and Baptist ministers officiating jointly. He worked at the refinery on the morning of his wedding day. Wanting to share the joy beyond the private wedding ceremony, he sponsored a lunchtime party for the twenty-six employees at the Kingsbury Run refinery. As he left to dress for the wedding, he reportedly told the refinery foreman, "Treat them well, but see that they work."

The month-long honeymoon included stops—some of them social visits with friends and relatives—at Buffalo, Niagara Falls, Montreal, Quebec, Boston, Worcester, Fairfield, New York City, and Albany. The devout newlyweds avoided travel on the Sabbath. When they returned to Cleveland, they made their home in a rental house on Cheshire Street, on the same block as Rockefeller's mother and his brother William and his bride.

The rental house sufficed for a while. The Rockefellers made themselves comfortable, to be sure, but they also focused on the less fortunate. They donated money, time, and compassion to numerous charities, including a mission house for vagrant children, a gathering place for Great Lakes seafarers, a local historical society, the Young Men's Christian Association, the Young Women's Christian Association, and the Women's Christian Temperance Union.

As profits from the oil refinery increased, the Rockefellers realized they could continue their philanthropy while purchasing a family home. In 1868, Rockefeller paid $40,000 for a house on Euclid Avenue, known in Cleveland as "the avenue of the affluent" and "millionaire's row." Manicured lawns, gardens dotted with fountains, and elm trees graced both sides of the thoroughfare. Previously owned by the wholesale dry goods magnate Francis C. Keith, the house had sunny, high-ceilinged rooms featuring decor by a New York City designer. The mansard roof and rounded dormer windows gave it something of a French flavor; other window groups reflected Victorian style; and a columned portico provided a classic flair. John and Cettie moved in with their two-year-old daughter, Elizabeth (Bessie). The remaining children would all be born at the Euclid Avenue residence—Alice in 1869 (she died the next year), Alta in 1871, Edith in 1872, and the long-awaited heir, a son, John D. Jr., in 1874.

An appreciator of horses, Rockefeller built a stone stable on the lot, which extended an entire block to Prospect Street. He sometimes raced his trotters against those of his neighbors, using the expensively paved Euclid Avenue right-of-way as the track. Because he wanted a great expanse of open space, he purchased the lot and house to the east of his own and paid to move the house to another part of Cleveland, where it became an expensive private school for young ladies. The newly created double lot along Euclid Avenue pleased Rockefeller immensely. Thinking even further ahead about Cleveland's growth, he also bought seventy-nine acres four miles east of his Euclid Avenue mansion, a tract known as Forest Hill.

As the 1870s began, Rockefeller and his four primary partners officially christened a new entity called the Standard Oil Company. Assets included two refineries, a barrel-making shop, railroad tank cars, lakefront docks, and land, some of it yet to be developed. A local newspaper disseminated the notice: John D. Rockefeller would serve as president and hold the largest number of the 10,000 shares, though not a majority. William Rockefeller would serve as vice president, Flagler as secretary-treasurer, Andrews as refinery superintendent, and Harkness as director without portfolio. Oliver B. Jennings, William Rockefeller's brother-in-law, served as the only nonexecutive stockholder. He had earned his fortune in California selling equipment to prospectors during the gold rush of 1848.

Flagler's biographer Edward Akin has noted that from its founding, Standard Oil depended heavily on the decisionmaking of Rockefeller and Flagler. In fact, for years they served as the only members of the executive committee. The two men created operational committees lower on the organizational chart as needed to solve problems or explore new opportunities. Akin also points out the degree to which Standard

Oil operated on trust at the top. Neither Rockefeller nor Flagler nor any other individual owned a majority of the stock. Rockefeller excelled at finding consensus within the Standard Oil hierarchy.

As the company grew and reorganized into what came to be known as a trust, Rockefeller, Flagler, and the corporate lawyer, Samuel C. T. Dodd, filled in the blanks after researching laws and customs in various states. They decided to create a Standard Oil entity in each state as business needs arose, with a trust (derived from the term "trustee") connecting those companies through a management structure at the top. Akin came to believe that neither Flagler nor Rockefeller thought they were committing legal or ethical violations. As the American economy transformed rapidly after the Civil War, "there was no clear-cut definition of ethical business practices," Akin said. "Flagler and his fellow Standard officers saw the economy as a war zone; anything that was legal was ethical." As for the state-by-state organizations answering to a small group at the top, Akin believed the arrangement made sense during an era when "American business had outgrown state boundaries. Because the states lacked the ability and Congress lacked the will to control these businesses, Standard and other large business combinations emerged."

In 1870, as Rockefeller made what turned out to be momentous decisions about his business and personal lives, so did Franklin and Esther Tarbell. They relocated the family to the town of Titusville, a center of railroad transportation that was growing as the region's oil industry stabilized (the transcontinental laying of track had been completed the year before). Eleven years earlier, when Franklin Tarbell learned about the nearby Drake Well, Titusville had had a population of just 300. In 1870, Crawford County's population reached 63,000, with Titusville earning the designation of county seat.

About to turn thirteen at the time of the move, Ida would consider Titusville home for the rest of her life, even when she lived in New York City and Connecticut and visited only occasionally. She quickly came to appreciate the civilized atmosphere compared to the oil boomtowns where she had lived until then.

The town took its name from Jonathan Titus, a surveyor for the Dutch-owned Holland Land Company. Titus had arrived in 1796, attracted by the waters of Oil Creek. Titusville formally organized as a town in 1809 and incorporated as a borough in 1847, long before the discovery of oil. Thus it had developed some infrastructure and as a result avoided the haphazard, lawless nature of the towns created nearly overnight in 1859 and 1860. Before the Drake Well started pumping oil, Titusville had developed a diversified economy anchored by lumber, coal, and retailing, trained a police force, installed drains and built wooden walkways to reduce mud, constructed a sewer system for sanitation, installed gas lights along the roadways, became home to at least a dozen churches, and staffed comparatively good schools.

It was to this teeming young city that the Tarbells decided to move. Anticipating their departure from Rouseville, Franklin and Esther had purchased two lots on Titusville's Main Street in 1868, spending a total of $1,000. Their new house at 324 East Main Street stood out because of its large size and attractive architecture. Modest compared to the home Rockefeller had purchased for his family in Cleveland, the Tarbell house suggested comfort. It did not, however, necessarily constitute a sign of increased financial fortune for the family. As the Pennsylvania oil industry suffered one of its periodic downturns, Franklin Tarbell decided he needed to shutter his Pithole shop. The Pithole wells were drying up. The owners of a Pithole hotel called the Bonta House, opened in 1866, posted a distress sale. Knowing that his family would be moving to Titusville and wanting to construct a stylish home on a tight budget, Franklin paid $600 for the hotel, which had earlier been valued at $60,000. He then tore down the hotel and hauled some of the salvaged materials—French windows, woodwork, iron brackets—10 miles to Titusville.

Although Esther and Franklin harbored few pretensions, they did believe, along with many others, that a large home meant its occupants possessed good character. Titusville was large enough for its residents to stay abreast of national trends. America was entering the Gilded Age, which got its name from the widespread opulence (and sometimes pseudo-opulence) of residential and commercial buildings. At this time architects compiled house pattern books; popular magazines published excerpts from those books for a mass audience. One architectural philosophy encouraged eliminating barriers between interior living spaces and the outdoors. Thus homes in the 1870s began to feature more numerous and larger windows, plants growing in public rooms, rustic chairs and tables made from tree limbs. Porches surrounding two or more sides of the house became common; wicker furniture for the porches grew in popularity. Those who liked to eat meals on the porch invested in mesh screens. A screening manufacturer commented, "There is nothing that a just and right-feeling man rejoices in more than to see a mosquito imposed on and put down, and browbeaten and aggravated—and this ingenious contrivance will do it. It is a rare thing to worry a fly with, too. A fly will stand off and curse this invention till language utterly fails him."

Ida, a curious student just entering her teen years, was not averse to the bourgeois aspirations of her parents. She treasured the stability represented by the family's Titusville home. She enjoyed browsing in her father's study, on the top floor, under the cupola. His desk overflowed with papers and books, especially books about his passions—religion, Middle Eastern holy sites, and, slightly later, Henry Stanley's African travels. Esther and Franklin had a Bradbury square piano placed in the great room, and a music teacher began visiting. Although Ida never found transcendent joy in her five-finger exercises, she practiced dutifully. She eventually learned piano well enough to perform regularly in high school, playing show pieces and leading less accomplished students through morning musical exercises.

Undoubtedly owing in large part to her precocity, Ida realized at an early age that she did not want to live the traditional life of a homebody. In that respect, she and Rockefeller were opposites. While Rockefeller used the accumulating wealth stemming from his precocity to establish the stable family life he had lacked as a youngster, Ida yearned to break away. Although helpful around the house, she showed no interest in traditional woman's work such as cleaning, doing laundry, ironing, sewing, cooking, and taking care of children. Nor did Esther force that role upon her. During her teenage years in Titusville, Ida was delighted by her mother's intellect and awareness of current events, including the burgeoning women's rights movement.

It seemed as if everything fed Ida's intellectual fires. Franklin would routinely gather sewing scraps from Esther; Ida would watch as he burned them in the back yard, then scattered the ashes in his garden as fertilizer. "I always sat on the back steps and watched the remnants of the process which had meant so much going up in smoke," she later recalled. Her father remarked pleasantly about his recycling, "Nothing lost but the smoke." For Ida, not even the smoke was lost. "I had dreamed dreams as it went up . . . Who can say that smoke which evokes dreams is lost?"

Ida Tarbell was obviously not a typical adolescent. She believed that other women should be the best possible mothers and housekeepers. Her entire life, she advocated those roles for women other than herself. She wished to live as an independent woman—independent from marriage and even romance, independent financially, independent occupationally and intellectually.

As a teenager, Ida anticipated the changing demands on women. More women were entering the workforce as advances in technology eliminated the need for certain home-based chores; for instance, because manufactured clothing was easier to buy, sewing became less and less necessary. She did not know how, as an adult, she would fit into the changing economy, but she did know that she wanted to explore the world beyond her one small swath of Pennsylvania, even beyond bustling Titusville.

The family did get out of Pennsylvania more than many other residents. The Tarbells often journeyed to Chautauqua Lake, New York, for picnics. They reached the lake, about fifty miles from Titusville, by boarding an early train to Mayville, then transferring to a small white steamer. They ate lunch en route from baskets filled with tin cups and plates, steel knives and forks; the menu included veal loaf, cold tongue, hard-boiled eggs, cucumber pickles, spiced peaches, doughnuts, cookies, and cake. They drank soda bottled in Jamestown, New York, where Franklin had studied to become a schoolteacher, and returned to Titusville "exhausted by pleasure," having eaten to the point of satiation, Ida recalled.

Ida possessed an unusually brilliant young mind, but she lacked discipline in the classroom at first, having become accustomed to roaming freely around Rouseville. At Drake Street primary school in Titusville, by her own account, she started poorly, paying little attention to her lessons and occasionally playing truant. A teacher who saw her potential confronted the recalcitrant student. "She told me the plain and ugly truth about myself that day," Ida recalled, "and I sat there, looking her straight in the face, too proud to show any feeling, but shamed as I never had been before and never have been since." Ida, who loved learning, started taking classroom exercises seriously. By the time she left the Drake Street school to enter high school, she ranked first in her class academically.

Given her ambitions, she was fortunate to attend a public high school that allowed girls to concentrate on intellectual instruction rather than forcing them into classes on motherhood and domestic management. Memorable among her textbooks were Joseph Hutchins Colton's *Common School Geography* and William Smith's *History of Rome*. A book from her father's shelf, John Clark Ridpath's *A Popular History of the United States from the Aboriginal Times to the Present Day*, sparked an interest in Abraham Lincoln, which later played a significant role in her career. Louis Figuier's *The World Before the Deluge*, translated from the French and with illustrations of extinct animals and plants, stimulated the girl's interest in natural history.

Ida's curiosity transcended Figuier's geology; she also became fascinated by zoology, botany, chemistry, and natural philosophy. By the 1870s, Charles Darwin's thinking about evolution, published as *Origin of Species* in 1859, had begun to find its way into American classrooms. As Janet Browne, a Darwin biographer, has noted, "The tidal wave of comment began almost immediately. Despite all Darwin's carefully amassed evidence . . . Victorians found it nearly impossible to accept the idea of gradual change in animals and plants, and equally hard to displace God from the creative process." Ida, however, was able to remain a churchgoer while forming an understanding that perhaps not everything about life and death could be explained by the biblical account of creation.

Using Darwin's theory as a touchstone, Ida could relate her youthful days spent exploring the landscapes around her Pennsylvania homes to what she was learning in school. "Here I was suddenly on a ground which meant something to me," she later recalled. "From childhood, plants, insects, stones were what I saw when I went abroad, what I brought home to press, to put into bottles, to litter up the house . . . I had never realized that they were subjects for study . . . School suddenly became exciting."

When Ida graduated from Titusville's high school on June 25, 1875, with a 99 percent grade average, she felt sad about moving away from her parents. Although few young women left home for college in 1875, she knew that a college education would help her achieve her idealistic vision of a better world. She began to gather college application materials, knowing that she would indeed go away.

Ida's outer world had been defined by the influences of the oil industry. The industry, however, was in the throes of an economic upheaval, in which monopolies and oligopolies were emerging, eliminating the role of the speculator and the small vendor. The consequences of these economic disturbances would be felt throughout American society. Despite his oil-field savvy, not even Franklin Tarbell completely understood the great forces, and great men, about to be unleashed on the oil industry. As the final quarter of the nineteenth century began, men like Jay Gould, Jim Fisk, Cornelius Vanderbilt, and especially John D. Rockefeller began changing the American economic landscape forever.

Before the Civil War, America's economy had been built on small agrarian units. By the 1870s, the economy was becoming ever more dependent on corporations that in certain industries verged on monopolies. The move toward consolidation offended the sensibilities of many independent oilmen, who had helped build the oil industry from basically nothing in just a decade. These men had looked ahead with confidence to its gradual maturation; the strangling impact of the trusts seemed profoundly unfair. "Life ran swift and ruddy and joyous in these men," Ida Tarbell would later recall. "They were still young, most of them under forty, and they looked forward with all the eagerness of the young who have just learned their powers to years of struggle and development." Then, suddenly, Rockefeller and Standard Oil could not be ignored. Ida Tarbell would write, dramatically, in muckraking prose, that a "big hand reached out from nobody knew where, to steal their conquest and throttle their future. The suddenness and the blackness of the assault on their business stirred to the bottom their manhood and their sense of fair play."

For those who had paid attention to the business maneuvers of the stern young man from Ohio, Rockefeller's sudden dominance came as no surprise. For most, however, he seemed to have appeared from nowhere to command a great deal of respect in the oil industry. During the previous decade he had quietly consolidated his businesses into one corporation, the Standard Oil Company. Rockefeller was shrewdly looking for ways to absorb or otherwise eliminate competitors to increase profit margins on each gallon of refined oil sold within the United States and overseas. He eliminated middlemen and direct competitors such as purchasing agents, barrel manufacturers, shippers, and wholesalers of consumer products such as kerosene. Each new acquisition became integrated vertically into Standard Oil.

Because Standard Oil was expanding so rapidly, Rockefeller used its volume and efficiency to squeeze down railroad shipping rates. Railroad executives often charged what they wished on the routes where their line was the sole carrier; they successfully rejected the populist notion that railroads receiving government land grants owed taxpayers a duty to charge all shippers and passengers equal prices, serving as a public utility of sorts. Unlike most businessmen, Rockefeller refused to act submissively with these executives. He knew they needed products to haul, and needed them at reliable intervals in reliable quantities. Standard Oil could supply lots of products, in large quantities. Understanding that lower rates could serve as a decisive competitive advantage, Rockefeller insisted on shipping at a discount, and brazenly also received a separate, secretly negotiated, unpublicized rebate from the railroads for every barrel of competitors' oil they carried. Pushing his advantage, he persuaded railroad executives to disclose market information about the activities of competing shippers as part of the deal.

In exchange for the bargain rates and competitive intelligence, Rockefeller offered railroad executives a large, reliable stream of oil products to haul, enabling the carriers to operate in a stable environment. As an added inducement, he lent the railroads train cars owned by Standard Oil to supplement the carriers' overburdened rolling stock. To the detriment of shippers other than Standard Oil, the railroads tried to make up income lost because of granted rebates by charging higher than necessary rates on local stretches of track where no competitors impinged.

The combination of Rockefeller's legitimate business acumen and the preferential shipping rates offered to his company by railroads worried Franklin Tarbell and other Pennsylvania oilmen. It turned out that their worries were well founded.

Rockefeller not only negotiated shipping rates in new ways but also used new laws to form an offshoot corporation, Standard Oil Company (Ohio); the parentheses suggested that he planned to expand to other states. The corporate model he instituted would simplify execution of a plan to consolidate control over competing refineries. He could offer stock instead of cash to struggling refiners. He could also boost Standard Oil's capitalization on short notice. In 1871 and the early portion of 1872, Rockefeller completed what came to be called, admiringly or bitterly, depending on the commentator's viewpoint, the "Cleveland massacre."

Rockefeller's biographer Allan Nevins placed the Cleveland refinery consolidation and other Rockefeller acquisitions in a positive context. "Everyone who looks at the record of industry and commerce from the Civil War to the First World War sees that the economy underwent the most sweeping transformation. The business realm changed from 'small, weak, highly competitive units' to one of 'concentration, efficiency and highly organized power.'" The process meant "destruction and reconstruction," according to Nevins. "Great business aggregations are not built without frustrating, crushing or absorbing multitudinous small enterprises." If the leaders of the transformation looked like robber barons to those being crushed, Nevins maintained, "the constructive aspects of the transformation were in the long run more important than the destructive; the development of new wealth far outweighed the wastes of existing wealth."

It seems reasonable to assume, without endorsing Nevins's enthusiasm, that a certain amount of oil industry consolidation almost certainly would have occurred without Rockefeller's initiative, as happened in many other industries. Local, small refiners started falling behind regional competitors with the advent of widespread railroad transportation. Furthermore, new technologies for efficient extraction of usable petroleum products called for costly upgrades of existing refineries and considerably higher startup investments for new refineries. In Cleveland, a dozen or more refineries seemed to be nearing bankruptcy. If Rockefeller had not begun his refinery-purchasing spree, voluntary shutdowns probably would have occurred. Rockefeller took advantage of his competitors' distress, and within five years he controlled twenty-one of the twenty-six previously competing refineries around the city. Standard's refining output increased from about 1500 barrels of oil per day to about 11,000. That capacity reportedly topped the output of the entire Pennsylvania oil region.

Probably the biggest coup during the "Cleveland massacre" occurred when Rockefeller approached Oliver H. Payne, the director of a Standard Oil refinery competitor partially owned by Maurice and James Clark, Rockefeller's former partners. Rockefeller inquired whether the college-educated Payne, the son of Henry B. Payne, an influential Ohio member of Congress, would like to sell the Walworth Run refinery in exchange for joining Standard Oil management, complete with newly issued shares of stock. Payne, a Perry on his mother's side and thus a descendant of one of Cleveland's founding families, had little need for money but favored the thought of helping manage an enterprise with such promise. As a result, he said yes; as Rockefeller had done before and would do later, he turned a competitor into an ally.

Parlaying Payne's local prestige into other overtures, Rockefeller easily persuaded John Stanley to sell his refinery. As he approached additional refiners, he suggested that they accept Standard Oil stock rather than cash. Those who accepted stock and held on to it for a while tended to accumulate substantial wealth. When Rockefeller purchased a refinery from the brothers Hugh and John Huntington, John accepted stock and Hugh insisted on cash. John Huntington became a rich man who made significant charitable contributions in Cleveland. Hugh never became wealthy.

Some of Rockefeller's competitors alleged that he had stated they would fall into financial ruin if they refused to sell their refineries for cash, Standard Oil stock, or a combination. Isaac Hewitt, who had hired Rockefeller as a teenaged bookkeeper, made such an allegation. Hewitt and his partners apparently valued their business at about $150,000, yet an angry and chagrined Hewitt accepted $65,000 under pressure from Rockefeller.

Unsurprisingly, Rockefeller chose to view himself as an accommodator rather than as a predator. In his memoir, he commented, "Late in 1871, we began the purchase of some of the more important of the refinery interests of Cleveland. The conditions were so chaotic and uncertain that most of the refiners were very desirous to get out of the business." He insisted that Standard Oil "invariably offered those who wanted to sell the option of taking cash or stock in the company . . . All these purchases of refineries were conducted with the utmost fairness and good faith on our part." Rockefeller knew about the nasty gossip, commenting that "in many quarters the stories of certain of these transactions have been told in such form as to give the impression that the sales were made most unwillingly and only because the sellers were forced to make them by the most ruthless exertion of superior power."

Perhaps the most unfortunate consequence of the purchases for Rockefeller involved the worsening of his already volatile relationship with his brother Frank. In 1870, Frank had married Helen E. Scofield, who belonged to a well-known Cleveland family. Her father, William, held an interest in Alexander, Scofield and Company, a refining competitor of John D.'s. No matter how legitimate Frank's love for Helen, marrying into a family competing with the Rockefellers signaled potential trouble. John D. purchased the Alexander, Scofield refinery two years after Frank's wedding. Frank later said publicly that his brother had obtained ownership by exerting pressure unethically, despite evidence to the contrary. From time to time, John D. offered Frank opportunities within

Standard Oil, lent him money for new ventures, or bailed him out of financial shortfalls. Sometimes Frank expressed gratitude; other times he lashed out, perhaps from anger at his own ineptitude.

Within Cleveland business and social circles, the uneasy relationship between the Rockefeller brothers became the grist of conversation, as local historian Grace Goulder made clear. Goulder's research into Cleveland's history led her to side with John D. rather than Frank, but she understood the appeal of the seemingly put-upon Frank: "Despite John D.'s clear vindication, Clevelanders chose to view him as a rich man who had ground down his brother. Everywhere the public was ready at this time to think the worst of the Standard Oil head." A member of the local Union Club, Frank, with his "jovial and outgoing" manner, formed a coterie of businessmen and their wives "who were ready to overlook his faults," according to Goulder.

John D. had to deal not only with Frank's outbursts but also with the questionable business ethics of Frank's father-in-law. Scofield started a new refinery operation after the 1872 sale, apparently in violation of a promise. That new refinery spawned litigation between John D. and Scofield that eventually sullied the reputations of both men. Although John D. rarely spoke ill about anybody in public, he openly castigated Scofield as an unsavory businessman.

As for the railroad rebates, Rockefeller conceded elliptically in his memoir that the Standard Oil Company "did receive rebates from the railroads prior to 1880, but received no advantages for which it did not give full compensation." Perhaps for good measure, he added an everybody-did-it rationale: "The reason for rebates was that such was the railroads' method of business. A public rate was made and collected by the railroad companies, but, so far as my knowledge extends, was seldom retained in full; a portion of it was repaid to the shippers as a rebate." Rockefeller insisted that "each shipper made the best bargain that he could, but whether he was doing better than his competitor was only a matter of conjecture. Much depended upon whether the shipper had the advantage of competition of carriers." Whatever rebates Standard Oil received, Rockefeller said, railroads still came out ahead by doing business according to "the natural laws of trade." The Standard Oil Company's shipping using rail-road tracks "was far more profitable to the railroad companies than the smaller and irregular traffic, which might have paid a higher rate."

No matter how wise his own decisions or Flagler's, especially regard-ing transportation alternatives, Rockefeller rarely took his own judg-ment for granted about businesses viewed from a distance. As a result, he undertook the journey between Cleveland and Titusville more than once to make sure his initial faith in the long-term flow of oil to his refineries would prove well founded. The more he saw of the Titus-ville works, the more confidence he gained that the flow of oil would not cease. Refining capacity looked satisfactory too. Consumer demand became the wild card in Rockefeller's calculations. Without growing consumer demand, the profit margin between the crude oil flowing up from the earth and the refined oil ready to market would drop. For the short run, Rockefeller and Flagler decided to place their hope in market forces—increasing demand for oil products refined from crude—as they built their business.

Rockefeller's biographer Ron Chernow makes the case that by 1872 the youthful tycoon had reached a turning point: "For his admirers, 1872 was the annus mirabilis of John D. Rockefeller's life, while for his critics it constituted the darkest chapter." According to Chernow, that year revealed Rockefeller the businessman in all his contradictions—"his visionary leadership, his courageous persistence, his capacity to think in strategic terms, but also his lust for domination, his messianic self-righteousness, and his contempt for those shortsighted mortals who made the mistake of standing in his way." Chernow's research led him to believe that "what rivals saw as a naked power grab, Rockefeller regarded as a heroic act of salvation, nothing less than the rescue of the oil business."

At first Rockefeller's corporate innovations attracted little attention. That changed, and thirteen years after the discovery of the Drake Well, Rockefeller had become well known throughout the oil region. The rev-elation of an entity called the South Improvement Company seemed to bring him into especially sharp focus. Three major railroads and the Standard Oil refineries constituted the backbone of the South Improvement Company, which existed to secretly institute anti-competitive shipping rates meant to harm smaller competitors. While helping to formulate the company in 1871 and early 1872, Rockefeller spent long stretches in New York City, away from his Cleveland home. Some of his letters to Cettie from those months can be found in the Rockefeller archives. The letters reveal plainly that he understood the questionable nature of the South Improvement Company. The secret leaked out only because of a mistake made by a lowly railroad clerk.

On February 27, 1872, after the leaked information spread, about 3,000 individuals, including Franklin Tarbell, rallied at the Titusville Opera House, carrying placards with phrases such as "Down with the conspirators." Soon they organized their own group, the Petroleum Producers Union, their answer to what they viewed as the refiners' cartel devised by Rockefeller. The producers—most of them fiercely independent, some greedy or otherwise unsavory—pledged to withhold oil from anybody known to be affiliated with Standard Oil. Vandalism aimed at the big railroads' tanker cars and tracks as well as at the barrels belonging to Standard Oil spread throughout Pennsylvania.

The independents won the attention of Pennsylvania state legislators in Harrisburg and of U.S. congressmen, and a committee held a hearing at the Capitol in Washington, D.C. During the session, evidence of Standard Oil's practices surfaced; the testimony featured terms like "restraint of trade," "antitrust," "unfair competition," and even "monopoly." But the congressional committee took no action to halt Rockefeller.

The day after the hearing, Rockefeller visited the oil region, demonstrating his fearlessness and his determination to win through persuasion what he had failed so far to win through secret dealings or outright force—the absorption of the area's relatively small independent producers and refiners into his operation. By 1872, Rockefeller, though still a young man at thirty-three, had acquired a reputation, at times legendary, for being a shrewd and heartless businessman. A traditional religious fundamentalist who opposed the consumption of alcohol and other signs of dissolute living, he found it difficult to mask his disapproval of intemperate day-to-day life in the oil region, and his distaste for the local life-style made him even more unpopular.

A year after the hearing, an economic depression that would last six years began. The downturn helped Rockefeller work his will on the oil industry as he pushed for consolidation of oil drilling, refining, sales, and transportation. Widespread unemployment and bankruptcies gave him the opportunity to consolidate his empire by purchasing competing businesses at bargain prices or merely watching as economic conditions eliminated them. Regarding refineries specifically, Rockefeller extended the "Cleveland massacre" to other geographic areas, acquiring facilities in Pittsburgh, Philadelphia, and New York. In the oil region, *The Derrick Handbook of Petroleum* published this brief item on June 2, 1876: "The Standard Oil Company has purchased the Deming, McLaughlin & Company refinery at Rouseville, and also the refinery at Miller Farm. The company now owns or controls nearly every oil refinery in the region."

Many of the acquisitions came after Rockefeller persuaded accomplished entrepreneurs accustomed to taking orders from nobody to enter the Standard Oil family, where he alone issued orders. He often insisted on secret negotiations and secret closings, so that the few competitors remaining would be unable to react in time. He promised the executives selling their assets that eventually their Standard Oil stock would make them wealthy. Usually that promise came true.

As a result of Rockefeller's stealth negotiations, many of the acquired companies retained their own names and longtime executives, at least in the short run, so it looked to outsiders as if nothing had changed. Sometimes Standard Oil competitors, determined to avoid being swallowed by Rockefeller, sold their businesses to companies with names like Charles Pratt and Company and Camden Consolidated Oil Company, unaware that Pratt and Camden had already become part of the Standard Oil empire. At intervals Rockefeller acquired competitors simply because he found the executive particularly impressive. He hoped to add such men's knowledge to his trust's pool of expertise, often for the long term. At least two men who would become vitally important, Henry H. Rogers and John D. Archbold, joined Standard management as a result

At age eight, Ida Tarbell found the oil fields of northwestern Pennsylvania, fascinating and dangerous. Her life and career were shaped by her experiences growing up in the oil region. *Ida M. Tarbell Collection, Pelletier Library, Allegheny College*

After Ida's parents decided to remain in northwestern Pennsylvania, the family moved from home to home to accommodate Franklin Tarbell's barrel-making business. In 1870 they made their final move, to a residence they built on the main street of Titusville with materials salvaged from a fancy hotel in one of the failed oil boomtowns. *Courtesy of the Pennsylvania Historical and Museum Commission, Drake Well Museum, Titusville*

This rare image of Franklin S. Tarbell shows him with Ida, his eldest daughter. She was inspired by his eclectic reading, his storytelling, and his brave struggle to remain independent of Rockefeller and the Standard Oil empire. *Ida M. Tarbell Collection, Pelletier Library, Allegheny College*

As Ida Tarbell was growing up amid the oil fields, John D. Rockefeller, eighteen years older, traveled to see the Pennsylvania wells for himself. He is seated on the lower right, facing left, in dark clothes and wide-brimmed hat, the central figure in the group. This picture depicts the mud and the haphazard construction so common during the boom. *Courtesy of the Pennsylvania Historical and Museum Commission, Drake Well Museum, Titusville*

Tarbell graduated from Allegheny College in 1880. She was the only woman in her class. *Ida M. Tarbell Collection, Pelletier Library, Allegheny College*

After a brief stint as a teacher in Poland, Ohio, Tarbell by chance began working at a magazine called *The Chautauquan*. She had never considered journalism as a career, and women almost never received meaningful assignments from newspapers or magazines during the 1880s. Against those odds, she began to make a name for herself as a journalist. She is on the far left, pictured with other staff members in 1888. *Ida M. Tarbell Collection, Pelletier Library, Allegheny College*

This rare view of Tarbell in profile was probably taken in 1898. Tarbell did not think of herself as attractive, but she was tall and striking. She never married; her work took precedence over her social life, and she preferred to live independently. *Ida M. Tarbell Collection, Pelletier Library, Allegheny College*

Finding a satisfying niche at *McClure's Magazine* in New York City, Tarbell worked long hours as a reporter and an editor. Her portraits of Napoleon Bonaparte and Abraham Lincoln made her a household name and set the stage for the biggest investigation of her career. *Ida M. Tarbell Collection, Pelletier Library, Allegheny College*

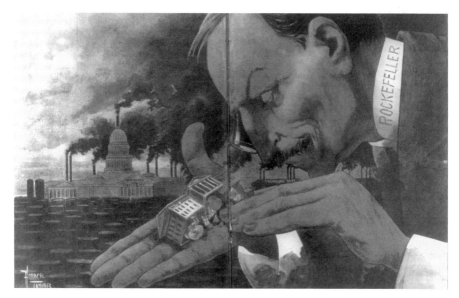

Tarbell's first years at *McClure's* coincided with an unprecedented rise in the power held by trusts. As the twentieth century began, it appeared that the Standard Oil Company would dominate the national economy for many years to come. Naturally, commentators, including editorial cartoonists, harbored strong opinions about the company's products, tactics, and bottom line. "The Giant Trust's Point of View," by Horace Taylor, originally appeared in *Verdict* magazine. *Courtesy of the Library of Congress*

Samuel Sidney McClure was the same age as Ida Tarbell but followed a very different path to journalistic renown. After emigrating from Ireland with his impoverished family as a young boy, he worked hard to earn enough money to feed himself and eventually to attend Knox College, in Galesburg, Illinois. Like Tarbell, McClure never thought of journalism as a career until he backed into it shortly after leaving college. *Ida M. Tarbell Collection, Pelletier Library, Allegheny College*

The cover of *McClure's Magazine* in November 1903 listed articles by Ray Stannard Baker and Lincoln Steffens, among others. This historic issue signaled a new era of muckraking and what is now called "investigative journalism." Tarbell sometimes edited her colleagues' work, including that of Baker and Steffens.

Courtesy of the Library of Congress

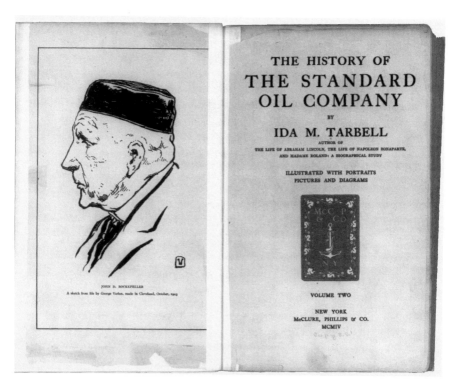

This is the title page of the first edition of Tarbell's exposé of the Standard Oil Company, which filled two thick volumes. George Varian's sketch of John D. Rockefeller led Tarbell to comment on the "power and pathos" of her protagonist.

Courtesy of the Library of Congress

Miss Tarbell Has the Distinction.

Rockefeller and other Standard Oil executives refused to comment on Tarbell's exposé. Many felt that Rockefeller's silence hurt him. In this cartoon, which appeared in the *Pittsburgh Gazette* on July 14, 1905, Rockefeller and his "Traditional Policy of Silence" are burned by the fire kindled by Tarbell's pages. *Courtesy of the Pennsylvania Historical and Museum Commission, Drake Well Museum, Titusville*

Ida Tarbell's history of Standard Oil appeared in book form in 1904, when this picture was taken. Though she was exhausted by finishing the book and the unwanted publicity it generated, she continued her research into John D. Rockefeller's character and other controversial topics, including workplace safety and federal tariff policy. *Copyright © J. E. Purdy / Courtesy of the Library of Congress*

The July 1905 cover of *McClure's Magazine* featured Tarbell's character sketch of Rockefeller. Tarbell's detractors called the article character assassination, while her supporters thought it was an especially revealing portrait. *Courtesy of the Pennsylvania Historical and Museum Commission, Drake Well Museum, Titusville*

By the middle of the first decade of the twentieth century, magazines practicing the journalism of exposure had proliferated. The February 21, 1906, issue of *Puck* illustrated "the crusaders marching embattled 'gainst the Saracens of graft." Ida Tarbell and her colleague Lincoln Steffens are among those pictured. *Courtesy of the Library of Congress*

of Rockefeller's depression buyouts during the 1870s. Both of them later assumed prominent roles in the collision course between Rockefeller and Tarbell.

No matter how many valuable managers Rockefeller acquired during the 1870s, however, his own brilliance as the manager of a far-flung corporation served as the linchpin of success. Long before e-mail and cell phones made long-distance communications easy, Rockefeller calculated how to unify the management of a gigantic decentralized corporation. No procedure at a distant refinery seemed too small for scrutiny; as a result, each refinery found ways to operate more efficiently because of his attention. He then spread word about the efficient innovation to all the refineries.

Years later, as Ida Tarbell studied the phenomenon, she shared her realization with readers: "In the investigation of 1879, when the oil producers were trying to find out the real nature of the Standard alliance, they were much puzzled by the sworn testimony of certain Standard men that the factories they controlled were competing, and competing hard, with the Standard Oil Company of Cleveland. How could this be?" It turned out that the statements of the Standard Oil executives constituted the literal truth. "Each refinery in the alliance was required to make each month a detailed statement of its operations," Tarbell explained. "These statements were compared and the results made known. If the Acme at Titusville had refined cheaper that month than any other member of the alliance, the fact was made known. If the cheapness continued to show, the others were sent to study the Acme methods." When the results were tabulated, Tarbell discovered, any improvement "received credit, and the others were sent to find the secret. The keenest rivalry resulted—each factory was on its mettle."

Operating efficiently saved Standard Oil—helped it thrive, in fact, during the economic depression of the 1870s. While many banks failed as the collateral they held to secure loans lost a significant percentage of its value during the long downturn, Rockefeller could still borrow money readily at low interest rates from the relatively healthy institutions that remained open. While some railroads failed because the industry had grown more quickly than the demand for shipping, Rockefeller could still transport materials to and from Standard Oil's refineries at favorable rates on the surviving carriers.

Although many knew of his shrewdness and respected his power, Rockefeller escaped widespread calumny over three decades for what his detractors saw as predatory business behavior, in part because everybody involved wanted to believe he would engage in fair play. As Tarbell explained after the deed was done, Rockefeller cultivated an aura of goodness as a shield against criticism:

"There was no more faithful Baptist in Cleveland than he. Every enterprise of that church he had supported liberally from his youth. He gave to its poor. He visited its sick. He wept with its suffering. Moreover, he gave unostentatiously to many outside charities of whose worthiness he was satisfied. He was simple and frugal in his habits. He never went to the theater, never drank wine. He gave much time to the training of his children, seeking to develop in them his own habits of economy and of charity." Yet, Tarbell would conclude, Rockefeller secretly "was willing to strain every nerve to obtain for himself special and unjust privileges from the railroads which were bound to ruin every man in the oil business not sharing them with him. He was willing to array himself against the combined better sentiment of a whole industry, to oppose a popular movement aimed at righting an injustice so revolting to one's sense of fair play as that of railroad discriminations."

The adolescent Ida listened carefully to the talk about Standard Oil at home, on the street, and at the anti-monopoly gatherings. She internalized impressions of Rockefeller based on his visits to the Titusville area: "The men who had fought [Rockefeller] so desperately now stared in amazement at the smiling, unruffled countenance with which he greeted them. Did not the man know when he was beaten? Did he not realize the opinion the Oil Regions held of him? His placid demeanor in the very teeth of their violence was disconcerting."

Ida watched her father turn from an easygoing companion into a somber and even depressed man. She wondered whether the family would lose its Titusville home, the fruit of her father's oil industry prowess:

"I remember a night when my father came home with a grim look on his face and told how he with scores of other producers had signed a pledge not to sell to the Cleveland ogre that alone had profited from the scheme." Ida noticed that many other nights, her father seemed silent and stern, even following his after-dinner cigar, "which had come to stand in my mind as the sign of his relaxation after a hard day." Sadly, she recalled how he "no longer told of the funny things he had seen and heard during the day; he no longer played his jew's harp, nor sang to my little sister on the arm of his chair the verses we had been brought up on."

Franklin Tarbell could have cast his lot with the Standard Oil trust, as so many independent oilmen from the oil region eventually did. But mindless conformity was not his way, just as it would never become his daughter's way. Ida wrote later: "Dignity and success lay in being your own master, owning your own home. I am sure my father would rather have grubbed corn meal and bacon from a piece of stony land which was his own than have had all the luxuries on a salary." One of Franklin's complaints against the Standard Oil Company was that "it was turning the men of the Oil Region into hired men—mighty prosperous hired men, some of them, but nevertheless taking orders."

The anti-monopoly talk around the Tarbell home and around greater Titusville started Ida thinking deeply about a larger American world. "There was born in me a hatred of privilege—privilege of any sort. It was all pretty hazy, to be sure, but it still was well, at fifteen, to have one definite plan based on things seen and heard, ready for a future platform of social and economic justice if I should ever awake to my need of one."

Ida Tarbell felt a distinct calling at an early age, albeit in a different manner from John D. Rockefeller. She did not yet see how she could make her views heard across the country. But her ambition was every bit as consuming as that of the oil tycoon from Cleveland. Further education provided her with at least part of the answer. Yet few colleges accepted women in 1875. As Rockefeller consolidated his grip on the oil business, finding a college that would enroll a woman became seventeen-year-old Ida's first challenge.

||||||||||||||||||||||||||||||||||||||||||||||||||||||||||||||||||||||||

CHAPTER FIVE

Lost, and Found

The second half of the 1870s featured a duel between the forces of corruption—in politics and in the business sector—and a fledgling reform movement that would become full-blown populism only thirty years later.

The Civil War hero Ulysses S. Grant was leaving the White House. The Democratic Party hoped to replace the Republican Party's Grant with Samuel J. Tilden, the governor of New York State. Tilden had been involved in combating political corruption since his teenage years, and the Grant administration had earned a reputation for being especially corrupt. Despite his public service, Tilden struck even many of his supporters as cold and aloof. Not many people seemed to like him, but almost everybody seemed to respect him. Rutherford B. Hayes, the governor of Ohio, Rockefeller's home state, won the Republican nomination. Although he had held a Civil War command and earned his law degree, Hayes seemed to be an intellectual lightweight. His extroverted nature had always won him many friends, however, so when he had first sought a seat in the U.S. House of Representatives and later the Ohio governorship, he had won handily.

A decade after the Civil War, the country was still grappling with the status of former slaves and the treatment of the former Confederate states. The nasty Tilden-Hayes campaign did nothing to heal wounds. The election results caused further tension: Tilden won the popular vote and apparently a majority of Electoral College votes, but Hayes ended up occupying the White House after a specially created commission sorted out the validity of competing ballots from Florida, Louisiana, and South Carolina. The Democrats and the press labeled this "the stolen election."

Although Ida Tarbell was still young and removed from the centers of power, she followed the election closely, finding the unprecedented process fascinating. Rockefeller, with eighteen years' more experience, a sharp mind, but a narrower range of interests than Tarbell, appeared to view politicians such as Hayes and Tilden primarily as the means to an end, the end being greater reach and fortune for Standard Oil. Rockefeller maintained a low profile in electoral politics, leaving it to other Standard Oil executives to contribute openly to pro-business candidates. During the last half of the 1870s, Standard Oil kept growing rapidly. But Rockefeller managed to operate the company pretty much out of sight of government and journalists, thus avoiding an outcry about what might have been considered predatory practices.

At age seventeen, Tarbell wanted desperately to get involved in the political and business worlds. Her father's travails, plus those of his compatriots in the Petroleum Producers Union, had given her a sobering glimpse of corporate power and its ability to destroy the dreams of individual entrepreneurs. Idealistic as well as gifted, the teenage Tarbell had a vague notion that she wanted somehow to right those wrongs. Her diaries from the period and her autobiography reveal a sense that she wanted to make the world a better place.

She believed that completing a college degree would serve as a vital first step—in becoming independent, in moving away from home (no matter how loving), in studying with worldly professors. She worried, however, that her father's cyclical earnings, tied to the vagaries of oil production, might be unable to pay for her education. Furthermore, few colleges accepted women, and those that did rarely accepted them on an equal basis with men.

Tarbell hoped to attend Cornell University, in Ithaca, New York, which had opened its doors to women in 1872, after five decades of male-only education. As she prepared her application, she met a man named Lucius Bugbee at her parents' home. A college graduate, professor, banker, minister, and former president of schools for women in Cincinnati, Evanston, and Cooperstown, Bugbee had been hired to lead Allegheny College in Meadville, Pennsylvania, only 30 miles from Titusville. Affiliated with the Methodist Church, Allegheny had started admitting women in 1870, many decades after its founding in 1815 and just before Cornell. Matthew Simpson, the church's most influential bishop and an early Allegheny faculty member, supported Susan B. Anthony and Elizabeth Cady Stanton as they campaigned for women's suffrage. Simpson wanted to admit women to Allegheny not only to rescue the college financially, but also because he sincerely believed in equality.

A generation earlier, Esther Tarbell had hoped to attend Allegheny College but had not been able to because of the ban on women. She thought Allegheny would be an excellent choice for her daughter. Franklin Tarbell expressed concern about the tuition, but Bugbee helped sway him, emphasizing that Ida would be only one day's buggy ride from home.

Impressed by Bugbee, Ida relegated Cornell to the back of her mind, working out a rationale favoring Allegheny. "It was near home, it was a ward of our church," she reasoned. "It had responded to the cry of women for educational opportunity and had opened its doors before the institution I had chosen. Was not here an opportunity for a serious young woman interested in the advancement of her sex? Had I not a responsibility in the matter? If the few colleges that had opened their doors were to keep them open, if others were to imitate their example, two things were essential— women must prove they wanted a college education by supporting those in their vicinity, and they must prove by their scholarship what many doubted, that they had minds as capable of development as young men. Allegheny had not a large territory to draw from. I must be a pioneer." She began preparing for the entrance examinations, which required proficiency in Latin, Greek, modern languages, English grammar, algebra, geometry, history, natural philosophy, botany, and physiology.

Before Tarbell's enrollment in 1876, nineteen women had attended Allegheny over six years—a smaller number than Bugbee had hoped, and only two had graduated. Adelle Williams served as one of the pioneers. The daughter of a faculty member, she had formed friendships with male students at her parents' campus residence before she enrolled. Jonathan E. Helmreich, an Allegheny College professor who acted as the institution's historian, commented that the young men "at first resisted the entrance of women as degenerating their institution into a 'bloomin' female seminary.'" But because "they already knew one of the interlopers, their resistance soon evanesced." Mary Chesbro, a Meadville native, entered with Williams. Her physical beauty "dispelled the notion that female students were 'blue stockings,' dull and unattractive," Helmreich said. Williams and Chesbro found it aggravating to accept "the sharp supervision by the elders of their gender," Helmreich noted. "These ladies—faculty wives and others—kept a firm eye on the girls, admonishing them if they saw their glances straying toward the boys or if they laughed too loudly, did anything to attract attention or dawdled after class to mingle. Yet within a term or so, mingle they did. And graduate they did."

Six years later, Tarbell was the only woman in her freshman class of thirty-two; none had entered the year before. The junior class included two women among its fifteen members, and the senior class had two women out of twelve total. Every professor was male.

The trip to the college took a full day, either by horse-drawn carriage or by railroad, because Tarbell had to switch trains at Corry. This meant that she needed lodging, but the college provided a dormitory for men only. As a result, she moved from private home to private home at the invitation of faculty wives, even lodging briefly with President and Mrs. Bugbee. She appreciated the hospitality but found it difficult to relax. "To sit at the table daily beside a president of a college was a trial that no kindness could quite assuage," she commented.

At Allegheny, Ammi B. Hyde turned out to be the most memorable professor she stayed with. Hyde, who taught English and the classics, was "so queer we were inclined to laugh at him, so full of knowledge we revered him," Tarbell recalled. A physical fitness devotee as well as a raconteur, a minister as well as a professor, he intimidated the young woman, no matter how hard he tried to put her at ease: "He lived largely among the Greeks, the Latins and the philosophers, and I was still too frightened to follow with my meager equipment into his fields." Hyde's wife and young daughter befriended Tarbell, but she never felt totally comfortable.

Finally, a seven-room boardinghouse, informally called the Snow-flake because of its white paint, opened for Tarbell and other women, including a few who had enrolled in Allegheny's new preparatory school. The Snowflake faced the back of Culver Hall, the men's dormitory, with about one hundred residents. Curfew kicked in at 10 P.M. but could be difficult for campus authorities to enforce. "If we had not been fairly well brought-up girls and our housekeeper had not been a good deal of a dragon, we might have made much more mischief for the faculty than we did," Tarbell recalled. Men sometimes entered the building and remained there undetected by college staff. Wayne Whipple, a contemporary of Tarbell's, recalled sneaking in on one occasion, aided by his sister, who lived at the Snowflake. "A tall prep miss named Ida Tarbell warned me that I must instantly evaporate" because a faculty member was patrolling the hallways, Whipple said. Tarbell's memoirs reveal that she apparently refrained from physical contact with men, partly because of shyness, partly because of fear that even the appearance of impropriety could lead to expulsion.

During sophomore year, Tarbell and about twenty other women moved into a rundown building called the Black Maria. Its inadequacies were so painfully obvious that college administrators moved quickly to find a substitute. They bought Bunce House, actually an aggregation of small houses connected to one another. Tarbell lived in a corner room on the first floor, with a side window that helped her see the comings and goings of the female residents as well as the occasional unauthorized male visitor.

Moving onto a college campus focused Tarbell's attention on national and world affairs during the centennial of the United States, in 1876.

But although the campus served as an excellent place to discuss current events, for the most part Tarbell found it a tranquil environment to expand her mind through classical education in the classroom. She found Bentley Hall's architecture wondrous: "It was the first really beautiful building I had seen, a revelation, something I had never dreamed of." Ruter Hall impressed her less architecturally, but, she said, "in this stern structure I was able to find a second deep satisfaction—the library. In a room on the top floor, the library displayed not only the splendid Bentley collection, but also one even more valuable, from Judge James Winthrop of Cambridge, Massachusetts, rare volumes from the great presses of Europe . . . They lined the great unbroken inside wall, as well as every space between openings." Tarbell enjoyed "looking out on the town in the valley, its roofs and towers half hidden by a wealth of trees, and beyond it to a circle of round-breasted hills. Before I left Allegheny I had found a very precious thing in that severe room—the companionship there is in the silent presence of books."

Adopting a positive outlook, Tarbell decided to make the best of her conspicuousness as a woman on campus. Instead of trying to downplay her gender—a difficult task given her height, at least five feet eight inches—she wore clothes that stood out. She and her mother designed and sewed the outfits. Later she recalled a dress she wore to classes during freshman year, "a tightly fitting black alpaca redingote, down to my instep in front, a tiny train behind. It was trimmed with forty-eight white pearl buttons." She wore a scarlet felt petticoat with black silk scallops and embroidery. The petticoat became public knowledge because poorly maintained walkways on campus forced Tarbell to lift her hem while negotiating the uneven terrain.

The men designated portions of the Allegheny campus as their domain, and Tarbell decided to respect those restrictions. "From the first," she recalled, "I was dimly conscious that I was an invader, that there was abroad a spirit of masculinity challenging my right to be there, and there were taboos not to be disregarded." She learned about one of the taboos when, between classes on a warm day, she sat under a tree on the campus green below Bentley Hall. One of the few senior women at the college noticed her and caught her attention from afar. "You mustn't go on that side of the walk," the beckoner said. "Only men go there."

Male and female students suffered alike through the long winters in unheated classroom buildings. Sometimes they wore mufflers to chapel to ward off the chill. Tarbell tried to treat the cold stoically, focusing on her studies. Bugbee had increased the faculty and the course offerings. By the year of her matriculation, students could choose courses from the Schools of Liberal Arts, Science, Latin and Modern Languages, and Hebrew and Biblical Literature. Tarbell's freshman curriculum covered botany, zoology, chemistry, geometry, trigonometry, Greek and Roman history, and literature. Before graduating, she also studied calculus, geology, mineralogy, physics, logic, astronomy, meteorology, art criticism, international law, U.S. history, and economics. Her book learning, supplementing her real-world experience to come, placed her at an advantage over the less formally educated Rockefeller.

Most of the Allegheny professors treated female and male students equally, as long as they took their studies seriously—or at least Tarbell left the college with that perception. Jeremiah Tingley, head of the natural science department, became her chief inspiration among the faculty. Born in 1826, he had taught at three other colleges before joining the Allegheny faculty during the Civil War. He had also accompanied the renowned scientist Louis Agassiz on field expeditions. Tingley's outlook led Tarbell to label herself a pantheist, at least for a time, as she searched for a way to meld her mainstream religious beliefs with emerging scientific theories. Pantheism would eventually color her outlook about Rockefeller's fundamentalist Baptist beliefs and how he translated them into his worlds of business and philanthropy. As expressed by Alfred, Lord Tennyson, her pantheistic creed went like this:

> Flower in the crannied wall,
> I pluck you out of the crannies,
> I hold you here, root and all, in my hand
> Little flower—but if I could understand
> What you are, root and all, and all in all,
> I should know what God and man is.

Tarbell looked forward to invitations from Tingley and his wife for suppers of venison or duck accompanied by stimulating conversation. A childless couple who had traveled all over the world, collected beautiful objects, and constantly sought new knowledge, the Tingleys inspired her to live enthusiastically while learning. She visited the couple often in Bentley Hall; the Tingleys had converted some of the spacious classrooms to their living quarters. "The people I had known—teachers, preachers, doctors, businessmen—all went through their day's work either with a stubborn, often sullen, determination to do their whole duty, or with an undercurrent of uneasiness," Tarbell observed. They radiated the message, based in the Puritan ethic, that labor is a necessary curse. "It had never seemed so to me," Tarbell said, "but I did not dare gloat over it. And here was a teacher who did gloat over his job in all its ramifications."

Understanding the educational opportunities available at the 1876 Centennial Exposition, Tingley granted Ida time away from the classroom so that Franklin could take her across the state to Philadelphia's Fairmount Park, along the Schuylkill River. The 200-acre extravaganza drew huge crowds to 30,000 exhibits spread over 167 buildings. Ida, whose political and social awareness was developing at a rapid rate on campus, visited the Woman's Building, featuring "the results of woman's labors." Exhibit after exhibit fed her interest in the sciences; she found the Corliss steam engine, powered by separate intake and exhaust valves for each cylinder, especially fascinating.

When Tarbell returned to campus, Tingley asked whether she had seen a newfangled invention called a telephone, whose possibilities had been demonstrated by competing inventors Alexander Graham Bell and Asa Gray only months earlier. When she said she had not viewed that exhibit, Tingley expressed disappointment. As he explained the telephone's potential to his class, Tarbell thought him a dreamer. He turned out to be correct. "How often I heard it said later, 'If I'd bought that telephone stock!'" she commented wryly.

When Tingley learned that Tarbell enjoyed using microscopes, he allowed her to experiment with the binocular version owned by the college. She studied mudpuppies taken from local streams, believing that the foot-long, slimy animal might be a missing link in the evolutionary chain, given its ability to use its gills and one lung to survive in either mud or water.

Latin professor George Haskins provided another strong influence. An Allegheny College alumnus who held a law degree, he labored to convey the relevance of the Roman Empire's rise and fall. Haskins could be searing in the classroom—not in a destructive way, but using sarcasm to bring slothful students to attention, hoping to motivate them. His "contempt for our lack of understanding, for our slack preparation, was something utterly new to me in human intercourse," Tarbell recalled. The people she knew tended to avoid candid criticism as a social courtesy. "I had come to consider that a superior grace," Tarbell said. "You must be kind [even] if you lied for it. But here was a man who turned on indifference, neglect, carelessness with bitter and caustic contempt . . . If it had not been for George Haskins, I doubt if I . . . [would] ever have become the steady, rather dogged worker I am."

Although she studied diligently in college, Tarbell also looked for friendship, and maybe romance. She found college men fascinating. At Allegheny they were everywhere, yet she knew so little about them as a species. "I had come to college at eighteen without ever having dared to look fully into the face of any boy of my age," she recalled, reflecting the naiveté so common among young women her age. "To be sure, I had from childhood nourished secret passions for a succession of individuals whom I never saw except at a distance, and with whom I never exchanged a word."

Whether Tarbell became romantically involved—no credible evidence has emerged of an attachment—she was never at ease with the notion of falling in love. Fraternity members offered her their pins. Unsure what etiquette should prevail, she handled the situation awkwardly. "I resented the effort to tag me," she said. "Why should I not have friends in all the fraternities? And I had; I accumulated four pins and then, one disastrous morning, went into chapel with the four pins on my coat. There were a few months after that when, if it had not been for two or three non-fraternity friends, I should have been a social outcast." Women constituted some of her non-fraternity friends. Tarbell bonded with a few of the women ahead of her in college. Then, during her sophomore year, seven young women entered the freshman class, providing companionship.

A quiet but natural leader, Tarbell decided that her class should place a boulder on campus as a monument to learning. She organized the search for an appropriate rock, supervised the difficult transport, rallied her classmates after the freshmen unkindly rolled the boulder to the bottom of a steep ravine, and then, after it had been restored to its campus spot, helped choose the Latin phrase that would distinguish it. "Spes sibi quisque" has been translated as "Everyone is his/her own hope," but Tarbell preferred the variation "Your hope lies within."

Finding other talents, Tarbell joined a campus women's literary society named for Margaret Fuller Ossoli, an adventurous thinker and writer who had died in 1850. The social life of the male students revolved around competing literary societies—the Allegheny and the Philo-Franklin. The societies fielded competitive debating teams, met on a regular basis to hear orations from members, and studied parliamentary procedure. Neither opened its membership to women, so the women formed the Ossoli group. The Ossoli society invited male students to an annual formal gathering with faculty chaperones. Tarbell seemed to feel more at ease during the all-female occasions, on some of which the women dressed as men. At one gathering, she wore her brother's military clothes.

Tarbell wrote for the Ossoli society's publication, *The Mosaic*, and she contributed articles to the campus newspaper, which previously had an all-male staff. Her presentations to the Ossoli group won her its prize for excellence during her sophomore year. Tarbell believed her calling to be science, not writing or public speaking, but she wanted to excel at everything available to her in college. For her senior oration, she explained and praised the realistic fiction of Charles Dickens, an excellent writing model, for its ability to "teach human nature and how to understand it," while dismissing romantic fiction as a "grotesque collection of fancies."

"It was in Ossoli that we found our best opportunity for free discussion and free exercise of whatever little talent we might have as writers," she said. Studying Elizabeth Barrett Browning's life for an Ossoli presentation, Tarbell realized that sometimes fame was bestowed on those who never sought it—even women in a male-dominated society. Such a thought gave her hope that she too might have a greater impact than ordinary individuals.

The campus newspaper summarized a Tarbell presentation in the moralistic language she would use all her life: "She showed that our present results had been brought about by toil and perseverance. That to every age had been entrusted something to develop whose light has been the peculiar work of that period. She spoke of the great interest manifested in women's education and how variously this subject has been viewed in the ages. She touched a chord in every true man or woman's heart when she said 'teach woman that she must be educated, not for man, but for her Creator.'"

Tarbell's reference to the Creator both suggested and masked the turmoil in her mind about organized religion. Her parents taught Sunday school, and in Meadville she herself taught at the local Methodist church. She attended chapel regularly at the college as required, including the evangelical revival meetings. She appeared compliant to those attending the gatherings, but inwardly—unlike her parents and unlike Rockefeller—she found herself doubting the details of the creation story. It might work as a bedrock for faith, but as a matter of logic she found it riddled with holes. Tarbell's mixture of traditional thought and independent reasoning almost always served her well during her long life. Thus, when the time came to research Rockefeller, she could respect his devotion to the Baptist Church while explaining how he relied on that devotion as a questionable rationale for his rapacious business practices.

Unlike some other Allegheny students, Tarbell did not resent the cognitive dissonance flowing from a more or less secular education on a church-affiliated campus. She remained loyal to the college for the next sixty years, serving on the board of trustees, helping to mediate faculty controversies behind the scenes, donating books and manuscripts, and speaking to classes. When the first women's dormitory opened, it carried her name.

By the time Tarbell graduated from Allegheny College, on June 24, 1880, she found herself thinking frequently about society's problems and solutions. But she felt unsure how to proceed. Teaching school was a standard choice for a college-educated woman in 1880 who wanted to work outside the home. Aching to make a difference on a major scale but uncertain how to do so, Tarbell had never seriously explored alternatives to classroom teaching.

During her senior year, she received a visit from three men serving as the search committee to hire a teacher at a Presbyterian-affiliated private school in Poland, Ohio, near the Pennsylvania border, a day's journey from her family home. In contrast to Esther Tarbell's teaching experience during the 1850s, by the 1880s many towns had developed public school systems financed by a combination of local property taxes and funds from the state legislature. The learning tended to be rudimentary, however, leading many families to prefer private, often church-affiliated schooling from grades one through twelve. Poland had become the site of a Presbyterian-affiliated school in 1830, but that school closed in 1845 because of financial difficulties. Four years later, B. F. Lee, an Allegheny College graduate, decided to start the school anew, first with no church affiliation, then with help from the Methodists, and later with assistance from the Presbyterians. Coincidentally, William McKinley was an early student, whom Ida Tarbell wrote about when he became president of the United States.

Lee was seeking a teacher in 1880 because Miss E. M. Blakelee, the preceptress, who had taught there since 1849, had retired. Tarbell agreed to accept the position, but she failed to understand how difficult it would be to satisfy the school's trustees, parents, and students, who believed Blakelee could do no wrong. Nor did she grasp that the trustees intended to save money with their offer of a $500 annual wage, a reduction of $300 from Blakelee's earnings.

When Tarbell visited Poland, she recalled, "I found the village delightful. It had an air of having been long in existence, as it had. Here there was no noise or railroads, no sign of the coal and steel and iron industries which encircled it but had never passed its boundaries. Here all people seemed to me to live tranquilly in roomy houses with pleasant yards or on nearby farms where there were fine horses and fat blooded sheep, and where planning and harvesting went ahead year in and year out in orderly fashion."

She received the employment offer on July 9, 1880. She taught her first class on August 23. Poland Union Seminary was a combination high school and junior college by today's standards, offering continuing education for area teachers too. As the lead teacher, Tarbell had to offer lessons in geology, botany, arithmetic, geometry, trigonometry, English grammar, Greek, Latin, French, and German. The burden turned out to be so crushing that she suppressed her pride and asked the seminary president to assist in the classroom. He refused, limiting his role to "conducting the chapel with more or less grandiloquent remarks," Tarbell said. The teaching load seemed weightier still as she heard comments like these about her predecessor: "So it's you that's taking Miss Blakelee's place. You have no idea how badly we feel about her resigning. I went to school to her, my father and mother went to school to her. I had hoped all my children would go to her. She was a wonderful teacher, a beautiful character. You look pretty young. You haven't had much experience, have you?"

Within a month, Tarbell decided to resign. She confided in Clara (Dot) Walker, the daughter of a seminary trustee named Robert Walker, a prominent banker, who talked to her in private and persuaded her to stay. Newly determined to succeed, she found solace in how much she learned while preparing her courses. She hoped the school would serve as a way station for a career as a biologist. At that point, she could not have predicted that the confidence she gained by mastering so many disparate subjects would prepare her so well for a career as a nonfiction writer.

Living in Mahoning County, Ohio, taught Tarbell other lessons that would eventually influence her muckraking. Poland, dependent on agriculture rather than oil, began to decline environmentally as industry moved in. The iron mills and the coal mines brought "the destruction of beauty, the breaking down of standards of conduct, the growth of the love of money for money's sake, the grist of social problems facing the countryside from the inflow of foreigners and the instability of work," she wrote. She saw the beginnings of slum housing in Poland and in the larger Youngstown, 10 miles away: "Strange that [one substandard area] should be in a place such as Poland, but here it was—a disreputable fringe where a group of men and women had long been living together with or without marriage. You heard strange tales of incest and lust, of complete moral and social irresponsibility." She learned about unsafe factories when a nearby iron furnace blew up, spewing molten metal that burned workers to death.

Despite her education inside and outside the classroom, despite the accolades she began hearing from her students and their parents, Tarbell left Poland after two years. She could not live easily on the low wage and sometimes found herself forced to borrow money from her parents. Her exhausting schedule left little time for her own microscope work. She no longer felt that her stay in Poland was having a significant impact. Unsure about what to do, she began looking into graduate schools of biology. Meanwhile, at age twenty-four, she returned to her parents' home in Titusville. She busied herself by helping to care for the property; nursing her ailing maternal grandfather, whose wife had died; reading in the Titusville Shakespeare Club; watching the infant children of her brother Will, who had married and was beginning his climb in the oil industry. Like his father, Will refused to join Rockefeller's Standard Oil juggernaut, joining up instead with an independent producer trying to beat the odds.

During Tarbell's four years of college during the last half of the 1870s, the world of drilling, Rockefeller, and Standard Oil never seemed far away. When the Tarbells got together as a family, Ida's mother, father, and brother discussed Standard Oil's increasing dominance and Rockefeller's leadership incessantly. The encroaching quasi-monopoly in the twenty-year-old industry impinged daily on their livelihoods.

As Ida Tarbell was leaving college behind, John D. Rockefeller had just passed his fortieth birthday. Tarbell's place in the world seemed uncertain. Rockefeller, in contrast, knew his place well. He would continue increasing his company's dominance. He would continue accumulating personal wealth as his deserved reward from the Almighty. Never completely self-centered, he would also serve as a steward of that wealth to help the less fortunate in accord with bedrock Baptist principles, to care for his wife, and to make sure that their four children understood the importance of hard work combined with devotion to God.

Not all independents quaked at the thought of competing with Rockefeller. Given Standard Oil's ability to demand favorable transportation rates from the railroads, independent producers and refiners hoping to escape the behemoth's embrace explored pipelines as a transportation alternative. Pipelines could not be laid easily. It was exorbitantly expensive to lay pipe across miles of rugged terrain, especially considering the frozen ground during the winter months, opposition from the teamster wagon drivers who would lose their employment, and political deals that had to be consummated in state legislatures holding the power to grant or withhold franchises.

Rockefeller, confident that Pennsylvania oil would continue flowing from the ground, overcame the obstacles by lobbying key legislators and getting construction money from his sterling relationship with bankers, until he had crisscrossed the region with well-financed Standard pipelines, signing up operators of wells as soon as each new gusher became known. He understood, perhaps more perceptively than anybody else in the business, that moving oil in barrels could not continue to generate maximum profits. "The package often cost more than the contents, and the forests of the country were not sufficient to supply cheaply the necessary material for an extended time. Hence we devoted attention to other methods of transportation . . . and found capital for pipeline construction," he explained matter-of-factly.

In hindsight, Rockefeller lauded the fellow capitalists who financed the pipeline system, noting that it meant cheaper prices for U.S. consumers and enabled America "to utilize the bounty which its land pours forth, and to furnish the world with light." The pipeline construction sometimes masked a dark side, however. If a producer resisted transporting the crude oil through a Standard pipeline at the price Standard named, Rockefeller's lieutenants might refuse to connect the well. If the producer could not afford to store the crude product and if he could not find a transportation alternative, the oil from the well might seep back into the earth.

Meanwhile, two separate pipeline construction plans emerged from the independents. One pipeline would transport oil to Buffalo, New York, where it would then be loaded onto barges bound for the Erie Canal. That route would take only a little business from Rockefeller, but Standard Oil nonetheless moved to impede construction by trying to persuade producers, refiners, and pipe manufacturers not to conduct business with the independent operation. Rockefeller hated competition of any sort; he considered the term "monopolist" a compliment.

The second independent route came from the Tidewater Pipe Line Company, which hoped to carry oil all the way to the coast, first to Baltimore, then to a site near Philadelphia. The Tidewater Pipe Line plan struck Rockefeller as a threat to Standard's hegemony. While building a near monopoly, he had served as a champion of oil industry innovation, spending corporate funds generously to improve storage, refining, and transportation. He felt entitled to respect. But a pipeline to Williamsport in central Pennsylvania connecting to a renegade railroad that would carry crude and refined products to an ocean port meant innovation that Rockefeller could not control, innovation that would harm Standard Oil's profitability.

During the late 1870s, Standard Oil operatives played the xenophobia game, spreading the message that refiners in European nations backed the Tidewater plan, hoping to wrest business from American refiners. Standard Oil operatives also suggested to farmers who granted permission for the pipeline to cross their land that spillage would poison the ground and harm buildings. Rockefeller acted to hamper the pipeline construction by contributing to state legislators who might be willing to halt progress by purchasing land across Pennsylvania to block the right of way. Tidewater refused to cave in, however, and in 1879 began transporting oil despite the unpleasant tactics ordered or allowed by Rockefeller.

The competition did not last long. Tidewater's chief executive, Byron Benson, decided that cooperation with Standard Oil would enrich him more quickly than competition. Soon Standard Oil acquired the stock of the previously independently operated pipeline.

Commenting decades later on allegations that Standard Oil was an octopus extending its tentacles to crush every competitor, Rockefeller said, "Only the uninformed could make such an assertion. It has and always had and always will have hundreds of active competitors. It has lived only because it has managed its affairs well and economically with great vigor." But Rockefeller's biographer Ron Chernow was not so sure. He wrote: "When Standard Oil subdued Tidewater, it again demoralized the independents and suggested that all opposition to the behemoth was a foolish, chimerical dream." It seemed that competitors could exist only if Rockefeller decreed they could.

||||||||||||||||||||||||||||||||||||||||||||||||||||||||||

Discovering the Power of the Printed Word

In 1880, John D.Rockefeller, having just passed age forty, found himself honing a plan not only to dominate the oil industry but also to change the very structure of American corporations. This new corporate entity, termed a vertically integrated trust, looked unstoppable.

The 1870s had been dubbed "the Gilded Age" by Samuel Clemens (better known as Mark Twain). Rockefeller and other men born at about the same time, such as Andrew Carnegie, Jay Gould, and John Pierpont (J. P.) Morgan, were becoming household names because of their corporate predations and the personal wealth that resulted. A culture of technological innovation featuring the "prudent, penniless beginner," as Abraham Lincoln had phrased the phenomenon, was turning into a culture of unregulated corporate growth, often tied to improved technology.

At the office, Rockefeller could not let anything go unremarked. He obsessed over the welfare of Standard Oil day and night, sometimes to the point of insomnia. At his desk, he studied documents divided into two piles. One contained matters already debated by his underlings, who had reached a tentative decision, which they expected Rockefeller to review. The other pile contained matters that needed basic consideration from Rockefeller, who would convey his thinking before the underlings made a decision.

Rockefeller expected detailed reports. In return he offered economical replies, devoid of as many names and other specifics as possible. He knew from the reports he received that sometimes those he hired used unsavory and maybe illegal tactics against Standard Oil's competitors. His language would never allow anybody to link him directly to such tactics. He delegated wisely, and that gave him the ability to deny involvement when attorneys general, prosecutors, and legislators began investigating who did what to whom as the Standard Oil trust extended its reach.

Lewis Emery, Jr., one of the oil region's successful independent oil producers and pipeline operators, regarded Rockefeller as a demon and used his considerable wealth to pursue evidence meant to prove Rockefeller's misconduct in railroad rates, refinery purchases, pipeline construction, and other business transactions. Yet despite his decades of opposition, which included attempts to schedule meetings with the demon himself, Emery never met Rockefeller. John D. insulated himself from unwanted outsiders at Standard Oil headquarters and rarely left his family home when the workday ended.

If Emery could have gained access to Standard Oil files, he would have found memos addressed to Rockefeller that implicated the trust in wrongdoing. William G. Warden, a senior executive at Standard Oil, wrote a telling memo to Rockefeller on May 24, 1887. Although Warden refrained from enumerating specific transgressions, he expressed concern about the trust's unpopularity. "Our public character is not to be envied," he said. "We are quoted as the representative of all that is evil, hard hearted, oppressive, cruel . . . While some good men flatter us, it's only for our money and we scorn them for it and it leads to a further hardness of heart." Warden pleaded with Rockefeller to discuss the situation with Mrs. Rockefeller: "She is the salt of the earth. How happy she would be to see a change in public opinion and see her husband honored and blessed . . . The whole world will rejoice to see such an effort made for the people, the working people." Rockefeller replied in a typically vague way, defusing the expression of concern with a memo that said nothing about the specifics and promised nothing at all.

Rockefeller's ability to spot talented executives (including Warden), his command of human nature, which inspired loyalty, and a near absence of autocratic tendencies enabled him to excel as a manager when Standard Oil was small, and later too, when its vastness strained the imagination. He listened respectfully to dissenting opinions and did not feel that he needed to prevail overtly each time disagreement arose. If he felt strongly about prevailing, he could do so later, privately, thus avoiding open conflict and helping others in the company save face.

Rockefeller believed that every employee performed important work, and he advanced those within the company who demonstrated efficiency, enthusiasm, discretion, and loyalty. The rare outsiders who observed him around his employees remarked how he seemed to know the name of each person without prompting. He had no patience with employees who favored labor unions, but he generally offered wages, salaries, fringe benefits, and pensions higher than the industry norm.

Standard Oil continued to expand throughout the 1880s, sweeping aside the hostility of independent producers, refiners, and transporters in Pennsylvania, where the Tarbell family members still depended primarily on the oil industry for their livelihood. As part of his incentive program, Rockefeller encouraged Standard employees to own as much stock in his company as possible and lent some of them money to purchase shares. Employee ownership spurred further expansion and loyalty to Rockefeller's leadership. Every year Standard Oil bought out more independent producers. Selling out to Standard was a tempting option for independents worried about whether they could continue to survive the reality of a near-monopoly, especially when so many former independents were prospering under Rockefeller's corporate umbrella.

With so much oil and so many byproducts to sell, Rockefeller now faced a new problem—how to dispose of everything profitably. He understood that corporate muscle could win at the well and at the refinery, allowing him to buy competitors or force them to quit by undercutting their prices. It could win when selling to other large corporations, such as railroads. Economies of scale and other efficiencies enabled him to market oil-based lubricants for the moving parts in train engines as well as the passenger and freight cars at the lowest prices. But Standard Oil could not force retail merchants and individual consumers in cities and farm towns to choose its products for home use. To increase the attractiveness of his products, Rockefeller insisted on both reasonable pricing and high quality. He could brush off the label "robber baron," but he would not be labeled "fraud." The memory of his father's swindles was too fresh.

John D. Rockefeller had begun to market kerosene for use in lamps as early as the mid-1860s. Lamp technology had improved over two decades, but low-quality, impure kerosene could cause them to explode, sometimes with fatal consequences. Rockefeller wanted Standard Oil to be known for selling clean kerosene, the kind that would never cause explosions. Tank cars drawn by horses—a Standard Oil innovation that replaced leaky and bulky wooden barrels—could dispense kerosene as needed by the country general store owner or urban retailer.

Looked at strictly as a manager, Rockefeller must be seen as a marvel. Historian Charles R. Morris, after studying the Rockefeller era, concluded in his book *The Tycoons: How Andrew Carnegie, John D. Rockefeller, Jay Gould and J. P. Morgan Invented the American Supereconomy* that the Standard Oil leader "has a claim to be not only the first great corporate executive but one of the greatest ever. He had the rarest of talents for adjusting to each new stage of the Standard's growth . . . He also seemed to see the future plain, and drove relentlessly to put the Standard at the head of the pack, quickly adjusting tactics to each sudden turn in the road . . . He managed to delegate well, but also to remain in close touch with operations . . . building a modern organization that was both highly decentralized and highly unified."

As Standard Oil moved increasing amounts of kerosene and other products, dominating wholesale and resale sales as it had previously dominated refining and transportation, local, state, and federal officials grew more aware of Rockefeller's strength. He felt increasing pressure to account to legislators and government regulators for the corporate tactics he often conceived. Hiding behind corporate secrecy, evasive answers, and occasional outright lies under oath, Rockefeller survived legislative and executive branch hearings about alleged predatory tactics.

Over and over throughout the decades, Rockefeller parried official inquiries with denials about a corporate monopoly or about his hegemony within the corporation. Standard Oil, he said, "always will have hundreds of active competitors. It has lived only because it has managed its affairs well and economically with great vigor . . . The Standard has not now, and never did have, a royal road to supremacy, nor is its success due to any one man, but to the multitude of able men who are working together."

A Clarion County, Pennsylvania, grand jury issued an indictment on April 29, 1879. The charges against Standard Oil read like a litany of generalizations composed by independent oil producers, refiners, and transporters, including price manipulation with intent to create a monopoly. Rockefeller decided to avoid going into Clarion County so he would not run the risk of arrest. As an added precaution, he won a promise from the governor of New York State to refuse any extradition requests made by Pennsylvania officials. In the end, the grand jury ran out of steam when Standard Oil agreed to an out-of-court deal that sounded like a capitulation on shipping rates. In fact the company gave up no advantages, because future rates could still be adjusted for volume, and Rockefeller's company shipped far more products than any of its competitors.

Based on extensive documentation, Tarbell would later write vivid scenes about Rockefeller's refusal to testify frankly about anything involving Standard Oil. For example, during a New York State Senate investigation of trusts, Rockefeller appeared reluctantly and probably resentfully at the committee hearing, "flanked by Joseph H. Choate, [later] ambassador to the Court of King Edward and the most eminent lawyer of the day, and S.C.T. Dodd, a no less able if a less well-known lawyer." Tarbell analyzed Rockefeller's demeanor as well as his words: "With a wealth of polite phrases—'You are very good,' 'I beg with all respect'—Mr. Rockefeller bowed himself to the will of the committee. With an air of eager frankness, he told them nothing he did not wish them to know."

A New York State legislative committee chaired by Alonzo Barton Hepburn labeled Standard Oil "a mysterious organization whose business and transactions are of such a character that its members decline giving a history or description of it lest this testimony be used to convict them of a crime." Rockefeller refused to appear in front of the Hepburn committee. Standard Oil executive John D. Archbold did appear, but refused to reveal the ownership structure of the company, fended off questions by citing advice from corporate lawyers to remain silent, and declined to appear as a witness for a second day. Despite his important duties at Standard Oil, Archbold minimized them by stating, "I am a clamorer for dividends. That is the only function I have in connection with the Standard Oil Company." He and other company executives cited the pending criminal investigation in Clarion County, Pennsylvania, as part of the reason for their silence. After all, they did not want testimony presented in New York to be used against them in an incriminating manner by the Clarion County prosecutor directing the grand jury.

Locating Rockefeller to testify during the Hepburn hearings would not have taxed a detective. He remained at home in Cleveland. Rockefeller managed to devote considerable time to his family despite his deep involvement with every aspect of Standard Oil's business. Haunted by his childhood, he was determined to provide a stable family life for his wife and four children. Cettie was an attentive, loving mother, although her conservative ways, grounded in religious fervor, could make her seem stern. John D.'s religious fervor quite likely equaled Cettie's, but he loosened up around the children. Because he hired associates he trusted at Standard Oil, he sometimes returned from the office during business hours to eat a meal and enjoy family time.

The family lived grandly but not ostentatiously on their Cleveland estate. John D. rode bicycles with the children, taught them how to ice-skate and swim, and played games like blind man's bluff with abandon. Each child learned to play a musical instrument: violin for Bessie and John Jr., piano for Alta, cello for Edith. Cettie and John D. often formed an attentive audience for the quartet.

The estate featured landscaping that had been supervised and sometimes even designed by Rockefeller. Among the many pleasures of his life, other than earning money through the creation of an unparalleled corporation, developing the vast grounds on his residential properties— "the making of paths, the planting of trees and the setting out of little forests of seedlings," as he phrased it—was something he often spoke of. Because he enjoyed the outdoors, he did some of the manual labor himself.

Jules Abels, an insightful Rockefeller biographer whose book *The Rockefeller Billions: The Story of the World's Most Stupendous Fortune* appeared in 1965, harbored no doubt that Rockefeller indeed enjoyed the landscaping. But, Abels noted, even though in Rockefeller's memoir he presents the discussion of landscaping as a diversion from the Standard Oil saga, the bookkeeper portion of his brain "cannot get away from his figures, plung[ing] immediately into a discussion as to how his Pocantico estate makes a bookkeeping profit by growing young trees for a few cents each and selling them to his Lakewood estate for . . . two dollars each."

Already one of the wealthiest individuals in the United States, Rockefeller remained assiduous at accounting for every penny. He might also have kept the lowest society profile of any corporate titan. Primarily because of his religious beliefs, he did not attend the theater or other cultural events or charity balls, leaving society columnists and others trafficking in gossip with nothing to say about him. He remained at home with his family, with a few close friends or church associates occasionally visiting for an early dinner.

Rockefeller rarely generated headlines for his behavior outside the workplace, even though he sometimes surprised those who thought they knew him well. For example, a woman doctor delivered the Rockefeller children, and in return the patriarch financed a clinic for that physician to assist low-income women, an unusual commitment to the downtrodden. After receiving a plea through his beloved Baptist church to help an Atlanta school for oppressed young black women, Rockefeller became the financial angel of what would eventually be Spelman College. Those contributions, starting in the early 1880s, proved Rockefeller to be very much the philanthropist.

Meanwhile, Franklin and Esther Tarbell did their best to thrive financially in Titusville as independent operators while the increasingly dominant Standard Oil Company made it more and more difficult to do so. Their daughter, Ida, the newly minted college graduate and teacher, paid close attention to Rockefeller's tactics while sensing the futility of her life so far. Her ambitions outstripped her opportunities.

At the age of twenty-five, she was approaching old-maid status by the standards of that era—no husband, no children, no wealth, not even gainful employment.

Feeling like a failure after leaving her teaching position, she tried to find comfort at her parents' home. During the 1880s, many unmarried women lived with or near their parents. Ida felt boundless affection for her mother and father as well as her younger brother and sister, both still living in Titusville. But she disliked being a stay-at-home daughter. Despite her love for her parents, she did not want to spend her life caring for them.

In a personal scrapbook, Ida pasted this item clipped from a newspaper: "A saint in church and something else at home is a not uncommon character. But a saint at home is sure to furnish a genuine saint to the sanctuary. The family is a severe test of Christian character." Yet despite her restlessness concerning her family, it was a meeting with a guest in her parents' home that not only changed her life in the short term but also set her on an unexpected path leading to a confrontation with Rockefeller.

Theodore L. Flood, then forty years old, a Methodist minister who sometimes filled in as the preacher at the Tarbells' church, arrived for a meal. He made the bulk of his livelihood editing the national magazine of the Chautauqua Assembly. Ida had never thought about working on a magazine, or even about editing or writing professionally. But she had experienced Chautauqua self-improvement gatherings since adolescence. It "had been almost as much a part of my life as the oil business," she would reflect, "and in its way it was as typically American."

Chautauqua had started as the vision of Lewis Miller, born in 1829 in Greentown, Ohio. A devout Methodist, Miller earned a fortune as a farm implement manufacturer in Akron. Wanting to expand religious education outside the church sanctuary and the Sunday school classroom, Miller conceived of a family retreat that would allow children and parents to bond away from home while expanding their minds within a Christian ethic. It would be a college without walls, providing lifelong learning to nontraditional students. No longer would the bulk of the population need to accept the conventional wisdom that education ended with high school graduation. Studies could continue at home, about one hour per day for nine months to complete one course. Students would organize into local discussion groups, called circles. Those too distant from neighbors to participate in a circle, such as the woman on a Dakota ranch sixty miles from the nearest post office, could still find satisfaction in receiving a certificate after completing a prescribed course of study. Miller persuaded John Heyl Vincent, editor of the *Sunday School Journal*, to share a site in New York State as the joint headquarters of the Chautauqua Assembly and the National Interdenominational Sunday School Institute.

The first educational gathering on the shore of Chautauqua Lake occurred during two weeks in August 1874, the year Ida turned seventeen. Still a schoolgirl, she did not attend that first year. Most of the five hundred or so who did were Sunday school teachers, a significant percentage of them quite likely from the Methodist denomination. Speakers arrived from afar to lecture on a variety of topics as the attentive throng sat on benches under the trees by the lake. Musicians presented concerts, some of them educational in nature, some of them for respite from the lessons. Lodging consisted mostly of tents.

Word of these gatherings spread across the nation, and Vincent and Miller developed the property. Soon families of modest income could stay in furnished cottages along the lake and visitors with more money could reside at the first-class Athenaeum Hotel. When President Ulysses S. Grant visited in 1875, journalists related the Chautauqua saga in story after story. The amenities received publicity, but they were not just for show. Everything at Chautauqua promoted learning. "What they wanted us to have there was the excellent training given in the Bible with all sorts of inviting accessories," Tarbell recalled. "I shall never forget a relief map of Palestine that ran for many rods along the lakefront. We used to romp from Baalbec to Beersheba, shouting out the points of interest, and, when we dared, wading in the Dead Sea. No youngster who knew that map was ever wanting in a Biblical geography examination."

Handsome, charismatic, a powerful speaker, and unrelentingly serious about the educational benefits of Chautauqua gatherings, Vincent captivated hundreds of thousands of citizens seeking knowledge, especially women—the youthful Ida included. The centerpiece of the continuing education program became a four-year commitment to a study circle, the Chautauqua Literary and Scientific Circle. Its members, mostly women, paid for books sent to their homes and then paid for tests about the reading. "Women of that generation had had their natural desire for knowledge intensified by the woman's rights movement," Tarbell recalled, "in which the strongest plank had been a demand for the opportunity for higher education. These women were now beyond the day when they could go to college, but here was something which they intuitively saw as practical. The immediacy of their response was in a degree accounted for by their devotion to Dr. Vincent. I suppose most of the women who frequented Chautauqua were more or less in love with him . . . but most of his audience would have preferred to die rather than reveal their secret passion."

When Tarbell met Flood at her parents' home in 1882, he had recently moved the magazine, with a circulation of about 50,000, and its editorial office from Jamestown, New York, to Meadville, where the printer kept his shop. Flood needed editorial help and found himself impressed with Ida's college-educated mind as well as her familiarity with the Chautauqua philosophy.

She did not warm to the idea of working on the magazine immediately. Still, she needed to earn a salary. She liked the flexibility promised by Flood—two weeks per month in Meadville, leaving the other two weeks with her parents and her microscope in Titusville. Microscopy continued to entrance her: "Never had anything so thrilled me as chasing the protean amoeba. Never had I so gloated over any achievement as discovering under the microscope the delicate foraminifera and mounting them on slides." So she accepted Flood's offer, thinking the arrangement would end quickly when she found a more suitable post. Flood announced the hiring in the magazine: "This unique little paper will be enriched by . . . Miss Ida M. Tarbell . . . of fine literary mind, endowed with the peculiar gift of a clear and forcible expression . . . Her wide ranging and versatile brain, together with her love for children and lively sympathies for Christianity, will make her services of rare value to young people."

One of Tarbell's responsibilities involved helping readers who had joined the Chautauqua Literary and Scientific Circle understand the books they read. Many readers could not afford dictionaries or encyclopedias and lived hours away from libraries. Some of the books on the reading list would have challenged college graduates, such as John Richard Green's *A Short History of the English People* and W. C. Brownell's *French Traits: An Essay in Comparative Criticism.* Vincent and Flood decided to publish partial texts in the magazine, with annotations. Tarbell welcomed the challenge: "I had known from childhood homes and towns where there were practically no books beyond the Bible and the children's spellers. As books had always come after bread in our household, I naturally pitied those who did not have time. So I undertook the notes with the determination to make them as helpful as I could."

In her early months at the magazine, Tarbell recalled preparing "what were called notes on the required readings, translating foreign phrases, writing little biographical sketches, explaining allusions of all sorts—scientific, philosophical, literary. Our efforts to aid brought us an enormous correspondence. There passed through our office day by day hundreds of letters." Always the perfectionist, she could not relax until she had read every proof page. "What if the accent was in the wrong place? What if I brought somebody into the world in the wrong year? Something of that kind happened occasionally, and when it did I quickly discovered that, while there might be many Chautauqua readers who did not have books of reference, there were more that did and knew how to use them."

Working part of the week at home in Titusville, Tarbell quickly realized that she too needed better reference materials close by, so she stayed in Meadville more and more often, relying on the Allegheny College library. At first she slept in the guest room at Flood's home. Later she shared a house with female work colleagues. They spent such long hours at the magazine that they paid the mother of one tenant to clean. Tarbell cooked, but only halfheartedly. Reminiscing about those years later, she said, "I could make three or four things very well. I could make a pie crust as flaky as any you ever saw . . . delicious waffles and Scotch woodcock. These accomplishments were in the nature of parlor tricks; I did them occasionally to show off."

Because Tarbell intended to leave the magazine as soon as she could, she might have performed at a minimal level. That was not her nature, however. "I began to see things to do," she recalled. "Dr. Flood had little interest in detail. The magazine was made up in a casual and, to my mind, a disorderly fashion . . . A woman is a natural executive; that has been her business through the ages. Intuitively she picks up, sets to rights, establishes order. I began at once to exercise my inheritance." Soon she was laying out the magazine, trying to make it look better while increasing its ease of use. She tackled letters from readers, which were being handled perfunctorily by Flood with already formatted replies. That bothered Tarbell, especially because many of the letters came from women "who laid their troubles and hopes on our shoulders, confident of understanding and counsel . . . I felt strongly that such an appeal . . . should have a personal, sympathetic letter, and I began producing them, pouring out counsel and pity. I shudder now to think of the ignorant sentiment I probably spilled."

For several months Flood knew nothing of Tarbell's missives, even though she had been signing his name. The secret exploded, however, when a male contributor to the magazine arrived without warning in Meadville to see Flood, to thank him for the understanding expressed in the letters. When he learned that a woman had been his correspondent, he groaned and departed. Tarbell refrained from dispensing advice after that.

In 1885, on her twenty-eighth birthday, despondent about her daily duties and acutely aware that her minor role at the magazine was having minimal impact on the world, Tarbell noted in her diary, "For the first time in my life I am beginning to doubt the blessing that I have always claimed lay in work." She thought about romance but rejected pursuing it or being pursued, writing, "I dislike these men of forty and upwards who persist in flattering girls with remarks like 'a lady who has so many admirers as you,' etc. The best compliment a man can pay me is a willingness to talk sense with me."

Confused about how to move her life forward, she remained at the magazine. Unsurprisingly, Flood became a topic of discussion among Tarbell and her coworkers. Born in 1842 in Blair County, Pennsylvania, he had received his formal education at a local academy, then at Dickson Seminary and Concord Bible Institute. He earned his license to serve as a Methodist Episcopal Church minister. During the Civil War, he reached the rank of lieutenant while fighting for the Union. He served at churches in New England, New York, and northwestern Pennsylvania after the war and wrote a book about Methodist bishops.

Flood could easily see Tarbell's value as an employee. Much like Rockefeller at Standard Oil, with his preternatural calm and polite demeanor, Flood developed his own techniques to make his employees feel appreciated, encouraging them to suggest ever more efficient ways of operating. Both Rockefeller and Flood passed negative judgment on employees who demonstrated less than faithful church attendance, but this was not a problem for Tarbell, who attended church regularly in Meadville and Titusville.

Flood allowed Tarbell to expand her job description pretty much as she pleased. As a result, she received a liberal education, taking her beyond what she had learned in Allegheny College classrooms and in her teaching at the Poland, Ohio, preparatory school. Surprisingly undoctrinaire, Flood opened the pages to many, and sometimes conflicting, viewpoints. Articles by some contributors, female and male, favored work for women outside the home, equal pay for equal work, and untrammeled access to public schools. Other articles advocated opposite positions. During her seven years on the staff, Tarbell edited many of those articles, so she was forced to consider the divergent arguments carefully and come to her own conclusions.

Although she had not been hired to report or write stories, Tarbell's ambition and intellectual curiosity and her desire to change the world led her to develop those skills. During the 1880s, almost no magazine or newspaper allowed women to practice serious-minded journalism. Flood, to his credit, encouraged Tarbell to report for the magazine's pages. She started with brief items for the magazine's standing column, "Editor's Note Book," and worked up to longer features. Her first signed article, "The Arts and Industries of Cincinnati," appeared in the December 1886 issue of *The Chautauquan*. As expected from an upbeat magazine, it praised the city's industries and cultural offerings. Her penchant for recognizing telling details showed up early. Many reporters would have written, as Tarbell did, that "money has been put freely into public works." Not all of them would have then provided specific examples, including dollar amounts of donations for the music hall, museum, and art school. The most vivid details came from her direct observations. Visiting an exposition hall, Tarbell commented how it was "a trial, to temperance people, to find beer bottling the first exhibit . . . and really horrifying to discover that the only sign outside the exposition building was for the same beverage . . . but the brewing and bottling of beer is a leading industry of the city, and the managers of the business, notorious for their worldly wisdom, succeeded in securing the best position in the hall for their display."

For the remainder of her long career as a writer, Tarbell would imbue her articles, essays, and books with moral content, grounded in her unwavering rectitude. That rectitude, while sometimes suggesting inflexibility, drove her instinct for reform, a vital element in her future confrontation with Rockefeller.

Tarbell received an unforgettable lesson about reliability and accuracy while employed at the magazine. The lesson opened with a visit to Meadville by a man who identified himself as Captain Dutton, U.S. Army. An Allegheny College professor impressed by Dutton's supposed connections in Washington, D.C., introduced the officer to Flood and Tarbell, and Dutton ended up as the guest of honor at several Meadville functions. Furthermore, he received two assignments to write for *The Chautauquan*. He submitted the articles, received his payment, and cashed the check quickly. Only then did Tarbell and Flood discover that he was a fraud; furthermore, he had plagiarized the articles. His real identity has never been established.

During the remainder of her employment at *The Chautauquan*, Tarbell grew exponentially as an editor and reporter. She developed her own writer's voice, built on a foundation of impressive detail and undergirded by a core philosophy that "the central principle of things is beneficence," a conclusion she reached from her study of Charles Darwin's controversial theory of evolution. Darwinian theory had begun to take hold as the conventional wisdom in the educated strata of American society. Considered blasphemy by many Christians, it made sense to Tarbell. Rockefeller ignored the spiritual crisis of the Gilded Age by repeating and taking refuge in his religious doctrine. Tarbell, ever the scientist, embraced the spiritual crisis, using it to teach herself and her readers. She viewed the evolutionary process as "the divine method or process by which the beneficent spirit in the universe was to work out its intent."

Because Chautauqua was primarily a Christian enterprise, the organizers could have banned discussion of Darwinian theory in the magazine, the classrooms, and lectures. But, surprisingly, open discussion was encouraged. Education trumped all other values with Chautauqua.

Tarbell soaked up the educational content; in fact, the magazine cut back on its features during July and August so its staff could attend the classroom and stage lectures. The staff produced an eight-page daily newspaper during the height of the learning season, helping to inform the approximately 400,000 visitors who attended Chautauqua summer sessions. Tarbell churned out two columns daily, based mostly on the activities of the previous twenty-four hours. She also assisted the Chautauqua faculty in adapting their spoken lectures for the printed page. She was helped by an intern named John Houston Finley, a Johns Hopkins University student. He reentered Tarbell's life later, as president of Knox College and as editor of the *New York Times*.

Two other Chatauquans came from Johns Hopkins University. Both served as lecturers whose thoughts about history and economics stayed with Tarbell the rest of her life. One, Herbert Baxter Adams, pushed for the acceptance of United States history as an academic discipline. He taught history in seminar style, which was an innovation during the 1880s, and founded the American Historical Association. His students included future U.S. President Woodrow Wilson and scholar Frederick Jackson Turner. Turner's theories of vanishing frontiers as the United States expanded westward would prove tremendously influential at the turn of the twentieth century.

The other Hopkins professor at Chautauqua, Richard Theodore Ely, specialized in labor movements and industrial trusts. Attracted by socialism, Ely believed that the most serious problem facing the American economy was worker-management polarization. Tarbell cared deeply about a level playing field for all laborers, managers, and owners. Although she was no ideologue, she found Ely's research compelling. Ely led her to think about trusts, helping make sense of the experiences of her father and brother as independent oilmen. In a sarcastic letter, Tarbell wrote, "There will come to exist a set of families with common interests. We'll have an Order of the Oyster, an Order of the Olive, the Order of the Poultry, according to the article which it controls. The wealth, policy and privileges of order will descend from father to son. We will have at least a heraldry worthy of the nation of everlasting accumulation. In the Order of Zinc, for instance, we shall have Smith I, Smith II, Smith III and so on from generation to generation."

As Tarbell expanded her intellectual horizons and gained confidence in her writing skills, she made her initial, tentative foray into journalism that explored and sometimes contravened the conventional wisdom. The immediate instigation came from an 1886 article in *The Chautauquan* by Mary Lowe Dickinson, suggesting that women would never become successful inventors. Dickinson based her assertion partly on the small number of patents—334—held by women. Most of those, she noted, had been granted for household articles.

Tarbell could have taken Dickinson's article on faith, but its wrongheadedness spurred her to action. "I had been disturbed for some time," she wrote, "by what seemed to me the calculated belittling of the past of women by many active in the campaign for suffrage . . . I had seen so much of women's ingenuity on the farm and in the kitchen that I questioned the figures." She decided to examine Dickinson's claim for herself by conducting research at a government agency. Her journey to Washington, D.C., to gather facts was the first of many fact-finding trips.

Tarbell located six times more patents held by women than Dickinson had reported. To strengthen her case, she commented that surely some of the most ingenious inventions had never been patented: "If a woman does contrive a useful article, it is ordinarily for her own wants, or doing something 'original.' Her ingenuity usually has no higher ambition. Her life is so circumscribed that she does not see the advantages to herself and family of a patent on her device."

The tone of controlled outrage found throughout her patent story reveals the evolution of Tarbell's unusual brand of female individuality, which would bring her legions of fans when she began writing for national publications. In "Women as Inventors," she made the point that homemakers could be feminists too. Women did not have to shine in the liberal arts or sciences to reach equality with men. The concentration of female inventors in the realms of clothing and household items, she wrote, "is interesting, but scarcely as forcible as it is ordinarily accounted. For if it be true . . . it is no disparagement of [women's] ability. An invention is an invention whether it be for housework or millwork, and the kind of mental quality it requires is the same."

Like Rockefeller, Tarbell grounded her decisionmaking in hard evidence, not in emotionalism. At Standard Oil, Rockefeller insisted that ledgers be maintained precisely. He based his business decisions on a careful analysis of the accumulated evidence. Similarly, Tarbell's articles derived their authority from the government and corporate documents she studied as well as the interviews she conducted. Both Tarbell and Rockefeller established new paradigms for their callings in life. Their reliance on facts was born of the rationalism and scientific outlook that had arisen during the industrial revolution.

Unfortunately, the heavy workload at the magazine meant fewer opportunities to publish in-depth journalism than Tarbell would have liked. After "Women as Inventors," she went fifteen months before publishing her next journalistic account, an unusual piece of reporting about the slow evolution of a government bureaucracy, the Agriculture Department. Single and independent, she became restless. If she left the magazine, however, how should she proceed professionally?

The emotional and sexual lives of well-educated, ambitious single women seemed confusing not just to Tarbell but also to others in the same category. Many professional, unmarried women suffered severe loneliness, but the subject was taboo for women of Tarbell's social class. Some turned to other women for companionship, forming "Boston marriages," a term coined by Henry James in his novel *The Bostonians*, first published as a serial during 1885. But Tarbell felt constrained by almost all companionship, female or male. She was so focused on her work and on improving the lot of humanity that she worried a deep commitment to a specific human being—other than her parents and siblings—would create a burden as she continued her career. Despite the substantial amount of her preserved correspondence, she was extremely discreet when discussing intimacy, and as far as it can be known, she always lived alone or with her sister.

Scholars of womanhood during the nineteenth and early twentieth centuries tend to agree that independent women such as Tarbell felt no need to keep heterosexual romances confidential unless the male was married or a workplace supervisor. As for women who sought out other women, they tended to keep those relationships secret from an intolerant society. Women sexually involved with other women avoided not only public displays of affection but also public displays of what could be called feminism, expecting that if they did not flaunt their personal beliefs while doing their jobs, they would escape judgmental episodes. One conclusion that can be drawn from these trends is not that same-sex love increased during this time, but rather that an increasing number of educated, talented women decided to become less reliant on men.

Whether to become emotionally involved with a nonfamily member, female or male, was no doubt intertwined for Tarbell with complicated feelings about financial security. After attending a church sermon, probably sometime in 1890, she began to think more deeply than before about her need for financial security during her employment at *The Chautauquan*. As she later recalled, the elderly Presbyterian minister had leaned over the pulpit, shaking his fist at the congregation while shouting, "You're dying of respectability." He had tapped into Tarbell's most repressed fear—that she was sacrificing intellectual growth in an endeavor important to her in exchange for the financial security of a job she had never intended to keep for more than a few months.

Tarbell began noticing how vulnerable secure-seeming individuals and families could be. She saw stately homes in Titusville auctioned in public because the occupants had failed to make their payments. She saw Wallace Delamater lose what she thought would be an easy run for Pennsylvania governor, then watched as the electoral defeat caused a run on his Meadville bank. Tarbell even participated in the bank run by withdrawing her own meager savings, a lemminglike reaction that caused her shame. She came to the disturbing realization that her reluctance to leave the magazine had become bound up in receiving a regular paycheck.

Striving to assess her situation wisely, Tarbell saw that "my early absorption in rocks and plants had veered to as intense an interest in human beings. I was feeling the same passion to understand men and women, the same eagerness to collect and to classify information about them." Understanding men and women meant writing about their successes and failures and how those successes and failures accumulated to define American society.

Editing features for *The Chautauquan* helped Tarbell to absorb fresh thinking, as when Frances Willard, a high-profile suffragist and prohibitionist, wrote about journalism careers for women in the July 1886 issue. Willard stressed that next to philanthropy, journalism seemed to be the best professional field for women, because of the opportunities to write about individuals undertaking progressive projects. Until then, Tarbell had not thought of herself primarily as a journalist. She considered the job at *The Chautauquan* a stopgap, a convenient way to make a living until she found a true calling. Willard's article caused her to reflect more deeply about her devotion to writing and editing, to consider applying her missionary and intellectual zeal to the printed word as a career rather than a stopgap.

Tarbell continued the conversation by writing an article on women in journalism for the April 1887 issue of the magazine. The article mixed recent history, details of contemporary practice, and advice. It also provided insights, conscious or otherwise, into her views about gender roles, societal ills, and—ultimately most important for understanding her—how journalists could change the world.

In the article, Tarbell demonstrated wisdom beyond her relatively brief experience. She explained that a journalist must absorb a broad education because story subjects are so varied and sometimes so deep. She also argued eloquently for the connection between 100 percent accuracy and journalistic credibility, a linkage poorly practiced and poorly understood by a significant percentage of reporters and editors during the 1880s and well into the next century. It would take many years for Tarbell's conviction to become the reporting standard, with herself at the forefront.

Concerning gender roles, Tarbell sent mixed messages in the article. Journalism jobs seemed open to women with a modicum of talent and a strong work ethic, she suggested. But she warned that women should avoid abusing their femininity ("presumed on their womanhood," in her phrasing), just as men should not trade on their masculinity, and that they should refrain from shedding tears too easily, thus appearing weak.

An important attribute of Tarbell's article is the attention she calls to numerous accomplished reporters and editors. Among the dozen female journalists she mentions are Jeannette Leonard Gilder (1849–1916), editor of *The Critic* magazine and novelist, and Helen Campbell (1839–1918) of the *New York Tribune*. Gilder, eight years older than Tarbell, became a vocational role model and a soulmate in the realm of political philosophy. Although well educated at a female seminary in southern New Jersey, Gilder did not go to college. Her father died in the Civil War, which led her to enter the salaried workforce to help support the family. Because of a combination of considerable intelligence, capacity for long hours in an office, and a flair for the arts, Gilder made her mark quickly as a writer and editor. Her brother Richard Watson Gilder helped her secure a respectable position at the *Newark Morning Register* and at *Scribner's*, a monthly magazine based in New York City. Jeannette and her brother Joseph B. Gilder served as coeditors of *The Critic* before she assumed sole editorship. A whirlwind of intellect and curiosity, like Tarbell, Jeannette Gilder also composed successful stage plays, translated French literature into English, and wrote essays.

Gilder, and later Tarbell, decided to eschew winning the right to vote for women, using the printed word instead to institute societal change. In "Why I Am Opposed to Woman Suffrage," Gilder wrote, "In politics I do not think women have any place. The life is too public, too wearing, and too unfitted to the nature of women. It is bad enough for men . . . Many of the women who are enthusiastic in the cause of suffrage seem to think that if they are given the power to vote, every vexed question will be settled, every wrong righted . . . If women vote they must hold office, they must attend primaries, they must sit on juries . . . What will become of home life? . . . Who will look after the children? . . . Read the life of any great man, and you will see how much of his greatness he owed to his mother . . . Open every field of learning, every avenue of industry to her, but keep her out of politics."

Campbell's influence on Tarbell was more directly connected to the exposé of Rockefeller. Born the same year as Rockefeller and thus eighteen years older than Tarbell, Campbell wrote about two distinct subjects. Many of her articles delved into the role of women as homemakers—how they tended to act, how they could act differently, and the differences they could make in society by performing their tethered responsibilities creatively. "Every science is learned but domestic science," she wrote. But many of Campbell's pieces explored the ills of society away from the family hearth. In 1882, Campbell published *The Problem of the Poor: Quiet Work in Unquiet Places*, a collection of articles which had originally appeared in the magazines *Sunday Afternoon* and *Lippincott's*. The preface says, "Our poor are fast becoming our criminal class and more and more it is apparent that something beyond preaching is required to bring order out of the chaos which threatens us. Industrial education seems the only solution to the problem." During her research, Campbell visited slums and followed those who could find employment to their workplaces to understand the conditions as well as to humanize those normally out of sight to the wealthy. Five years later, Campbell published *Prisoners of Poverty: Women Wage Earners, Their Trades and Their Lives.*

Tarbell described Campbell's reporting as "thrilling pictures of the life of the poor of New York City . . . It is the duty of one-half of the world to find out how the other half is living, and no means can be more effective and far-reaching than that which Mrs. Campbell is using." In her estimation, the best journalists viewed the craft as a calling, offering "large opportunities for doing good, for influencing public opinion, and for purifying the atmosphere of the times." Moral reform could be achieved better by female journalists than by male journalists, Tarbell believed. She began seriously considering becoming one of those women journalists.

Tarbell expanded her argument in the August 9, 1890, issue of *The Critic,* writing, "There is hardly a single issue of a single newspaper in which the most erroneous opinions in regard to vital matters do not find expression." Such erroneous opinions needed to be counteracted, she said, noting that "there is not a single missionary field upon which a woman can enter that is more promising or more important than that of establishing among plain people throughout the country the habit of thinking clearly and soundly on the one thousand and one questions on which they are forced to give their opinion, either directly or indirectly by their vote." She called on women to train well for the task: "A woman who holds a ready pen and who is so fortunate as not to be obliged to rush into journalism for her support should feel, it seems to me, a strong sense of obligation, first, to fit herself for entering journalism, and then, if she still feels the desire to do so, to enter it as a very sacred calling."

There were many requirements to becoming a good journalist, according to Tarbell. Writing talent helped but would not be sufficient.

Education, including at least two years of studying political economy at a first-rate university, mattered most. Additional qualities Tarbell described fit herself—no mistaken thoughts about glamour, an ability to thrive despite periods of drudgery, a large capacity for work, good health, versatility, dependability, a never-flagging curiosity, logic, and devotion to accuracy of fact as well as to context. As Tarbell so often did throughout her career, she warned women against trading on their gender while suggesting that they might be their own worst enemy: "Tears are not a part of the journalistic capital. An editor . . . has no leisure for 'feelings' . . . When a woman enters journalism she must not put forward her femininity to such an extent as to demand that the habits of the office be changed on her account."

As the 1880s neared an end, Tarbell, battling her restlessness at the magazine while evaluating whether to venture out as an independent journalist, recalled her father's idea that it is better to control one's own destiny than to become a hired hand. "I suspect [my father's] philosophy working in me was at least partially responsible for my revolt against the kind of security I had achieved on *The Chautauquan*," she reflected. "I was a hired girl."

Tarbell compiled a list of women from history "who seemed to offer food for reflection." Among those was Germaine Necker de Stael, who had lived through the French Revolution and died in 1817. Her intellect, lively salon, and influential friends had made her a celebrity in France, and increasingly throughout Europe. Tarbell profiled her in the July 1889 issue of *The Chautauquan*. The profile, though not altogether approving, revealed Tarbell's skill in portraying strong women. It includes passages about de Stael's superiority to her husband ("The baron's chief claim on posterity's attention is that he was the husband of his wife") and to Napoleon Bonaparte ("He was a muscle, she an intellect. He had no guns for riddling ideas").

Tarbell decided after extensive research that de Stael, though admirable in many ways, was too self-centered to serve as the ultimate role model. She turned next to the life of Madame Manon Marie-Jeanne Philipon Roland (1754–1793), of French Revolution renown. Roland had distinguished herself not only by her actions but also by the words she left behind. Her extensive correspondence during the bloodshed opened a rich vein for historians. In Roland, Tarbell met a female historical figure worthy of lavish attention: a revolutionary killed by political opponents, the suicide six days later of her husband, the futile death the next year of Roland's fellow revolutionary and lover. Tarbell began with a brief profile in the March 1891 issue of *The Chautauquan,* "The Queen of the Gironde," then made a momentous personal decision to continue mining the rich material. Finally, at age thirty-three, Tarbell had found her intellectual reason to seriously consider departing from the magazine—to research and write a full-length biography of Roland.

A falling-out with Flood in 1890 contributed to this resolve. He first upset the usually self-effacing Tarbell by placing the name of his nineteen-year-old son, Ned Arden Flood, above hers on the masthead. Then something else, something unspeakable, occurred. The exact nature of that something is hidden. Tarbell held on to the secret the rest of her life, just as Rockefeller held on to the secret of his father's bigamy. The difference is that the bigamy surfaced anyway, while Tarbell's secret remains buried.

Although Tarbell's departure seemed amicable on the surface—Flood wrote her a letter of recommendation calling her "a high-minded, honorable Christian woman whose strength and force of character I have learned to admire"—she referred to the troubles after she left the magazine as "the affair" or "the Meadville incident." She mentioned her "disagreeable feelings about that episode." She feared Flood's influence, no matter where she landed. "What astonishes me," she wrote to her family, "is that the Lord evidently means to let me have a chance in spite of the doctor."

The incident was probably of a sexual nature rather than simply an accumulation of slights. Nowhere else in Tarbell's voluminous correspondence, on any subject, is there anything comparable to the fear of Flood and the vituperation leveled against him. She told her family not to let Flood "worry you into any kind of retaliation." Even after that general admonition, she was concerned that her brother might seek revenge.

When Flood ran for the U.S. House of Representatives, the year after she left the magazine, she wrote to her parents that her brother Will "must be careful not to let the personal side get a start. He at least must stay out of that for my sake, but on the grounds of decency, honesty, etc., [Will] surely can have all the material he'll have time to use. Work quietly, but keep it up." With uncharacteristic bitterness, Tarbell said of Flood, "I don't care if he does go to Congress, he'll break his neck as sure as there are moral laws governing things, sooner or later, and he might as well do it in Congress as anywhere. He is one of those men who don't need to be helped to destruction. He's bound to kill himself unless, indeed, he sees the evil of his ways."

Flood lost the congressional election. He lived into his mid-seventies, dying in 1915. Tarbell, wanting to avoid crossing his path, decided to cross the Atlantic Ocean in the summer of 1891. Her destination: Paris, the city of her dreams and the place where she could best research Madame Roland's life for her biography.

Tarbell wanted her independence, and the Chautauqua experience had further convinced her that she wanted to make an impact on the world around her. She still had no clear idea how that would happen—nor that Rockefeller would serve as both the vehicle and the subject matter.

Far from Home, Close to Home

By the time Ida Tarbell left the place of her upbringing, John D. Rockefeller had made a momentous decision to do the same—involving not Paris but New York City. Although he retained his family's beloved Euclid Avenue home in Cleveland, plus the 700-acre Forest Hill estate, originally constructed as a medicinal resort, Rockefeller relocated his wife and children to a new primary residence in New York City in 1883.

Business operations beckoned. His Standard Oil managers told Rockefeller that running the company from separate headquarters in Cleveland and New York City made little sense. Those he had hired and trusted to oversee the New York operation wanted his genius nearby. Rockefeller grasped that keeping track of a far-flung empire would be easier from the communications center of New York City than from the less well connected Cleveland; he felt sentimental about Cleveland but would not allow that sentimentalism to overrule wise business practice.

Other corporate leaders made the same decision around the same time. Edwin G. Burrows and Mike Wallace, in their book *Gotham: A History of New York City to 1898*, note that during the 1880s, New York City banks and Wall Street firms found the big trusts—with Standard Oil as the model—attractive investments compared to the smaller manufacturing enterprises that had previously received the bulk of financial backing. The New York financial institutions' relationships with the trusts provided plenty of rationale for the leaders of those trusts to live in Manhattan or close by. Furthermore, New York City offered experts, especially lawyers who devised new ways for the trusts to profit. Thus Andrew Carnegie relocated his family from Pittsburgh, Collis P. Huntington arrived from California, and the Armour family shifted from Chicago. Soon after his own move, Rockefeller enabled other Standard Oil executives to move from Cleveland to New York. A reserved railroad car delivered them to the metropolis. Rockefeller met them at the train terminal, treated them to a meal, then matched them with real estate guides, who took them to view houses for sale.

With his move to New York City, Rockefeller harbored no intention of becoming an absentee husband and father, as his own father had been. Before 1883, his wife and children had accompanied him to New York for stretches of weeks or even months, residing with him first in the Windsor Hotel, later in the Buckingham Hotel. It now felt like time to purchase a family home.

In consultation with his wife, Rockefeller bought a relatively modest four-story brownstone mansion on West Fifty-fourth Street near Fifth Avenue. Although he possessed great wealth, he shunned ostentation; unlike many of his fellow industrialists, he resisted owning a private railroad car and a yacht. He did not attend the opera or mingle in high society. He often rode the elevated train from his home to the Standard Oil office at 26 Broadway, a new building that opened in 1885 without a trace of the corporation's name on the exterior. Rockefeller did enjoy his recreation, however, so he spent money to create an ice-skating rink next to the family home. He also constructed a horse stable a few blocks from the family brownstone and took his trotters and carriage into Central Park for sightseeing and racing. In essence, he created opportunities for himself and his children to enjoy the same recreational pursuits they had come to enjoy in Cleveland.

In Cleveland, Rockefeller continued to support his elderly mother, his business associates, and the Baptist church attended by those who tended to idolize his religious fervor. As a practitioner of Baptist evangelism and egalitarianism, he never faltered in his philanthropy to Cleveland institutions, including those benefiting women, blacks, and downtrodden whites. According to his painstaking calculations, he increased his charitable giving from $61,000 in 1881 to $119,000 in 1884, much of it in and around Cleveland. Those amounts would keep rising, and the geographic spread would keep increasing.

Rockefeller decided to expand his horizons in other ways too. Normally content to travel within the United States, he visited Europe for the first time at age forty-seven. Accompanied by his family in what he intended as a well-deserved adventure vacation for all, Rockefeller tried to drive the daily operations of Standard Oil from his mind while crossing the Atlantic Ocean, but with little success. Before the ship even docked in England, he sent a message to one of his executives asking about the ups and downs of oil prices. He sent additional messages from land before the end of the vacation, which included stops in France, Germany, and Switzerland. Three months seemed like a long time to surrender control.

Worried about overspending on the vacation despite his vast wealth, Rockefeller dismissed the tour guide for overcharging. In the middle of the journey, he commandeered the financial arrangements. He did not speak French but possessed plenty of self-confidence, and his son recalled him studying each bill carefully, trying to determine whether each item had been added correctly. "Poulets," he would say. "What are poulets, John?"

As at home, Rockefeller stayed away from theaters and music halls, which represented weakness and sin to him. He preferred scenic views, consistent with his appreciation of natural settings at his estates, and religious shrines, consistent with his devout persona. A curious person, Rockefeller undoubtedly absorbed much useful information while traveling through Europe. What perhaps surprised him most, however, was the celebrity that followed him from country to country. Local newspapers announced his arrival. Letters from ordinary citizens awaited him

at the hotels he chose to lodge his family. The letters reportedly sought
money, or scolded him for business practices, or praised his business acumen. Both thoroughly and politely, Rockefeller shipped the letters back
to New York City, where he eventually read them and replied. As his
biographer Ron Chernow concluded, "For a man who had fled to Europe
for a peaceful interlude, it must have been startling to realize that his
fame and notoriety were now so widespread in a world dominated by
Standard Oil that he could no longer find refuge anywhere from his own
reputation."

Tarbell, in contrast, traveled to Paris anonymously, a celebrity to no
one. She started her adventure inauspiciously, nearly missing the departure of her ship on August 6, 1891. Reaching the New York City area
just hours before the scheduled launch, she boarded the wrong ferry and
ended up at a Jersey City pier two miles from the correct point. After a
last-minute scramble, she made it on board. She viewed the hectic, fascinating cavalcade as thousands of travelers and well-wishers crowded the
pier. The less fortunate passengers riding in the steerage portion of the
ship spoke at least a half-dozen languages. During the Atlantic crossing,
leaving her cabin in tourist class, she studied these passengers as unobtrusively as possible, her relentless curiosity in overdrive, noticing the
family togetherness that abounded despite their uncomfortable quarters
and their ability to entertain themselves with song and dance.

Within hours of embarking, Tarbell wrote the first of many letters
to her family, signing it "Your loving traveler, Ida M. Tarbell." Always
one to fill each day with projects, she was surprised by her indolence on
board: "I never knew the possibilities for laziness in my makeup before.
I am as entirely cut off from all sorts of interests as I am from the land.
I don't think, read, talk, care. I suppose it is good for me." She could not
push The Chautauquan and Flood from her mind, however, writing, "If I
needed anything more to cure me of my disagreeable feelings about that
episode, I've found it."

Although Tarbell had steeled herself against romantic involvement,
she did entertain such thoughts on ship. Three men voyaging with common purpose—a visit to Carrara, Italy, to select marble for a commercial

building—showed her pictures of their wives. The architect, the marble dealer, and the civil engineer treated her like a lady of great interest. She felt flattered. Tarbell wrote about one of them, "He is one of the most thoroughly refined and highly cultured men I have met in a long time. He is rich and of fine family and modest as a child. He has a wife and three boys, alas! But we are great cronies."

While sightseeing in Antwerp before boarding a boat for Paris, Tarbell characteristically tried to fill every minute with absorbing something new. She viewed the paintings at the prominent art museum, then rode a merry-go-round "to the music of a full orchestra, ate waffles, jumbles, hot candy and cakes [just made] by the hands of funny Flemish girls and boys . . . and pegged balls at the rag figures. It was a wild, jolly scene." Worried that her family might think her frivolous, she felt compelled to add, "Do not be horrified. I am seeing things, not changing my habits." Indeed, thoughts of home were never far removed from her mind. The job she had abandoned, relationships with men, not to mention the expansion of the Standard Oil trust and John D. Rockefeller's power base there—Tarbell thought about each on a regular basis. Describing the roofs of Belgian harbor city homes as seen from the boat, she said they looked "exactly like Standard Oil tanks." She then commented, "I grew pale to think of that combination swallowing Belgium, too."

On the trip to Paris, as fellow passengers from the United States began singing "Home Sweet Home," "Jesus, Lover of My Soul," and "America," the usually stoic Tarbell counted herself among those "weeping on everybody's bosom." Unconfidently calling herself a "middle-aged wanderer," she recounted how she "broke up worse" than when she had "kissed mama goodbye."

Keeping perspective, she told herself over and over how many Americans had made the journey to a new life in Paris, although single women in their midthirties constituted a relatively small percentage of them. Given the time and the significant expense required to cross the Atlantic Ocean by ship, a lot of the American visitors could fairly be called "idle rich." Unlike the idle rich, however, Ida Tarbell had saved almost no money and had no interest in meeting royalty or participating in late-night revelry. She wanted to sharpen her research skills and complete her proposed biography of Madame Roland.

Before she could begin researching, however, she needed a place to call home. She arrived in Paris with about $150. Less than a decade before she would start researching her exposé of perhaps the wealthiest individual in the world, she was living in self-imposed near-poverty. Tarbell had devised a budget, though: "In the ten years I had been trying to support myself, I had learned that the art of spending money is quite as important in a sound financial program as the art of earning it . . . I had applied my principles to my small salary on *The Chautauquan*, never over one hundred dollars a month, well enough to get myself to Paris." She was counting on a small reserve "while I was proving or disproving that I could convince a few American editors whom I had never seen that my goods were worth buying."

Tarbell had persuaded three friends from home to move to Paris to share rent (she could be remarkably persuasive). Josephine Henderson had also grown up in Titusville; like Tarbell, she had graduated from Allegheny College and worked at *The Chautauquan*. Tarbell described her as "a handsome woman with a humorous look on life—healthy for me. I have never had a friend who judged my balloons more shrewdly or pricked them so painlessly." Mary Henry, another coworker at *The Chautauquan*, had been raised in the Silver Lake, New York, household of a militant Women's Christian Temperance Union leader. Annie Towle completed the quartet. An Evanston, Illinois, friend of Henry's, Towle apparently made the move on a whim. The three women referred to the organized, take-charge Tarbell as "mammy," despite their similarity in age.

Before leaving the United States, Tarbell had researched Parisian lodging and decided that living in the Latin Quarter, on the left bank of the Seine, would be the most sensible choice. Rents seemed reasonable, and apartments bordered on the university campus. She decided to look for lodging near the Musée de Cluny: "Not that I knew a thing about the musée or what was in it; simply, Cluny was one of the words that had always pulled me." When she arrived in Paris, reality struck: finding affordable, suitable rental housing is rarely easy in any cosmopolitan city. After three days of searching, Tarbell wrote to her family that "we found bugs at one [apartment], odors at another, hard cases at another, endless stains in another." Eventually the four women moved into a relatively clean but cramped second-floor apartment on Rue du Sommerard, a quiet street a few blocks from the grand boulevards, the Pantheon, Notre Dame Cathedral, and the Sorbonne.

Moving quickly to generate income as a freelance writer, Tarbell sent dispatches from Paris to newspapers across the United States, hoping some of them would publish her words for pay. Normally a private person, she shared an unusual amount of detail about settling in Paris, from which it is possible to know a great deal about her day-to-day living. The *Sunday Oregonian* in Portland published one of those detailed dispatches under the headline "Four Girls in Paris/A Great Co-operative Success/ The Experience of Young Lady Students in Housekeeping in the French Metropolis."

"We had a liberal allowance for one year's study," Tarbell said of herself and her three companions. "We wanted to stay two [years], and we determined to do it by economy and good management." The unfurnished apartment they rented cost $15 a month for two bedrooms, a salon, a kitchen, a big closet, and a hall. The four women spent only $80 for furnishings, because, Tarbell explained, "a French room with its pretty ceiling and walls, its chimney-piece, always surrounded by a mirror, and its hardwood floor is not difficult to make look well with very little furniture. Your kitchen, too, is furnished entirely, save stew pans and the like." She lauded the secondhand shops of Paris and how the contents allowed her "to make wonderful articles from little or nothing." She and her roommates created "a marvel of a low couch" from four steamer trunks, a thin mattress, Turkish curtains purchased for two francs per yard at the Bon Marché, and four pillows "in artistic covers which at night in white slips served for the beds."

Just outside the entrance to the apartment, Tarbell found a breakfast of coffee and rolls for four cents at the milk shop. None of the women took much satisfaction in preparing the evening meal, but, Tarbell reported, "as we learned the habits of the Latin Quarter, we discovered that it was not necessary to do much or any cooking. The baker roasted our meat for two cents a time. At the bouillon shop we had vegetables cooked." Tasty fruit could be found easily and bought affordably. As for dessert, "no one ever bakes pies, cakes or bread in a private house in Paris," not with all the excellent patisseries dotting the city.

To improve their language skills, Tarbell and her roommates "adopted a French evening, when the young French girls who wanted to learn English came for exchange lessons—one hour in each language. We each took private lessons, too, and as we gained knowledge we gained determination, and after a few months we talked almost exclusively in French."

Madame Bonnet, the landlady, rented mostly to expatriate Egyptians, especially students of law, medicine, or diplomacy from well-to-do families. The proximity to Egyptians immediately expanded Tarbell's horizons; she wrote her family about the fascinating people also lodging at Bonnet's, including Prince Said Toussoum, a cousin of the khedive, Egypt's ruler: "We all shared the American flutter over titles, and when we caught a first glimpse of the prince and his friends we were still more excited. They were quite the most elegant looking male specimens so far as manners and clothes went that any of us had ever seen . . . We had come to study the French and had dropped into an Egyptian colony."

The Egyptian men—multilingual, well-educated, privileged, handsome, with playboy tendencies—returned the curiosity. Egyptian women of their class would not dare to live in Paris unescorted. Meeting the Tarbell contingent in Bonnet's salon on a Sunday, the Egyptians suggested dancing. The four women, reared as observant Methodists, expressed shock that anybody would dance on a Sunday. Tarbell heard the men whispering in French that these women must be very religious. "It was just as well," Tarbell recalled, "they should have that idea to start with. Better than starting with the degree of intimacy they might see in our dancing in their landlady's salon on a first meeting."

Bonnet began hosting a weekly gathering for her tenants, at which she served dinner. Tarbell's concern about respectability in her private life did not stop her from discussing her relationship with the Egyptians:

"We used them rather shamelessly to impress wandering Americans who looked with badly concealed scorn on the Latin Quarter and particularly on our narrow and stuffy rooms. A prince was our neighbor, we said loftily, and to prove it we could show an autographed photograph which the prince on his own notion had given me." Although the relationship apparently remained respectable even by Tarbell's strict standards, the talk could be frank. "They were eager to know all about our ways," Tarbell recalled, "particularly the life of women, their relation to men before and after marriage. There were would-be reformers of Egyptian marriage customs among them; especially did they resent the convention which prevented them looking at the face of the bride before the marriage ceremony."

While in Paris, Tarbell could have become romantically or sexually involved any number of times, but she almost certainly did not. She never wavered from the vow she had made as an adolescent to remain single. Perhaps because she wanted everybody she knew to understand the ironclad nature of her vow, she felt compelled to explain just about every professional relationship with a man. Writing to her family about collaborating with a freelance illustrator, Tarbell said, "I can work with this young man with propriety, for he is going home in May to be married. I hasten to assure you of that, for my past experience with young men has been so severe that I feared you might worry."

Tarbell enjoyed the companionship of men with sharp minds and was not oblivious to her femininity; she discussed her wardrobe, her hairstyle, and other matters of appearance with her sister Sara. She did not judge herself prudish, at least compared with some others. Referring to a potential roommate, she said the arrangement might fail "because she's too proper to stand in with us. She nearly fainted the other day because one of the girls was talking about one of the gentlemen being handsome. [She] seemed to think it highly improper for an unmarried woman to hold such an opinion."

Despite Tarbell's protestations, rumors floated about alleged romances. Most of them seemed to link her with Charles Downer Hazen, a graduate of Dartmouth College. At the time Hazen, a decade younger than

Tarbell, was a doctoral candidate in history at Johns Hopkins University studying at the Sorbonne. He later became a professor at Smith College and Columbia University.

Tarbell and Hazen shared a passion for Paris; Hazen became so enraptured by France that he would concentrate his research and teaching on the French Revolution and contemporary French culture for the remainder of his life. Tarbell's relationship with him—and the rumors—ripened in Paris, then continued even after both left the city. Tarbell knew about the rumors. As early as March 1, 1892, she wrote to her family that she had met Hazen through Mary Henry. Hazen is "Mary Henry's particular friend—you see, I am careful to explain that he isn't mine." In their written exchanges, Hazen usually addressed Tarbell by her first name, unlike her other male correspondents. She sometimes addressed him as "Downer," a departure from her usual formality.

After both returned to the United States, on December 30, 1894, Hazen wrote to her from Vermont, expressing his melancholy about the distance separating them: "I am doomed to the wretched expedient of writing . . . to you rather than handing over a slice of fried sweet potato for two hours of ceaseless and rapt conversation. What this country needs is a constant example of leisurely enjoyment and I know of few persons in the universe more competent to set such a glorious example than you and I." Referring to a recent rendezvous in New York, Hazen called it "a radiant success, distinctly one of the most notable of modern times . . . My heart has turned into ashes at the thought of having to wait months for another inning." He signed the letter "Sincerely yours, Charles D. Hazen."

They met in a Boston suburb during 1895; Hazen recalled moments "on that private porch in Newton." The next year they met at Clifton Springs, a sanatarium and health spa used by the Tarbell family. In 1897 they saw each other during travels in France. In 1898 they met again in the Boston area. When it appeared that they would fail to meet in 1899, Hazen wrote on August 14, "Fortunately, you are the one woman I have known to whom one does not need to explain things. You take things like a man, as they come and without seeking for avière-feusses and without endless analysis." That same year, Hazen sent a letter with an imagined dialogue:

> Miss Tarbell: Have you forgotten me?
> Mr. Hazen: Pensée mandite.
> Miss Tarbell: Has one of those Smith [College] girls captured you
> at last?

It is unclear whether Hazen and Tarbell ever discussed marriage directly. It is certain that Hazen wanted to marry and father children. On December 4, 1900, shortly after Tarbell turned forty-three, Hazen informed her, "The worst has happened and your faith in me is to be severely tested. I am engaged to Miss Sally Duryea of New York." It is difficult to discern from the remainder of the letter whether Hazen hoped for Tarbell's approval or hoped she would dissuade him. Hazen and Duryea married during 1901. They remained married until his death, in 1941.

Correspondence written by Tarbell's friends and acquaintances speculated about the possibility of romance with men other than Hazen. For example, Henry Wickham Steed, a young British scholar, earned an introduction to Tarbell, bonded with her almost instantly, and then found himself the subject of rumors that they were romantically involved. Whether they did connect romantically is uncertain; what is certain is that Steed and Tarbell remained in contact until her death. Rumors also arose about Tarbell and the Swiss legal scholar Charles Borgeaud. Perhaps most curiously, the name of George F. Southard, a former Titusville resident managing Standard Oil interests in France, also became publicly linked with Tarbell's. She commented about Southard, a married man, "It is the first time I've hobnobbed with a Standard Oil Company magnate," adding, "He's very nice even if he's a monopolist."

It is difficult to know whether the relationships with Hazen and other men in Paris are enlightening or misleading. They look like heterosexual courtships. Tarbell's former apartment mate, Jo Henderson, wrote to her in Paris from her Wisconsin home to say, "I wish you'd marry a foreigner; I want to come and stay a year with you. Hurry, I grow old." Thus it would seem that Henderson almost surely considered Tarbell heterosexual. But while in Paris, Tarbell received an introduction to Madame Jeanne Magre Dieulafoy, an archaeologist who dressed like a man—originally because trousers seemed practical for excavation work, later because she wished to make a social statement. Tarbell commented that her relationship with the married Madame Dieulafoy involved an "amusing flirtation," but never elaborated beyond saying, "She was such a pretty little man, so immaculate . . . that I could not keep admiring eyes off her. She used her eyes, too, and loved to pat me on the knee, partly, I suppose, because I always blushed when she did it."

Madame A, Tarbell's French language instructor, also seemed to be a subject of physical attraction for the expatriate American. (Tarbell never fully identified her tutor in print.) She considered her "a woman of great force, [who] takes unusual interest in her pupils." Tarbell described Madame A as an admitted "character," buxom and fortyish. Madame A, after exhibiting her temper, said, "When you get cross, mademoiselle, break something. You will be absolutely calm after." Tarbell seemed to find that philosophy charming.

Miss C, an American in Paris, formed a needy attachment with Tarbell. The woman, who seemed to be in her late thirties, exhibited a personality Tarbell described as "curiously repellent." Apparently a breakup with a fiancé had altered a happier disposition. In her despair, she began stealing from Parisian vendors. Authorities caught her. When Tarbell heard about the arrest, she exclaimed, "Blast this falling in love anyhow! It causes more trouble than it gives satisfaction. I feel better after that revolutionary expression." Unable to leave Miss C's situation alone, Tarbell got together with her French instructor to orchestrate a defense. They achieved partial success, as Miss C avoided prison. She paid a fine, accompanied by a promise that she would leave France. Tarbell herself could not fully understand why she threw herself into the cause when Miss C was so obviously guilty of criminal behavior. Perhaps the involvement stemmed from an emotional or maybe even a romantic attachment. In any case, Tarbell seemed unable or unwilling to address the question.

Tarbell's behavior with an American visitor to Paris raised questions about her sexual identity too. When Knox College student Elizabeth Wallace, a careful reader of Tarbell's freelance dispatches, visited Paris, Ida dressed in male garb as the two women went strolling along the boulevards. Wallace said later that neither wanted to explore the city without a male companion for safety—but that worry had not arisen before Wallace's visit.

Romance, real or rumored, contributed to some of Tarbell's early entertainment in Paris, but certainly not all of it. The Sorbonne proved to be central to her Parisian existence. As a place of higher learning, the Sorbonne differed drastically from Allegheny College. Whereas the American college kept to a rigid schedule, Sorbonne professors came and went as they pleased, making it difficult for students to predict when lectures would occur. They rarely introduced themselves to the assembled students, instead launching into their lectures without any formalities. Tarbell was patient with the chaos. She could not understand every word of the French she heard, but she usually absorbed the key themes. Professors and male French students generally tolerated women in the lecture halls but sometimes jeered them openly.

During her first term at the Sorbonne, Tarbell attended lecture classes covering political economy, French revolutionary history, eighteenth-century literature, and period painting. The specific information in those courses extended her knowledge base, to be sure. More importantly, she learned research methods practiced by the best historians in France. She heard how to puzzle through gaps in the historical record. She developed tools to weigh contradictory evidence. Accuracy checking became de rigueur. French historians exerted the greatest influence on Tarbell by demanding that she present the best possible evidence in a clear, compelling style; at many other universities, an accessible writing style would not have received emphasis. In Paris, Tarbell developed some of the most powerful tools as a writer of narrative nonfiction.

Given her choice, she would have preferred simply to attend lectures and continue her research into Madame Roland to the exclusion of everything else. The shortage of money, however, rendered that plan inoperable. To pay her bills and control her budget, she shopped for food and clothing bargains; she sought freelance editing and writing jobs as well as appointments to teach English to the French. To complicate matters, she experienced more ill health than she had expected—Parisian water upset her stomach, flulike symptoms hung on through weather to which she was unaccustomed, and her gums ached through periods of no dental care. On top of everything else, when May 1892 arrived, her three roommates left Paris; she had never counted on any of them staying long-term, but she had hoped she might be able to persuade one or more. Paying rent became more of a burden, so she moved to a smaller apartment, at 17 Rue Malebranche.

Despite her relentless work ethic, Tarbell allowed herself to explore Paris, its suburbs, and the French countryside. She could justify that much pleasure. Before she could write about a nation other than her own, she needed to know it better. Watching the cost of every journey because of her tight budget, she ventured somewhere new almost every weekend during her first year or so in France. "Every Saturday we were taking a bateau mouche or train or tram journey costing only a few of our precious sous, to Saint-Denis, the September fete at Saint-Cloud, Versailles. If the weather was bad we went to the museums, the churches, the monuments." In spring, the pleasant weather encouraged a greater range, including weekend trips to Fontainebleau as well as "the great cathedral and chateau towns—Chartres, Beauvais, Rheims, Pierrefonds, Compiègne." Feeling the need, as she would throughout her life, to explain any apparent frivolity, Tarbell wrote to her family after Sunday sightseeing, "You musn't think I am getting Frenchy in my morals because I do things here which I don't at home. I only do these things to see what the French life is really like."

To demonstrate seriousness of moral purpose rather than merely state it, Tarbell resumed churchgoing, complete with teaching Sunday school to children and playing the organ at the American Chapel of Paris. She felt torn between traditional Christian tenets and what for lack of a better term could be called the logic of common sense. She wrote to her brother, "I am just home from church where I heard a senseless sermon on heaven . . . If people who preach would only try to give a little more incentive to stay on earth and behave themselves for the sake of behaving themselves, instead of holding up heaven as a reward of merit, I'd have more hope for the church."

Already homesick, Tarbell felt great anxiety during her second year in Paris when she heard reports that Titusville had been decimated by raging fires that killed citizens and destroyed property. Unfortunately, the reports turned out to be accurate. A dam on Oil Creek, swollen with rainwater, burst, killing seventy-two residents from the Titusville area and fifty-seven from the nearby Oil City area. In the developed portion of Titusville, the fast-moving floodwaters overturned a tank of benzene at a refinery. The benzene mixed with oil leaking from other refineries, the mixture floated on the surface of the rushing water, and then a spark ignited it. The riverborne ribbon of fire swelled to half-a-mile wide. Homes and businesses built of wood caught fire readily. Along Main Street, buildings collapsed all the way from the highway to the creek. Sick with worry, Tarbell finally received a one-word telegram from her brother: "Safe."

Besides worrying about her parents and her siblings, she could do little to help materially except write regularly. She had no intention of giving birth, but she did serve the role of generous aunt to her nephew, Scott, and her two nieces, Esther and Clara, all fathered by her brother, Will. In her letters to the children from Paris, she addressed them as "my sweethearts." Sending a toy Parisian dog for Christmas, she commented "It was the Frenchiest thing I could find."

She wrote to her father separately from time to time, hoping to receive a letter back that did not filter everything through her mother. She was worrying from afar, and knew that her father was worrying at home, about the continuing adverse impact of Rockefeller's Standard Oil Company on the independent producers, refiners, and marketers. Although the Titusville fire had caused so many deaths and so much property damage, it had spared her family and their property, and its impact on Standard Oil operations—by then sprawled around the nation and outside the United States too—was negligible.

Standard Oil had come to epitomize the ways that unregulated commerce within an industry could lead to unfairness for competitors. Domination akin to Standard Oil's also existed in the sugar, beef, and whiskey industries, among others, but Rockefeller's company seemed to dominate the discussion about the large trusts. Potential competitors often failed to establish operations in underserved territories for fear that Rockefeller would outmaneuver and eventually bankrupt or control them.

Congress's creation of the federal Interstate Commerce Commission during the 1880s gave independents brief hope that Standard Oil's predatory tactics might be reined in and even punished by regulators. Congress, however, did not provide the ICC with powers adequate to halt objectionable anticompetitive practices by the trusts, the railroads, or any other powerful business institution. Existing documentation suggests that Rockefeller did not vigorously oppose creation of the Interstate Commerce Commission, realizing that its powers would be limited. In fact, compliance with weak ICC directives could serve as a convenient cover for corporate captains like Rockefeller, who could point out that they were complying with federal laws and regulations. The federal agency could conduct surveillance on transportation rates but could not set those rates on its own. The only remedy available to the agency was to use the federal courts, and lawsuits could drag on for years while the alleged unfair practices continued.

As Rockefeller's biographer Ron Chernow noted, given that Rockefeller "had figured out every conceivable way to restrain trade, rig markets and suppress competition, all reform-minded legislators had to do was study his career to draw up a comprehensive antitrust agenda." But legislators looked the other way. Rockefeller's successful avoidance of potentially onerous government regulation showed his adaptability as well as his dislike of rules aimed at Standard Oil by outsiders.

In 1888, small oil refiners tested the mettle of the Interstate Commerce Commission by complaining about a rate hike by railroads. Previously, the railroads had not charged refiners for the weight of barrels used to hold the oil. Suddenly they added the weight of the barrel to the weight of the oil inside. The practice favored Standard Oil, which could afford to ship its oil in modern tank cars, which were beyond the budgets of small refiners. After extensive hearings, the ICC ordered the railroads to equalize shipping rates for barrels and tanks. The railroads refused, and filed a lawsuit that delayed reckoning for another decade.

Knowing that he had little to fear from government regulators, Rockefeller encouraged a Standard Oil Company practice that paid employees of independent businesses to report proprietary information for the trust's benefit. Tarbell explained the twisted ethic decades later: "The marketing department of the Standard Oil Company is organized to cover the entire country . . . To forestall or meet competition it has organized an elaborate secret service for locating the quantity, quality and selling price of independent shipments." According to Tarbell's research, a Standard Oil operative, "having located an order for independent oil with a dealer," would try to persuade the consumer—a grocer, for example—to cancel the order. If the persuasion failed, the Standard Oil representative would threaten the independent producer or refiner with "predatory competition, that is, to sell at cost or less until the rival is worn out. If the dealer still is obstinate, it institutes an oil war . . . the cutting and the oil wars are often entrusted to so-called bogus companies, who retire when the real independent is put out of the way."

Standard Oil's predatory practices had expanded beyond northwestern Pennsylvania. In 1885, oil had begun to flow from wells in Ohio, where drillers previously had expected to find only natural gas in the fields. The discovery of oil outside northwestern Pennsylvania embarrassed geologists and business speculators, who had discounted the possibility of major deposits anywhere else. As a boomtown atmosphere developed around Lima, Ohio, questions that could not be answered definitively in the short term confronted Rockefeller: Were the Pennsylvania wells about to dry up? If not, how much oil would the Pennsylvania wells continue to produce? Could the smelly, sulfuric Ohio oil be cleansed enough to sell successfully, and even if it could, how long would the underground supply last?

Unlike other Standard executives, Rockefeller expressed no surprise at the Ohio yields, despite his previous concern that the company would run short of oil to market if it were dependent entirely on Pennsylvania wells. As he explained later to his authorized interviewer, Inglis, the oil must have surfaced in Ohio for a divine reason. Rockefeller mixed his religious faith and his business acumen so thoroughly that he could make himself believe that God had placed oil deposits for a deserving entrepreneur to find and then market for consumption by humankind.

In short, during the late 1880s Rockefeller needed to make the momentous, difficult decision about whether Standard Oil should become a major producer in addition to its role as the dominant refiner. He turned to science first. Understanding that the oil found in Ohio needed to be altered in odor and other properties to become widely marketable, he searched for a petroleum chemist, a rare occupation at that time, who could offer a solution. He promised to invest heavily in well-equipped laboratories and handsome incomes to attract the men he needed.

Herman Frasch, a German immigrant, led the effort. Rockefeller's research had informed him of Frasch's success in removing sulfur from oil located in Ontario, Canada. Perhaps the Ohio oil was similar enough in chemical makeup to the Ontario oil that Frasch could succeed again. Using copper oxide, Frasch indeed succeeded, after about two years of experimentation, in removing the rotten-egg stench. The news arrived in a memo dated October 13, 1888, from Frasch's laboratory, sent by a Standard Oil executive monitoring the research: "We are pleased to advise you that by experimenting with the Frasch process we have succeeded in producing a merchantable oil."

Once the odor from the Lima "skunk oil" could be removed, Rockefeller decided that the potential rewards of drilling in Ohio justified the substantial risks. After decades of avoiding the extraction of oil from beneath the earth's surface, Rockefeller proposed to enter Standard Oil in the production sweepstakes. At first he met resistance from other Standard Oil directors. "Our conservative brethren on the board [of directors] held up their hands in holy terror and desperately fought a few of us," Rockefeller recalled. Demonstrating his commitment to exploration in the Lima fields, he offered to invest millions of dollars from his personal account. Accustomed to winning within the board of directors, he had pushed the right button. His fellow directors decided that a financial commitment that passionate must be based on hard evidence. Rockefeller pressed his advantage, persuading his Standard Oil colleagues to develop not only Ohio oil land but also vast acreages in other states where drilling appeared promising. Soon, for example, Standard Oil owned entire counties in West Virginia.

Knowing that new supplies from the Lima fields would be coming to market, Rockefeller ordered the Standard Oil sales force to seek new uses for new customers. Those new markets emerged, with Rockefeller's approval, among commercial building owners switching from coal furnaces to oil heat and among railroad executives willing to switch to oil-burning locomotives from those using coal.

With the oil flowing from wells in more than one state and an enhanced marketing force in place, Rockefeller could turn his attention to building new pipelines and railroad tank cars for transporting the crude and building new refineries for processing the oil. A Standard Oil refinery at Whiting, Indiana, about twenty miles from Chicago, became the largest and most technologically advanced refinery in the industry. The company's directors expressed pride in what it took to achieve dominance, which they saw as a sign of progress, not predatory behavior.

As Tarbell would write, "There seemed to the independents no escape from Mr. Rockefeller in the market." Standard Oil's move into the production realm confirmed their worst fears. The Rockefeller legend grew, Tarbell said: "The ruthlessness and persistency with which he cut and continued to cut their prices drove them to despair." Anecdotes abounded. Tarbell said the independents "told of crippled men selling independent oil from a hand cart, whose trade had been wiped out by a Standard cart which followed . . . day by day, practically giving away oil. They told of grocers driven out of business [after] an attempt to stand by a refiner." Tarbell understood that "probably all" of the anecdotes had been exaggerated and perhaps some of them were false, yet "all of them believed . . . There came to be a popular conviction that the 'Standard would do anything.'"

Ruminating about the independence shown by her father and brother despite the pressures against them, especially those induced by the Standard Oil trust, Tarbell considered writing a novel about the impact of conglomerates. She dreamed up a corporation, M&M Vacuum, sketched specific characters, wrote a plot outline, and drafted two chapters. Midway, however, she decided she lacked the talent for fiction, calling her manuscript "poor stuff. Luckily I soon found out I was beyond my depth."

In addition to monitoring Rockefeller and Standard Oil from across the ocean, Tarbell absorbed horror stories of other American capitalists who seemed to place growth of market share above all else, including the well-being of their workforce. On July 5, 1892, at the Homestead steel factory in Pittsburgh, labor-management strife led to violence and death. Unlike Rockefeller, who tended to treat employees respectfully, Andrew Carnegie and Henry Clay Frick, who had profited immensely from the operation of Homestead and other factories in their industrial empire, bore the reputation of treating workers with disdain.

Much of the steel industry centered in and around Pittsburgh, where Carnegie, four years older than Rockefeller, had arrived as a Scottish immigrant in 1848 at age twelve. Frick, fourteen years younger than Carnegie, grew up in rural Pennsylvania and entered the steel industry through a cousin who owned coal-producing land. As Frick became more deeply involved in the iron and steel business through the energy supply pipeline, he obtained money from Thomas and Andrew Mellon, the powerful father and son Pittsburgh bankers who eventually joined Rockefeller among the wealthiest, most influential men in the nation.

Frick and Carnegie had stirred up resentments among union workers during contract negotiations in the summer of 1892. Anticipating trouble from union laborers, Frick hired approximately 300 gun-toting security guards from the Pinkerton company. Many of the union workers carried guns too. It is impossible to know precisely how the gunfire started on July 5, but the battle continued for hours. Although the number of fatalities is uncertain, twenty-one (perhaps on the high side) is an informed estimate. Whatever the precise death toll, the images of violence remained, influencing labor-management relations, including Tarbell's view, for many years into the next century.

Tarbell could not and did not ignore such dreadful behavior from the greedy men directing dominant corporate enterprises. But she had traveled to Paris for a different purpose—to begin her research in earnest for the Roland biography. Because of her relentless curiosity about all manner of topics, and because she needed to earn cash in the short term from her writing, the Roland book languished for a while.

To promote her writing career, Tarbell determined quickly that she would address an issue of significance to her—the mythical, potential, and actual evils of alcohol. She set the stage for publication of her findings about alcohol consumption with a personal essay in the October 1, 1891, *Union Signal*, the periodical of the Women's Christian Temperance Union. Although already persuaded that alcohol should be banned across the United States, she reported and wrote in a scrupulously fair manner. Alcohol consumption in France seemed benign compared to its effects in the United States. The more she learned while reporting on the issue from Paris, the more she found subtleties; to her credit, she conveyed those subtleties, no matter how unpopular they might be with her readers.

Tarbell could not resist adding moral commentary to her carefully researched journalism, however: "The effects are most difficult to estimate. They are much more subtle and hidden than in America. Reeling, brawling crowds are rare. Dissipated, haggard faces are not common in Paris . . . [But] it has been estimated that one-twentieth of the violent deaths in the country can be traced to alcohol, and one-tenth of the suicides." Tarbell reported that promiscuity among French women, including giving birth out of wedlock and prostitution, could be linked to their absinthe consumption. Furthermore, she speculated on a connection between alcohol consumption and what she termed the pornography available at newspaper kiosks, bookstalls, and photography shops.

Moralistic essays for the *Union Signal* were a publication outlet that Tarbell felt compelled to feed. But she had no intention of limiting herself. She wanted to share so much about the French way of life with American readers. Despite her bad experience at *The Chautauquan*, she carried Flood's letter of recommendation as she sought reporting and writing assignments that would allow her to disseminate her acute observations and defray her living expenses. In person, Flood had demeaned her Parisian plan: "You are not a writer" and "You'll starve," he had told her. In the recommendation letter, however, he termed Tarbell "an accomplished writer of scholarly habit."

Tarbell mailed her first self-syndicated essay from Paris in September 1891. Six newspapers received it—the *Boston Globe*, the *Chicago Tribune*, the *Cincinnati Times-Star*, the *Omaha Bee*, the *Buffalo Express*, and the *Pittsburgh Dispatch*. From the beginning of her efforts, she sold a respectable number of stories. But the pay was usually low. Newspaper editors tended to pay $5 per published piece without illustrations, $6 with illustrations, and gave no guarantee that anything would be accepted. Payment tended to take months, if the check arrived at all. She could not exercise control over the editing, the layout, or the quality of illustrations, which sometimes led to frustration when she finally saw the published version.

Many freelance writers would have considered Tarbell's accomplishments a success. Tarbell, however, did not, and considered giving up. Then, as she phrased it, "The unbelievable happened." Sale of a short story yielded $100 from *Scribner's Magazine*, one of the most prestigious fiction (and nonfiction) outlets anywhere, despite its relatively recent launch, in 1887. Writers from all over the world aspired to be published in *Scribner's*. Acceptance came all the more unexpectedly because when she had arrived in Paris, Tarbell had had no intention of writing fiction. For reasons she could not articulate fully, she wrote and submitted the short story anyway. The story had its genesis in her real-life tutoring sessions with an elderly French couple who lived in Titusville. (She called the man Claude but never mentioned the woman's name.)

After Tarbell decided to move to Paris, she thought that improving her spoken French would be helpful. She visited the couple three times each week before leaving home. "In this delightful association I discovered that the passion of Monsieur Claude, the longing of his heart, was to see France before he died. He had insisted that I learn and almost daily repeat [Pierre-Jean de] Beranger's 'France Adorée.' Once in Paris, I understood him, wrote his story, sent it—a trial balloon—to *Scribner's*

Magazine." It was not a literal tale. "There is only one thing in it which is recognizable, I think," Tarbell commented. "That is the story of the bell made from the French cannon. There is nothing in it which would give offense to Claude himself, I think, if he could read it."

Scribner's editors suggested substantial revisions; Tarbell's tone and pace were not right for fiction, they said. She underwent "mature deliberation for about one-fiftieth of a second" before agreeing to revise, she recalled. Her good fortune bolstered her confidence as well as her bank account. She wrote another short story, eventually published in *New England Magazine* as "A Compatriot," about the ambivalent treatment by American expatriates in Paris of a newcomer to their gatherings, a young female journalist from the United States. She also started sending more queries for her nonfiction.

As Tarbell received assignments and demonstrated the range of her interests, readers saw for themselves the revelatory nature of her insights. She showed special talent for exploring the world of work, rather than focusing, like so many expatriate freelancers before her, on royalty and the extremely wealthy of her adopted city. When still new to Paris, she said, "I had the American notion that the chief economic duty of the poor was to become well-to-do." She soon realized that Parisian workers viewed the situation differently, treasuring even lowly jobs as prideful obligations: "Serious workers in Paris seemed to give to the job the same kind of loyalty that serious men and women in America gave to the businesses they owned. You respected yourself and were respected in proportion to your fidelity to it. You might be advanced, but more probably not. Opportunity did not grow on every bush as at home." Yet the workers Tarbell came to know seemed neither restless nor envious of those in better jobs.

Tarbell's eye for detail and her ever-increasing ability to dig out telling facts came together for her report "In the Streets of Paris." She marveled at the way the French repaired minor imperfections in the streets before they became major problems, so unlike public works in Pennsylvania: "The city is admirably and entirely paved, but nearly four million dollars a year is expended simply in keeping it up. The principle followed is the old and often despised one of a 'stitch in time.' No broken or rough place is too small to receive attention."

Tarbell had no idea that one reader of her insightful dispatches, S. S. McClure, hoped to shake up the American way through an eponymous magazine—the magazine that would eventually allow her to expose Rockefeller to the world. On the other hand, she did sense from afar that as she sent her dispatches from Paris, Rockefeller sat secure. The devastating economic depression of 1893 demonstrated his uncanny anticipation. With other businesses and their owners facing major disruptions or even bankruptcy, with railroads ceasing operation and banks failing, Standard Oil remained cash rich. Rockefeller had reduced the corporation's debt, built up huge reserves, and then scattered the money among multiple banks, hedging against any one bank's failing. In fact, he had decided that Standard Oil needed to serve as a bank of sorts, lending money to other companies in the oil industry, which enabled them to discourage competition from upstarts. As the economic depression deepened, it appeared that all of the United States had grown too fast, shifting from an agricultural base to industrialization without a safety net, except for Standard Oil.

Rockefeller's biographer Ron Chernow concluded that the economic panic "showed him functioning less as a Standard Oil executive than as a sovereign power, endowed with resources rivaling those of government. He continued, however, to operate in the shadows, a spectral figure whose presence was mostly felt, not seen." That sovereign certainly could not have imagined that an upstart periodical called *McClure's Magazine* and a staff writer there named Ida Tarbell would become the bane of his life less than a decade later.

CHAPTER EIGHT

McClure's Magazine

S amuel Sidney McClure entered the world in 1857, the same year Ida Tarbell was born. The two would prove to be more than just contemporaries. McClure would become Ida's often exasperating friend. More importantly, he would provide the platform from which she would publish some of her greatest works.

Born in County Antrim, Northern Ireland, McClure grew up poor but never starving. His parents, Elizabeth and Thomas, tended a small farm near family members; Thomas supplemented his farming income by working as a carpenter. Samuel McClure began his formal education at age four, attending a rural schoolhouse Monday through Friday and half-day Saturday, fifty weeks each year. He enjoyed his school lessons from the start, and his hunger for book learning never abated, as he attests in his autobiography, and as verified by biographer Peter Lyon as well as in the extensive personal papers McClure left behind for researchers.

At age seven, McClure experienced the collapse of his happy world. His father left home to work in the big city of Belfast, because farming and carpentry could not support his growing family adequately. A few weeks after his father's departure, McClure's youngest brother, eighteen months of age, died from diphtheria. Before the year ended, McClure's father died too, after a freak accident in a Glasgow shipyard, to which he had been detailed by his employer. When he died, Thomas McClure was thirty-two years old. His wife was seven months pregnant. After her child was born, Elizabeth tried to support herself and her four sons by farming their nine acres, but without her husband's income she could not provide enough. She moved the family to her mother's home in another town. Samuel McClure, age eight, had to attend a different school, where he never felt comfortable intellectually or socially.

With her family's charity strained and poverty looming, Elizabeth McClure decided she might escape a pauper's existence by following her two sisters and two brothers to the United States. In 1866, when Samuel was nine, she gathered her children and started out for Indiana, where her siblings had settled, with money she had scraped together, primarily by selling the farm. They remained on the ocean for twelve days during the first portion of the journey, which involved passage to Quebec. Samuel Sidney alternated between seasickness and wonderment. On land, the seemingly interminable seven-day train ride to Valparaiso, Indiana, yielded little hope at first. They had used their meager savings for food on the ship and the train. Samuel Sidney and his family lodged with one of his aunts on a remote farm fourteen miles south of town. The small house already held his aunt and uncle, their six children, and his mother's two unmarried brothers.

To relieve the overcrowding, S.S., as the child was called, and one of his brothers moved to the home of Elizabeth's other married sister, north of Valparaiso. The only work Elizabeth could find was as a live-in servant at a household in town. S.S.'s aunt and uncle soon decided they could not bear the expense of feeding two boys, so dropped them off at the home of Elizabeth's employer without warning. Elizabeth could not expect her employer to house and feed two more people, so she had to quit the job. Homeless, she and the boys slept inside a vacant building under repair, squatters in the promised land. Improvising, Elizabeth found four families who hired her to do washing and ironing. With that meager income, she could afford to rent a room in the same block as the vacant building.

A local physician and his wife, learning of the McClure family's plight, offered to provide a room rent-free in exchange for Elizabeth's services as a washerwoman. The physician generously allowed the intellectually curious S.S. to read books from a well-stocked library. *Robinson Crusoe* especially stayed with him as an adventure tale not completely divorced from real-life drama. But the idyll ended within a few months when the physician's family relocated to Indianapolis. Forced to move away from town, the McClures settled on a rural rental property. Elizabeth found work only sporadically, prices for food and other necessities shot up in the booming post–Civil War economy, and the family fell into a state of constant malnourishment.

Within a year, Elizabeth met a man from a nearby farm. Thomas Simpson, also an Irish immigrant, was scraping by, trying to pay off the mortgage on his 100 acres. But he could provide shelter in a house of adequate comfort. S.S. suggests in his autobiography that his mother entered a marriage of convenience. Simpson was able to help provide for Elizabeth, while her growing sons provided ready labor in the fields.

As the eldest of the four brothers, S.S. worked nearly full-time; his stepfather placed earning his keep above schooling. During the winter Simpson relented a bit on some days, so the boy could obtain a hit-and-miss education. The only reading matter at home consisted of a bound volume containing agricultural reports sent from Washington, D.C., by the local congressman. In addition to farm chores, S.S. found his half-brothers and half-sisters distracting; Elizabeth gave birth to four children with Simpson, but three of them died in infancy from enlargement of the spleen.

Determined to finish his education without further interruptions, McClure left home at age fourteen, with his mother's blessing. The move relieved some of the financial pressure from his family, and it gave him the opportunity to attend the newly built high school in Valparaiso. McClure entered Valparaiso from the farm on foot, with only one dollar in his pocket. He had no idea where he would sleep the first night, or any other night. He stopped at each house in town, "asking whether anybody wanted a boy to do chores and go to school," according to his recollection. Someone finally said yes—a man believed to be the richest in the county. In exchange for lodging, food, and time for schooling, McClure arose at five o'clock each morning, built fires in four stoves, cared for the cow and horses, and bought provisions for the meals—all before classes commenced. After school, he cared for the proprietor's grounds until supper. Finally, as darkness arrived, he could usually concentrate on his schoolwork until he fell asleep.

During the summer, when school adjourned, McClure needed to find a steady job. At age fifteen, he could demonstrate enough learning to obtain a position as a teacher in a rural school near Valparaiso. He found the job boring, and disagreed with a policy that required students to recite lessons all day without the benefit of recess outdoors. He quit before the three-month appointment ended. He next worked as a grocery store clerk, then as a newspaper typesetter, then in an iron foundry. Restless, high-strung, and prone to depression, McClure found steady, routine employment difficult.

When his stepfather became gravely ill two years later, McClure felt obligated to abandon his studies and return to the farm to help his mother tend the land. Like so many poor young men of the 1870s, he lacked hope when it came to attending college. His father and his stepfather had died, his mother could not finance a college education, his family needed his earnings, and saving enough money for tuition under the circumstances seemed unlikely.

While doing his best to make the farm profitable, McClure received an unexpected visit from his uncle Joseph Gaston. Studying for the ministry at Knox College in Galesburg, Illinois, Gaston encouraged the young man to join him and seek higher education based on his intellectual prowess rather than formal schooling. Persuaded by his uncle that entry into Knox College was not impossible, McClure, shortly after turning seventeen, bought a train ticket to Galesburg. He arrived with fifteen cents in his pocket, not even enough money for a meal. But he noticed that fields of corn surrounded the campus and felt certain "that food was plenty and cheap."

Officials at Knox College agreed to accept McClure as a student if he completed preparatory lessons satisfactorily, given the gaps in his high school education and the absence of a high school diploma. That would take him three years of off-and-on study, interrupted by bursts of employment to raise cash for his rent and income for his mother back in Indiana.

While in Galesburg completing his preparatory studies, McClure met Harriet (Hattie) Hurd, the daughter of a Knox College Latin professor. The meeting occurred when the lady of the house where McClure was boarding, a minister's wife, sent him to deliver a luncheon invitation to Hattie. Smitten on the spot, McClure hoped to gain Hattie's attention, then to court her. He possessed little money, however, and failed to win the approval of Hattie's father, who envisioned better for his learned, beautiful daughter. Hattie became fond of McClure and did nothing to discourage him. But she feared the disapproval of her father, so usually kept her distance from her suitor.

Hattie graduated from Knox College in 1877 as valedictorian, then moved overseas to study. McClure wrote to her but received no reply. When she returned to Galesburg two years later, she refused to see him, perhaps of her own volition, perhaps on her father's orders. Infatuated, McClure could not stop thinking about her, despite the apparent hopelessness of the situation.

Hoping to quell his obsession, McClure studied hard at Knox College. He worked as many part-time jobs as humanly possible and met fellow students who would play a role in his career, as well as in Ida Tarbell's. When Albert Brady arrived at the college as a freshman, McClure was a sophomore nearing his mid-twenties because of his periodic departures from Galesburg. Brady and McClure first became friends because of their mutual fascination with solving mathematics problems presented in one of their classes. John S. Phillips grew up in a Galesburg family. McClure met him through classwork, then they became friends during student activities, including the *Knox College Student*, a campus newspaper. During his senior year, McClure, without having shown previous interest in journalism, became editor in chief of the newspaper. Phillips served as literary editor that year, Brady as business manager. Phillips and Brady never lost contact with McClure after graduation from Knox College, and eventually they reunited at *McClure's Magazine*.

Hattie Hurd returned to Galesburg during McClure's senior year, 1881–1882, but Professor Hurd continued to oppose a marriage. He persuaded his daughter to move to the East Coast, where a teaching job awaited. Refusing to give up his dream of marrying Hattie, McClure spent almost his entire savings for a train trip to Utica, New York, where she was visiting a friend. But she did not welcome him in Utica, believing the visit to be presumptuous. Certain he would never again see the woman he loved, McClure bought a railroad ticket to Boston on a whim. He had never visited Boston and knew nobody there except a former Knox College teacher, who took him in briefly when he showed up unannounced.

Searching for a job, McClure called at Pope Manufacturing Company, a bicycle maker that had placed an advertisement in a booklet about college newspapering that McClure had published while at Knox. The founder told McClure he had no need to hire anybody. McClure persisted until the founder doled out a one-day assignment—teaching bicycle riding on July 4 at a park on Huntington Avenue. Never having ridden a bicycle, McClure nonetheless showed up for the assignment and received the promised pay of one dollar. Learning quickly and working energetically, he showed up the next day and the day after that, until news of his industriousness reached the founder, who summoned him.

The company was going to start a national bicycling magazine, *The Wheelman*. Albert A. Pope wondered whether McClure felt confident enough to take charge of the effort. Relying on his college newspaper editorship, McClure answered yes. He received permission to hire a staff, and he quickly made offers to his brother John as well as to Phillips. They both accepted. The first issue of the magazine appeared in August 1882.

Finally earning a steady income, McClure tried again to win Hattie's love. He visited her at Andover, Massachusetts, where she was teaching at a private school. After six years of courtship, McClure, who could never be certain of how Hattie felt, learned that she had developed a fondness for him. Hattie informed her father that she had delayed and delayed because of his reservations but would delay no longer. The two were married on September 4, 1883, in Galesburg, despite the continuing disapproval of Professor Hurd.

The couple settled in Cambridge, adjacent to Boston. McClure grew restless at his job, however, when Pope hired a business manager with equal authority to the editor in chief. So S.S. and Hattie McClure decided to seek jobs in New York City, the center of the magazine and book worlds. In 1884, the year after they married, S.S. found a position at the De Vinne printing house, while Hattie took an editorial position at the Century Dictionary firm.

Within four months, McClure left De Vinne—he had learned a great deal about magazine production, but he disliked the chores associated with the printing side of magazines. He found an editorial job at *The Century Magazine*. Hattie left her job after becoming pregnant, and the couple moved from Manhattan to the more affordable East Orange, New Jersey. Their daughter Eleanor was born in July 1884.

During his two-week paternity leave, McClure devised a way of becoming independent of office routine dictated by supervisors. Instead of working for somebody else's magazine, he would launch a syndicate that would sell features to newspapers. The syndicate would target the nation's daily newspapers with short fiction commissioned by McClure. He would pay well-known writers by the story—say, $150—and an estimated one hundred newspaper clients would pay him $5 each to publish the story. McClure believed a number of newspapers would become permanent clients, willing to pay a flat fee of, say, $10 a week to publish whatever they liked from a range of stories he would offer.

McClure had noticed "a tentative experiment in that direction" by Charles Dana at the *New York Sun*, who had paid authors such as Henry James, William Dean Howells, and Bret Harte for publication in his newspaper and other newspapers simultaneously. "To be sure, the thing was in the air at the time," McClure recalled. "Somebody had to invent it."

Persuaded that he needed a New York City address for credibility, McClure, Hattie, and Eleanor left New Jersey after less than a year and returned to Manhattan. The plan did not succeed immediately, despite offerings from well-known writers such as Robert Louis Stevenson and Howells, who immediately liked McClure's plan when he approached them cold by letter. Acceptances from the *St. Paul Pioneer Press* and the *San Francisco Argonaut* gave McClure just enough hope to continue. Hattie did the marketing, edited submissions, and translated submissions from French and German into English. They paid themselves nothing.

Finally the business showed a small profit. After one year as a self-employed businessman, McClure hired a stenographer and rented a downtown office, removing the paperwork and supplies from the family flat. Hattie was pregnant with their second child; they would have a total of four children within six years. After two years in business, McClure could afford to employ his Knox College friend John Phillips, who had continued his studies at Harvard University and in Leipzig, Germany. Phillips knew that McClure's syndicate still suffered from cash-flow problems, but the founder's magnetism, energy, and optimism could not be denied.

Around 1890, with the syndicate earning money, McClure began planning an even riskier venture—an eponymous national magazine featuring quality fiction and narrative journalism. For inspiration, he looked to three magazines from England—*Strand, Country Life,* and *Review of Reviews*—plus *Ladies' Home Journal* in the United States. "They made me think that a cheap popular magazine would be possible in the United States," he recalled. The early 1890s seemed like a smart time to launch a national magazine. Photoengraving technology had lowered the cost of publishing from previous decades, when expensive wood engraving had served as the standard. The new technology would allow McClure to publish an attractively designed magazine while charging a cover price of fifteen cents, less than most of his competitors and affordable to readers hungry for factual accuracy, informed analysis, and memorable writing.

As national wealth grew in tandem with population increases and westward expansion during the 1880s, McClure felt confident that he could attract advertising dollars. He hired Albert Brady, his Knox College friend, away from the *Davenport* (Iowa) *Daily Times,* a thriving enterprise. Brady would serve as McClure's advertising manager. The optimism faded quickly, though, as a cyclical economic downturn led to bank closings, job layoffs, and overall anxiety across the nation during the early 1890s. The timing boded ill for McClure, who was about to retrieve the debut issue of his magazine from the printer.

The depression of 1893 did not come as a complete surprise. Baring Brothers, a large British bank, had already failed because of bad loans made in Argentina. Low crop yields across Europe helped American wheat farmers by providing overseas sales, but hard times in European nations dried up the orders. In February 1893, the Philadelphia and Reading Railroad collapsed financially after expanding imprudently. Then the National Cordage Company, sometimes called the "twine trust," collapsed, shaking confidence in other trusts that had looked so financially stable. Inevitably, Wall Street brokerage firms slipped as stocks dropped, with banks foundering next. Business loans dried up and bankruptcies followed—thousands of them. Businesses able to continue laid off workers, which engendered bitterness and labor-management altercations. Homelessness became epidemic across New York City and in many other cities across the United States. Haphazard government and somewhat more organized church-based relief efforts were largely ineffective in stemming the spread of poverty.

"The panic was like no other panic of recent years . . ." McClure said in retrospect. "As soon as the newspapers felt the pinch of the panic, they began to cut down expenses, and our syndicate service was one of the first things they could dispense with. One paper after another wrote us to say that they would have to discontinue taking syndicate matter."

Although worried about a collapse of the magazine before it could find its audience, McClure pressed on. Some of the magazine's content would come from syndicate contributors, he hoped, which would save money for production and distribution. Additional content would come from other writers McClure admired. Some of those writers would become employees, if McClure could find money to offer salaries. Hardly any magazines used that model in the 1890s. In fact, the practice of having full-time staff writers and editors was so unusual that McClure had no fix on what to call such an employee. He was considering terms such as "associate editor," "staff writer," and "staff associate."

McClure had singled out Tarbell as a potentially valuable contributor to the magazine. Shortly after her arrival in Paris, she had begun offering essays to the McClure syndicate. Her first sale to the syndicate was a piece on weddings held in public view, published under the headline "Marrying Day in Paris." But it was an essay several months later that really grabbed McClure's attention. Tarbell documented the French method of mounting large public works projects titled "The Paving of the Streets of Paris by Monsieur Alphand." After reading it, McClure remarked to Phillips, "This girl can write. I want to get her to do some work for the magazine." McClure asked whether Phillips knew anything about the author. "No idea," Phillips replied, "but from her handwriting I should guess she's a middle-aged New England schoolmarm."

Planning to visit Paris on syndicate-related business during the summer of 1892, McClure decided to meet with his promising contributor. As he remembered the visit, "I called upon her at her little apartment on the river, taking with me some newly discovered information about the Brontës upon which I wished her judgment. I went to see her, intending to stay twenty minutes, and I stayed three hours." McClure remarked how well Tarbell had learned research techniques and theory from French historians. The soundness of her judgments impressed him. Unlike many other male editors, McClure rarely distinguished invidiously between the women and the men who wrote and edited for him. He appreciated inquisitive minds, no matter the gender.

For her part, Tarbell recalled McClure finding her apartment on a "crooked and steep passage." After he entered, she noticed his "shock of tumbled sandy hair, blue eyes which glowed and sparkled. He was close to my own age, a vibrant, eager, indomitable personality that electrified even the experienced and the cynical. His utter simplicity, forthrightness, his enthusiasm and confidence captivated me." She found McClure so galvanizing, in fact, that when he realized he needed cash for the next leg of his journey, to Geneva, Switzerland, Tarbell lent him $40, nearly her total savings, for a train ticket. She despaired about being paid back almost as soon as McClure departed, but McClure returned the money as promised.

The visit settled nothing about Tarbell's role in the proposed magazine. It did, however, begin a professional and social relationship that would last for almost five decades. McClure so admired Tarbell's reporting and writing that he began to commission features from her for the syndicate. Those assignments meant that she was able to worry less about supporting herself in Paris.

"He is deeply interested in the question of French morality and its relation to America," Tarbell wrote to her family, "and we are talking of a series of articles which I am to edit to make a book. Altogether it looks like a good chance and it certainly means that you needn't worry any more about my money affairs . . . All this is at his request, so you see he is in earnest." McClure even agreed to pay Tarbell extra for translating French articles into English for the syndicate, and for finding new writers as the syndicate's Parisian editorial representative.

It was through her editorial duties that Tarbell met August F. Jaccaci, McClure's art director. Educated in Italy and Germany, a resident of Constantinople and London, Jaccaci visited Paris often for work and pleasure, and he impressed Tarbell with his worldliness. "He is a gentleman and very companionable," Tarbell wrote home. "We get on capitally together." She classified their friendship as "something quite apart in my relations with men. Jac had a certain superior appreciation and wisdom never quite put into words, but which you felt." A perfectionist, Jaccaci would express anger even at Tarbell from time to time if her work failed to meet his professional standards. "They came and went like terrible summer thunderstorms," she recalled. "He would roar down the corridor of the office where I sat and watched him, enthralled. Those rages, whether directed at me or somebody else, never made any other impression on me than that of some unusual natural phenomenon."

Tarbell's connection with Jaccaci and others in McClure's orbit linked her to a vast array of sources and subjects. She honed her research and interviewing skills with regular assignments, building her confidence as a journalist. For one *McClure's Magazine* story, she made contact with France's leading intellectuals, including Alphonse Daudet, Émile Zola, and Alexandre Dumas. Her stories for McClure and for other publishers sometimes focused on renowned intellectuals, to be sure, but they also concerned street cleaners and police officers. As a journalist, Tarbell crossed socioeconomic classes easily to learn what she wanted to learn—something a foreigner could accomplish more easily than a French journalist.

In Paris, various science-related stories for her magazine and newspaper clients returned Tarbell to her high school and college enthusiasm for the microscope. "I found that, little as I knew of all these things, I still had something of a vocabulary and knew enough to find my way about by hard work . . . There was Pasteur; there was Janssen, who was building an observatory on Mont Blanc; there was Bertillon, the inventor of the system of criminal identification then attracting the attention of the world." As never before, Tarbell's curiosity and intellect were being challenged, but they were also paying unimagined dividends.

Tarbell's profile of Louis Pasteur consumed thirteen pages of *McClure's Magazine* in September 1893. The reporting demonstrates a relentless curiosity, and although the story uncovers no wrongdoing in Pasteur's career, the piece is a precursor of her successful investigative form. She described complicated discoveries and cures precisely, with surging narrative skill. Tarbell believed she understood Pasteur well enough to relate what he was thinking at precise moments in the recent and distant past.

One of the stories Tarbell found herself tracking involved the global initiatives of Standard Oil. Rockefeller and his executives had finally turned their attention from Pennsylvania and Ohio oil production to international markets—not because they wanted to, but because they felt they had no choice. Just two years after the Drake Well discovery in Pennsylvania, oil entrepreneurs had found ships that would haul the cargo to Europe, despite the dangers from fires and explosions. Europeans wanted kerosene to light their homes and offices, wanted to lengthen their days and nights with manmade illuminants. Rockefeller-built refineries took advantage of favorable railroad shipping rebates to move kerosene to East Coast ports in large quantities. Standard Oil took its cut, then let other distributors profit across the ocean.

That strategy changed after the discovery of oil near the city of Baku in what had been considered an inaccessible region of Russia. The Nobel family, having settled in Russia from their native Sweden, determined how to extract, refine, ship, and sell oil in St. Petersburg and other quasi-European markets within the czarist empire. Rockefeller fretted about being cut out of the Russian market, especially after the Rothschild family from France also became involved in transporting Baku-area oil to European nations.

Standard Oil lacked private intelligence sources in Russia and Europe, but diplomatic consuls sometimes provided information informally or for a fee. As it had throughout the United States, Standard Oil used underhanded tactics overseas if it could not prevail through honest competition. Oil historian Daniel Yergin, in his book *The Prize: The Epic Quest for Oil, Money, and Power*, commented that Standard Oil's "local agents started rumor campaigns in various European countries about the quality and safety of Russian kerosenes. They also resorted to sabotage and bribery." Whatever Rockefeller's role in those tactics, he had no intention of surrendering even a small portion of the world's markets to the Nobels, the Rothschilds, or anyone else. He pushed the Standard Oil executive committee to establish marketing companies in foreign nations.

During the second half of the 1880s and the first half of the 1890s, Rockefeller and his colleagues tried various strategies to gain domination of oil markets outside the United States—negotiating with the Rothschilds, the Nobels, and independent Russian producers in the hope of absorbing them, undercutting prices of the competition, exploring transportation by a newly designed type of oil tanker. Standard Oil made inroads everywhere. But it never dominated overseas markets in the same way it dominated the U.S. oil industry. As the twentieth century approached, even Standard Oil's dominance at home seemed threatened—not by another oil company, but by Thomas Alva Edison's invention of functional light bulbs and the system that made electricity increasingly available to the owners of homes and commercial buildings, especially in big cities. On the other hand, the advent of gasoline-powered motorized vehicles in Europe and the United States—thanks to entrepreneurs such as Gottlieb

Daimler, Karl Benz, and Henry Ford—suggested a potentially lucrative new market, adding to the sales of kerosene.

As Tarbell took notes of the dealings from her Parisian outpost, she sensed that Standard Oil's vulnerability might make for a great story. In the short term, however, she focused on her work for McClure, the work that paid her bills. Nor had she forgotten her research about Madame Roland. Rereading Roland's memoirs in a Parisian setting had deepened Tarbell's understanding of the woman, and she never wavered in her conviction that Roland's life needed to be fully told.

Tarbell's walks to and from the National Library took her through the section of Paris where Roland's father had practiced his goldsmith trade, past the house in which Roland had been born, the church where she received her first communion, and the prison where she had spent her final days. At certain points, Tarbell's path even matched the route Roland had walked to her death by guillotine. "It was amazing how little things had changed," Tarbell remarked.

Like any serious biographer, Tarbell was trying to understand Roland's life as she lived it, not primarily as interpreted through the writer's own era. She felt fortunate that Roland (unlike her later subject Rockefeller) had been a prolific letter writer; those letters helped her understand how Roland had viewed herself. No other individual with such an important role in the French Revolution had left behind so many written insights about the thoughts behind their actions. Tarbell read widely and deeply about the era of the French Revolution. More than coming to know Roland herself, it was Tarbell's exhaustive period research that proved most taxing.

"I began to see the Revolution already well on its way when she was born," Tarbell revealed. "It was rising around her, sucking her in, using her when she thought it had gone far enough and should check its excesses." Tarbell began wondering whether the benefits of such upheaval ever outweigh the costs. Had Roland been heroic or foolish? Was her work of real social value? Then, as Tarbell uncovered information about Roland's personal life, she began to question Roland's motives: Had Roland become a revolutionary because of ideology or to please the man she loved?

Although Tarbell was becoming less enamored of the wisdom of revolution in general and Roland's role during the French Revolution in particular, she drew strength from "the brilliant and friendly intellectual circle into which my quest of Madame Roland had led me." While writing a feature about French women of letters, she received a referral to A. Mary F. Robinson, an English poet married to French scholar James Darmesteter, known for English and French translations of Zoroastrian scripture. When Darmesteter learned about Tarbell's interest in Roland, he wrote a letter of introduction to Leon Marillier, the revolutionary's great-great-grandson. That letter led to a dinner invitation. The dinner in turn took Tarbell into the Roland circle, including Leon's wife, Jeanne, Leon's mother, Madame Marillier, the Sorbonne history professor Charles Seignobos, and several others.

Suddenly Tarbell became part of a rarefied French salon. During Roland's lifetime, she discovered, the competing Parisian salons had drawn "women of fashion, young girls, a few dowagers, would-be poets, the curious, the intriguing." A century later, the similarities outstripped the differences. Tarbell found vibrant, calculating hostesses devoting energy to drawing in Parisians and foreign habitués with intellectual star power. Those special guests would dominate the conversation, perhaps even reading from unpublished writings or performing new musical compositions.

Tarbell enjoyed the intellectualism, the gossip, and the unhurried nature of the gatherings. Though stimulated, she did express mild criticism of French ethnocentrism: "One of the most surprising things to me among the French, high and low, was their utter indifference to the geography of the rest of the world. Why should they bother about the rest of the world? There was only one land about which they should know—that was France, and that they should know to the last corner."

More significant than Tarbell's social standing was the access to Roland's papers, especially the previously unpublished letters, which she gained through her acquaintance with Marillier. What she discovered in those letters gave her the ammunition to contradict previous Roland biographies. As she read further, Tarbell realized that the candid letters undermined portions of the revolutionary's published memoirs. Without any formal training as a biographer, she grasped that every word of the letters, every word of every document, needed to be evaluated. "It has been my business . . . to try to get at the exact truth of various historical events . . . [but] I almost never am able to get hold of material for my work which seems to me entirely trustworthy," she commented. She described trying to locate an accurate account of a riot at Champs de Mars, a Parisian meeting place for discussion about politics. The account by Roland differed significantly from that of the U.S. representative in Paris and of the official investigation. Tarbell decided that Roland, usually precise in her accounts, this time was so anxious to advance her cause "that truth-telling was a secondary consideration."

The more previously concealed information Tarbell read, the more clearly she realized that many of her early impressions had been misguided. The hagiography Tarbell had planned to write turned out to be indefensible. She had originally hoped to make the case, through Roland's life, that women in public service could be, and usually were, simultaneously dependable, opposed to violence, and intuitive. She had hoped to demonstrate that women tend to understand human nature better than men do, given the traditional female role as child-rearer and nurturer.

As Tarbell learned, however, instead of exhibiting these qualities, Roland harbored the grand idea that her fate would determine the revolution's fate. Her promotion of violence caused Tarbell to lose her belief in "revolution as a divine weapon." This would prove a profound revelation to the journalist. "Not since I discovered the world not to have been made in six days of twenty-four hours each had I been so intellectually and spiritually upset," she recalled. She now had to reenvision her biography and craft a new theme to explain Roland's life.

Always worried about paying her bills, Tarbell agreed irrevocably to complete the Roland biography only after a visit to Paris in 1892 by her *Scribner's Magazine* editor, Edward Livermore Burlingame. The son of an American ambassador to China, educated at Harvard University and in Germany, and the holder of a doctorate, Burlingame could seem intimidating. But he and the less pedigreed Tarbell liked each other personally and worked well together on paper. Tarbell asked Burlingame if he would consider printing an illustrated magazine profile of Roland. Burlingame said not only would the magazine be interested, but also that Scribner's book publishing arm would probably be eager for the entire manuscript.

Tarbell understood that the book she was finally set on finishing—as opposed to the book she had originally planned to write—would be unpopular with a large portion of American readers. "What woman in America seeking the vote as a sure cure for injustice and corruption would listen to such a message?" she wondered. She pressed on, though, undaunted by the prospect of controversy.

It was during this period that McClure offered to bring Tarbell to New York City to write for his magazine full-time. He told readers of the magazine's January 1894 issue that he considered the Parisian correspondent "a singularly interesting writer." Privately, McClure flattered Tarbell by saying she had "succeeded marvelously as a writer of special articles" whose information gathering "commends itself to all readers for its accuracy and human interest." He enticed her with the camaraderie of the magazine staff, an ample income, and the promise of an interested readership. McClure added, "We all hope you are not planning to get married and thus cut short your career." Tarbell entertained no marriage plans, but many male editors of McClure's era (and later eras) avoided hiring women, assuming that marriage would lead to a quick departure from the newsroom. It is unlikely that McClure knew about Tarbell's decision to remain romantically unattached. Still, he cared deeply about hiring and retaining extraordinary talent, so his offer to her was unconditional.

In April 1894, Tarbell finally gave in to McClure's persistence. She agreed to begin work at the magazine's New York City headquarters that coming October, before she could complete the Roland biography.

Tarbell took inspiration from Madame Charles Vincens, born Louise-Cecile Bouffe, who wrote under the pen name Arvède Barine (1840–1908). In a profile of Barine, Tarbell wondered why American journalists, especially women, avoided "sustained, brilliant, virile, authentic, biographical, historical or scientific articles." She believed the interest among readers existed, and felt certain that female journalists could conquer the genres, although not easily: "It demands the greatest patience, faith in the outcome of the efforts, and downright hard work. College training with a PhD is not sufficient. An apprenticeship as a reporter and editor is not enough. Severe study with constant writing are the only means."

By accepting McClure's offer, Tarbell was poised to become one of the few full-time magazine staff writers in the United States doing serious, in-depth articles—and almost certainly the only woman.

|||||||||||||||||||||||||||||||||||||||||||||||||||||||||||||||||||||||||

Napoleon

In the late summer of 1894, Ida Tarbell boarded a ship at Boulogne, bound for New York City. She had been out of the United States for three years. Her first stop would be Titusville, Pennsylvania. It had been an age since she had seen her parents, her sister, her brother and his family; had eaten her favorites, such as fresh strawberries, codfish, and toast; had turned the dirt in a flower garden; and had played aunt to Will's children. Before leaving Paris, she had asked her nieces what they wanted as gifts. Clara requested a French doll that could walk and talk. Decades later, Clara recalled that "to me at that time, Paris and Heaven were two adjacent states and Aunt Ida and God were closely related." Clara eventually learned that Ida had spent so much money on the doll that she found it difficult to cover her expenses aboard the transatlantic ship.

The reunion in Titusville was a joyous occasion, but after a few days at home, Ida could not help noticing the background of despair. One of Franklin Tarbell's business partners had died unexpectedly, an apparent suicide, and Ida's parents had been forced to take a mortgage on the family residence. The depressed business climate made it difficult for Franklin to generate the necessary cash for his oil field and oil barrel business operations. Esther had returned to classroom teaching after a thirty-year hiatus to help with the family's finances.

Laboring mightily to keep the Tarbell family and other independent operators afloat, Ida's brother Will had become secretary-treasurer of the Pure Oil Company, a vertically integrated cooperative of drillers, transporters, refiners, wholesalers, and retailers who resisted Rockefeller. Pure Oil, after years of financial uncertainty, became a rare long-term competitor to Standard, despite the huge disparity in operational size.

Ida had followed the oil industry as best she could while in Paris. Will's letters had told her about the regulatory recalcitrance of the Interstate Commerce Commission, from which independent oil enterprises had expected so much. He had described how businesses slid into ruins while they waited for government to act. He told Ida about the Ohio lawsuit that had ordered Standard Oil to reorganize, "a legal victory which in no way weakened its hold or crippled its growth."

Hearing all the talk about Rockefeller and Standard Oil during her family reunion in Titusville caused Ida to resurrect the manuscript of a novel she had begun while working at *The Chautauquan*. She had set the opening chapter in Pithole, the boom-and-bust oil town of her childhood. Back home in 1894, curious to explore the settlement as a journalist, she asked her brother to accompany her to Pithole.

What she saw was devastation. Where a settlement of 20,000 had thrived, she found "only stripped fields where no outline of a town remained." She and Will walked the area all day, "trying to place the famous wells, to fix my father's tank shops, so profitable while Pithole lasted, to trace the foundations of the Bonta House which had furnished the makings of our home in Titusville." The experience left her feeling melancholy about "the impermanence of human undertakings." Instead of being inspired, she despaired of ever being able to recreate the Pithole era effectively through fiction, despite her brief success with the form in *Scribner's Magazine*. "One must be an artist before he can create—that I knew. I was no artist," she recalled.

Tarbell's return to Titusville affected her personal life as much as it affected her professional life. She saw women of her youthful acquaintance, now married, many with children. It was clear to both Ida and her family that marriage would never make sense for her. She knew she was labeled a spinster, but for the first time in American history, educated women around the nation were openly rebelling against marriage, living well materially and emotionally.

Moving to New York City did not worry Tarbell, as it might her Titusville relatives. She felt accustomed to city living after negotiating Paris. Still, every city thrives on its uniqueness if it thrives at all, and she had plenty to learn about her new municipality. Large companies with huge numbers of employees, including Standard Oil, required office space that older buildings could not accommodate. Those companies wanted proximity also—to each other, to law firms, to Wall Street brokers, to bankers—which meant that the already cramped island of Manhattan needed to build up, not out. Four years before Tarbell moved to New York, the newspaper publisher Joseph Pulitzer opened the tallest skyscraper in the world, the World Building, 309 feet high, within walking distance of where Tarbell would write for S. S. McClure at 743 Broadway, third floor. Electricity for safe, clean, incandescent lighting had just become available in portions of the business district. New elevated trains helped hundreds of thousands of residents move around the island faster than they could have on foot and more cleanly than they could by horse-drawn car. The spread of affordable, dependable telephone service in residences and offices was just beginning as Tarbell made New York her home, increasing the efficiency of reporting, writing, and socializing after work.

Choosing to live alone, Tarbell resided in Manhattan apartments, first at 1519 Eighteenth Street, then at 40 West Ninth Street. In 1898, various government entities would consolidate into the boroughs—Manhattan, Brooklyn, the Bronx, Queens, and Staten Island. New York City had not yet become the financial and cultural center of the world—London certainly retained that title during the 1890s—but it was gaining. The city, for the moment, was still beset by economic depression, inadequate government services, unsightly utility poles carrying electricity and telephone services to customers, live wires falling from those poles and threatening electrocution, garbage in the streets, tuberculosis, cholera, typhoid, and diphtheria. Tarbell, hoping for a minimum of distraction, eventually found a stable, relatively quiet neighborhood near Gramercy Park to call home. She stayed at 120 East Nineteenth Street for the remainder of her life.

Perhaps the biggest adjustment for Tarbell was not finding the right neighborhood but figuring out how to please the unpredictable McClure. William Allen White, the Kansas newspaperman who found a national forum by writing for *McClure's Magazine*, met the proprietor about the same time that Tarbell did. White, with experience among outsized personalities, nonetheless felt overwhelmed. "Enter Sam McClure," he recalled. "Blond, tow-headed and mustached, blue-to-hazel eyes, oval face . . . with a wire voice which had come down from some Scotch or English ancestry. He talked like a pair of scissors, clipping his sentences, sometimes his words, [giving] the impression of a powerhouse of energy." Like almost every journalist who ever met McClure, White noted the avalanche of ideas coming from the publisher. "And a lot of them were excellent . . . We used to say that Sam had three hundred ideas a minute, but JSP [John S. Phillips, McClure's right-hand man] was the only man around who knew which one was not crazy."

At first Tarbell was thrilled at the idea of a generous salary and the knowledge that her name would appear prominently at the start of her features. But she felt daunted too, because of the responsibility combined with the added pressure of her gender. McClure had studied the magazine business carefully; he knew that hiring full-time staff writers and giving them bylines went against the tested practice of relying on poorly paid, often anonymous freelance journalists and academics. Always a visionary, McClure had never let protocols stop him. He believed that full-time, salaried writers and editors would produce more accurate, compelling, and entertaining material than a flock of stringers.

McClure's biographer, Peter Lyon, wrote about Tarbell's employment, "For a publisher plunged deep in debt to hire a relatively untried writer, and a woman at that, is as though the captain of a sinking ship were all at once to lay about him with an axe." Almost from the day she showed up at the office, rumors began about a personal relationship between her and McClure. Tarbell and McClure were about the same age, she was attractive and unattached, he was handsome and not monogamous. If a romantic involvement developed, however, it is well concealed in the existing correspondence of Tarbell, McClure, and others associated with the magazine. On the contrary, there is a good deal of evidence that Tarbell continued to avoid romantic love and sex steadfastly. Throughout her decades-long professional relationship with McClure, she disapproved of his extramarital liaisons. Sometimes she summoned the courage to lecture him about his actions and the importance of his marriage to Hattie, although she was reluctant to do so.

As Tarbell learned how to work smoothly with McClure, she realized that another person had as great a say as the owner in the magazine's daily operations: John S. Phillips. He "was the focus of every essential factor in the making of the magazine—circulation, finance, editing," she recalled. "He knew the supreme value of naturalness, detested fake style."

In 1895, with Tarbell feeling at home on the staff, McClure began pushing her further afield, to grander topics and more incisive pieces. He understood intuitively, as Tarbell did not, that he needed her, above all other journalists, to tackle the largest, most important subjects. Not only would the assignments demonstrate daring, but McClure also knew that Tarbell would quite likely succeed because of her relentless curiosity, her research skills, her perfectionism as a writer, and her reform instincts. Her first such assignment was a profile of Napoleon Bonaparte.

During the early 1890s, the deposed French ruler had become the object of renewed fascination throughout the world. While living in Paris, Tarbell had been caught up in the enthusiasm of the Napoleonic revival, as McClure had been in New York City. "I had been talking largely about devoting myself to French revolutionary history," Tarbell commented. "If this wasn't that, what was?" Another rationale occurred to her: Napoleon, she believed, "had pulled France out of the slough where she lay when Madame Roland lost her head. I had a terrific need of seeing the thing through, France on her feet. Napoleon had for a time set her there and brought back decency, order, common sense."

McClure mentioned the possibility of an originally researched, serialized life of Napoleon as early as December 6, 1893. "It seems to me," McClure wrote to Tarbell, "that we ought to take advantage of this present increased interest and publish something in *McClure's*. I wish we could get some very fresh, striking material, unpublished documents, letters or what not, something that has human interest." McClure approached Gardiner Green Hubbard, of Washington, D.C., a wealthy collector of Napoleon artifacts. Hubbard also happened to be a promoter of a potentially revolutionary device called the telephone, which was being developed by Alexander Graham Bell, who had married Gardiner's daughter Mabel. McClure had already published a profile of Bell in the magazine.

Impressed by the energetic, enthusiastic McClure, Hubbard offered never-before-published portraits of Napoleon for use in the magazine. He placed a condition on the offer, however—compelling, accurate, balanced text must accompany the artwork. McClure hired the British writer Robert H. Sherard to produce the text, but what he submitted had such a one-sided, anti-Napoleon tone that neither McClure nor Hubbard found it acceptable, McClure for journalistic reasons, Hubbard for personal ones. The rejection left McClure in a bind. He had already told readers that the first installment of the Napoleon saga would appear in the November 1894 issue. So he turned to Tarbell, insisting that she start Napoleon research without delay. He sent her a telegram in Titusville, where she was visiting her parents. "My telegram touched her sense of humor by its very improbability," McClure recalled, "and she replied that she would."

Tarbell found Napoleon fascinating but wrestled with misgivings, knowing that some of the best resources about the emperor were back in Paris. She also worried about the limitations placed on her candor by Hubbard's conditions. On the other hand, the research would link nicely to her Madame Roland biography.

Hubbard felt so proprietary about Napoleon that he insisted Tarbell board at his Twin Oaks estate in Washington as she conducted her research in 1894 and 1895, so they could talk regularly. Hubbard believed, and Tarbell agreed, that the engravings illustrated four distinct phases of

Napoleon's life: military general, 1796–1797; statesman/lawgiver, 1801–1804; emperor, 1804–1812; and man in decline, exiled after the defeat at Waterloo until his death in 1821.

Tarbell's temporary residence in the nation's capital provided her with a wealth of influential connections. Although Washington compared poorly to Paris in her estimation, her posting to the U.S. capital did not constitute hardship duty. Hubbard had not amassed holdings on the level of Rockefeller, but he was no pauper. Tarbell called the Hubbard residence "the finest country estate in the Washington district . . . Mrs. Hubbard herself was a woman of rare taste and cultivation . . . Maids, butlers, gardener—all took on something of her dignity and gentleness." Tarbell could not help feeling self-conscious in such surroundings, "a strange woman with a meager wardrobe and a preoccupied mind" who had invaded the Hubbards' "carefree, gaily bedecked society." But the Hubbards demonstrated such tolerance that soon she felt at ease more often than not. Gardiner Hubbard's respect for her grew to the point where he wrote about her Napoleon research, "You are a born lady and always will be one whom I will be glad to call a friend . . . I feel so much interest in you that I must make you a success."

Hubbard kept his promise, introducing Tarbell to his acquaintances in Washington. During her residency at the Hubbards', she met Samuel Pierpont Langley, the director of the Smithsonian Institution, who was laboring to invent a flying machine despite those who mocked the idea. Although McClure wanted Tarbell to push to complete the Napoleon assignment, he simultaneously wanted his new staff writer to collaborate with Langley on an account of the invention. Tarbell worried not only about the workload but also about how she would be perceived: "I think perhaps it was a little strain on Dr. Langley's good will to have a young woman come to him and say 'Now we want the whole story of how you have done this thing, what it means—but no scientific jargon, please. We want it told in language so simple that I can understand it, for if I can understand it all the world can.'" The Langley-Tarbell collaboration did eventually appear in *McClure's Magazine*.

While researching Napoleon's life, Tarbell spent long hours at the

Library of Congress and other Washington repositories. She practiced what would now be termed historical investigative reporting, relying heavily on original documents rather than trusting secondary sources. At the State Department, she located the full Napoleonic correspondence published by order of the French government. She searched files of French newspapers retained by American libraries.

After about six weeks, driven to discover more about Napoleon but feeling that she might become a burden on the Hubbard family, Tarbell moved to a rooming house on I Street Northwest, between Ninth and Tenth—an easy walk from the White House and other government buildings. The move yielded an unexpected intellectual relationship with George Frisbie Hoar, a U.S. senator from Massachusetts, who served as a sympathetic, encouraging friend to Tarbell while McClure was pressuring her to deliver drafts of the Napoleon manuscript. Although Tarbell was uncovering fascinating new material, McClure felt he was running out of time. Not only were his magazine's readers expecting the first installment, but now he had the distressing news that a competing magazine, *The Century*, was planning to publish its own Napoleon retrospective that fall, by William Milligan Sloane. McClure kept the pressure on Tarbell, and she responded by working nearly around the clock for weeks at a stretch. She considered "biography on the gallop" to be "impudence," but suppressed her doubts while striving to meet McClure's deadline.

The first part, appearing on schedule in November 1894—the same month as Sloane's competing version—covered the first twenty-six years of Napoleon's life in twenty-four magazine pages. Comparing her account to her competitor's, Tarbell felt triumphant, despite her late start. Sloane's version lacked the Hubbard engravings as well as the published explanation from the collector about how and why he had accumulated about three hundred Napoleonic treasures, the earliest dating from 1791, when the emperor-to-be was twenty-two years old. From the opening installment, Tarbell's account demonstrated exceptional research and lyrical writing, conveying the sweep of history built primarily on the "great man" theory. Like so many other biographers, Tarbell believed that extraordinary individuals could shape their society at least as much as society shaped them.

Not all professional and amateur historians subscribed, then or now, to this theory. Many believe that the emergence of an Abraham Lincoln or Napoleon Bonaparte or Andrew Carnegie or John D. Rockefeller is something of an inevitable accident related to the social structures of the time. If Rockefeller had died unexpectedly on his way to the Pennsylvania oil fields in the early 1860s, these people posit, some other entrepreneur surely would have devised a way to build an oil trust.

Readers apparently hungered for Tarbell's Napoleon rendition; circulation of the magazine jumped from 40,000 to 80,000 as the serial progressed. Tarbell shared her judgments with readers, working against the just-the-facts tradition. She understood that every person is complex— not all good, not all bad. Tarbell considered Napoleon a genius of war and government administration but flawed in his personal affairs. As she increased her knowledge of him, she placed greater emphasis on Josephine Bonaparte, who was thirty-two and widowed with two children when the younger Napoleon fell in love with her. Tarbell told Josephine's story dramatically, demonstrating to her readership, as with Roland, that biographies of women could be as compelling as those of men. Josephine's story, like Roland's, revealed layers of contradictions and half-truths.

The monthly serialization of the Napoleon biography in the magazine ended with the June 1895 issue. In book form, *A Short Life of Napoleon Bonaparte*, also published by McClure, sold well, and the 70,000 volumes of the first printing disappeared quickly. McClure sent the book back onto the presses for reprinting in 1896, 1901, 1903, 1905, and as late as 1923.

As more and more people came to recognize Tarbell's name because of the Napoleon biography, she felt increasing confidence that she could make a difference through journalism. Investigating Rockefeller and Standard Oil remained in the back of her mind, but in 1895 she was not quite ready for that task. As she wondered where to place her focus after the Napoleon research, McClure made the decision for her. She would write about Abraham Lincoln.

||||||||||||||||||||||||||||||||||||||||||||||||||||||||||||||||||

CHAPTER TEN

Unearthing Skeletons

In 1895, it seemed that nothing new could be said about the six-teenth president of the United States. Abraham Lincoln had been dead for three decades, and historians had produced voluminous works on every aspect of his life. S. S. McClure, however, saw the success of Ida Tarbell's Napoleon serialization and decided that a serialized life of Lincoln written by his best-selling reporter would provoke an equally passionate response.

Even before McClure began pushing Tarbell to write about Lincoln, the editor in chief had published two Lincoln-related features in his fledgling magazine: "How Allan Pinkerton Thwarted the First Plot to Assassinate Lincoln" and "Lincoln as Commander in Chief." McClure's original plan called for a Lincoln serialization with multiple authors; the common denominator would have been each author's personal acquain-tanceship with the dead president. Tarbell's role would have been to edit each part, then fill gaps with her own reporting. Eventually, McClure realized how unwieldy it might become to coordinate so many authors, so he abandoned the group approach.

Tarbell initially resisted McClure's plan, worrying that writing about Lincoln would derail her study of French history. After all, she was almost forty years old. "If you once get into American history, I told myself, you know well enough that it will finish France." Furthermore, after she completed her biography of Madame Roland, she hoped to start investigating the United States of the 1890s, including the impact of John D. Rockefeller and the Standard Oil Company. Why look back to Lincoln?

Still, McClure was offering her a comfortable salary to write about Lincoln. Furthermore, Lincoln had fascinated Tarbell since his assassination, when she was seven years old. She remembered her father trudging home from his shop the day news of the murder reached rural western Pennsylvania. She remembered her mother "burying her face in her apron, running into her room sobbing as if her heart would break." She remembered the crepe hung on the house, which was shut tight for mourning. She remembered attractive photographs of the dead president from issues of *Harper's Weekly*.

Tarbell decided to do McClure's bidding, and she devoted the remainder of 1895 to research that would allow the Lincoln serialization to begin before year's end. Simultaneously she was completing the Roland biography for Scribner's.

At this point in her career, Tarbell had developed a philosophy of biography. "One should start by wiping out of his mind all that he knows about the man, start as if you had never before heard of him," Tarbell would explain later in material she developed for a college course. "Everything then is fresh, new. Your mind, feeding on this fresh material, sees things in a new way. You are making an acquaintance of one who, if he is worth writing about, grows more interesting to you whatever he has done or not done as the time goes on."

The philosophy worked well for the Roland book. As Tarbell enjoyed praise for her Napoleon portrait, the Roland biography appeared in stores and libraries. An unsigned review in *The Dial*, a journal of literary criticism, ran on May 16, 1896. The reviewer congratulated Tarbell for a "terse, clear and literal biography," filled with "close researches among original documents." The documents plus interviews with Roland's descendants had enabled Tarbell "to present some new facts that throw additional light upon the career and character of her heroine." Two months later, in *The American Catholic Quarterly Review*, essayist James Field Spalding devoted eighteen pages to an account of Tarbell's effort. Tarbell "presents a most inviting subject for study, and in a way which cannot fail to gain attention," he said. "The book is charmingly written, the narrative is clear and strong, the story is well balanced, French life of the eighteenth century and events of the revolution are again distinctly before us." Tarbell had "indisputably" written the best biography of Roland.

In her biographical work, what Tarbell enjoyed most was discovering new material, as she had in the Roland and Napoleon archives. Still, she could not help wondering whether any researcher, no matter how skilled, could hope to find significant new information about Lincoln three decades after his death. She would have to work through thousands of books and articles about Lincoln, sorting fact from rumor, figuring out the accuracy or inaccuracy of conflicting accounts. She would also need to grapple with his legacy as the emancipator of slaves.

Early versions of Lincoln's life tended toward the eulogistic and hagiographic. By the 1890s, the increasing availability of material—mostly correspondence and memoirs—that had been kept private during their holders' lifetimes brought a new round of accounts to market. In that vein, *The Century Magazine* completed a Lincoln series in 1890, based on the ten-volume biography by John D. Nicolay and John Hay. Their study relied heavily on papers shown to them exclusively by Robert Todd, Lincoln's son, who then announced that the Lincoln papers would be unavailable again until at least twenty-six years after his own death.

Hoping to gain access to revealing information, Tarbell called on Nicolay in Washington, D.C. He treated her icily, hoping to discourage her. His rudeness at first surprised her, but she came to understand that his years of personal devotion as Lincoln's private secretary had made him territorial about the president's legacy. In fact, Nicolay's negative reaction proved valuable for Tarbell. By denying her access to Lincoln's personal papers, Nicolay forced her to improvise. "Mr. Nicolay's rebuff settled my plan of campaign," she recalled. "I would not begin at the end of the story with the great and known, but at the start in Kentucky with the humble and unknown. I would follow the trail chronologically."

Instead of conducting herself like a traditional biographer, Tarbell decided to pursue her historical inquiry as a journalist. Without the ability to see the story from Lincoln's perspective as set out in his papers, she devised a wholly new strategy to construct her narrative. She planned a tour of courthouses and county historical repositories and newspapers. "If I were lucky, somewhere on the trail I might turn up the important unpublished reminiscences which Mr. McClure was so certain existed."

Travel in 1895 meant putting up with sometimes undependable railroad schedules and with unheated horse-drawn carriages after arriving at the train depot. Tarbell began her trek in the first few months of the year. She found Kentucky's February weather freezing, and the boarding houses and hotels where she slept lacked heat. She never removed her socks, even under the quilts.

At first the documentary record seemed sparse. She persisted. Visiting little-used archives in several states, she slowly began to uncover new material in county histories, courthouse records, and yellowing newspaper accounts. To her surprise, an encouraging percentage of these archival details had not appeared in the Nicolay-Hay compendium.

Across the Midwest, Tarbell found statements by women and men who had known various members of the Lincoln family. Christopher Columbus Graham, a Kentucky physician, mentioned to a friend in 1882, at age ninety-eight, that he had attended the wedding of Abe's parents, Nancy and Thomas. Graham's friend, understanding the historical importance of the memory, quickly secured a sworn affidavit. After Tarbell located the affidavit, she knew she would be obliged to conduct further research before deciding how much credence to place in the memory of an elderly man. During that accuracy check, she located a second oral account from Graham, set down by a historian from Louisville just before the old man's death in 1884, at age one hundred. Tarbell located several of Graham's acquaintances who could tell her about his mental ability, and she finally decided to accept the two oral statements as substantially accurate. Most journalists during the nineteenth century took statements such as those made by Graham at face value. Tarbell's measures to determine veracity became her trademark decades before other journalists adopted the practice.

Interviewing living witnesses rather than relying on affidavits from dead ones did not necessarily make her fact-checking easier. Tarbell located Josiah Crawford, who said he recalled young Lincoln visiting the family home to borrow Parson Weems's well-known biography of George Washington. When Lincoln failed to protect the book from damage during a rainstorm, he had to shuck corn on the Crawford land for three days as penance. Tarbell was able to confirm that the incident had occurred, and it seemed she was the first to interview Crawford. But she experienced greater difficulty in determining whether the young Lincoln actually declared to Crawford that he intended to become president someday. He was rumored to have said to Crawford, "I do not always intend to delve, grub, shuck corn, split rails, and the like." Tarbell could not confirm the quotation, so she refrained from using it.

Encouraged that she had found previously untapped human sources, Tarbell found further encouragement when she received an unpublished daguerreotype of the president from Lincoln's son Robert Todd. The daguerreotype showed a handsome, confident-looking Abraham Lincoln, probably in his early thirties. McClure, in typically grandiose fashion, published it as "the earliest portrait of Abraham Lincoln."

Tarbell gained access to the president's son through a former Illinois woman whom she had befriended in Washington, D.C. "To be drinking tea with the son of Abraham Lincoln was so unbelievable to me that I could scarcely take note of his reply . . ." Tarbell recalled. "I devoured him with my eyes. He was very friendly." She realized that Robert Todd Lincoln could persuade other normally reluctant sources to assist. At least in part because of his influence, five private collectors of Lincoln materials— two in Philadelphia, one in Chicago, one in Louisville, and one in Washington, D.C.—opened their archives to Tarbell and the magazine.

Her interaction with Robert Lincoln proved invaluable for the serial about his father. It also taught Tarbell an invaluable lesson about sources. Robert Lincoln had declared research material off-limits, and yet he had already proven tremendously valuable as a source. Tarbell would remember that well while laboring to uncover the truth about Standard Oil and John D. Rockefeller.

She also learned that finding a dependable, enthusiastic, intelligent researcher in the subject's hometown could lead to extraordinary new material. For the Lincoln project, she found such an individual in J. McCan Davis, a lawyer and journalist in Springfield, Illinois. Tarbell credited Davis with unearthing Lincoln's initial public speech, a document recording the first time he voted, and his marriage certificate, among other papers. Forgeries and false leads abounded, but slowly Tarbell's careful courthouse searches and visits to the homes of various Lincoln acquaintances built upon Davis's discoveries. Throughout 1895, Tarbell, Davis, and other researchers looking on her behalf acquired at least three hundred previously unpublished items.

McClure found the material so compelling that he could not contain himself. He insisted that Tarbell start writing for publication even as she continued her research. Despite her protestations that she needed more time to uncover the real Lincoln, McClure made a business decision to publish in the November 1895 issue and would not back off. Tarbell's misgivings persisted, but the magazine's circulation increased immediately by tens of thousands of readers anxious to find out what she had discovered.

From the first installment, Tarbell portrayed Lincoln simultaneously as an example of a unique American type—the honest frontiersman come to greatness while refusing to compromise his principles—and a distinct individual, a figure who defied easy categorization. She was confident that her profile would stir up controversy, but she hoped it might have a positive impact on the general public's understanding of perhaps the most influential American ever. Above all, she insisted on accuracy, so that the myths spread by previous commentators would fade. For example, she established to her satisfaction that Lincoln's ancestry traced to Hingham, Massachusetts, rather than Kentucky. She considered that fact "a matter of great importance." It proved in her mind that the president came from a branch of the family "endowed with the spirit of adventure, of daring, of patriotism, and of thrift, that his ancestors were men who for nearly two hundred years before he was born were active and well-to-do citizens of Massachusetts, New Jersey, Pennsylvania or Virginia."

Although she emphasized the importance of her findings about Lincoln's lineage, Tarbell felt strongly that his upbringing, not solely his genealogy, explained much of his success. Perhaps most notably concerning the nature-versus-nurture paradigm, she presented a revisionist account of Thomas Lincoln, Abraham's father. "We believe the new documents we have found . . . justify us in it," Tarbell told readers of *McClure's Magazine*. "We have not made it a sign of shiftlessness that Thomas Lincoln dwelt in a log cabin at a date when there was scarcely anything else" throughout Kentucky and southern Indiana. Previous biographers had suggested that Abraham Lincoln "came from a home similar to those of the 'poor white trash' of the South," Tarbell reported. Those biographers told only part of the story, she said. "There is no attempt made here to deny the poverty of the Lincoln household, but it is insisted that this poverty was a temporary condition incident to pioneer life and the unfortunate death of Thomas Lincoln's father when he was but a boy."

A portion of the saga's credibility derived from Tarbell's own rugged experience growing up on the frontier. The oil-drilling frontier of Pennsylvania could not equate directly to the frontier Lincoln experienced farther west, but the mental state was much the same. With her parents as models, Tarbell understood how greatness could arise from rural isolation and hardship. Subtly, she helped readers see that rural individuals could achieve success in complicated, unexpected ways.

As a journalistic biographer, Tarbell wanted to construct an unambiguous chronology. Thus she told the story of Lincoln's youth through documents she had unearthed: the land plats he signed while working as a surveyor, papers he executed as a local postmaster, records of his service during the Black Hawk War, and more. She could not contain her excitement at documenting Lincoln's life in a new manner: "In telling the story of the six years of Lincoln's life in New Salem, we have attempted . . . to show the exact sequence of events, which has never been done before." She documented assiduously that Lincoln had labored to master many trades. She found suggestive "the persistency and courage with which he seized every opportunity and carried on simultaneously his business as storekeeper and postmaster and surveyor and at the same time studied law."

Unlike authors before her, Tarbell shared her sources with readers, presaging her technique in the Standard Oil exposé. For example, in the Lincoln text, she reproduced the poll book page recording his first vote, on August 1, 1831, in New Salem, where he had been assisting one of the election clerks. She explained how "in the early days in Illinois, elections were conducted by the viva voce method. The people did try voting by ballot, but the experiment was unpopular. It required too much 'book larnin', and in 1829 the viva voce method of voting was restored." Election clerks would sit in plain view with the poll book. As each voter arrived, he announced his candidate, and the clerk recorded the vote in his presence. "To this simple system we are indebted for the record of Lincoln's first vote," Tarbell commented.

She went further than previous biographers in portraying the depth of Lincoln's feelings at the premature death, in 1835, of Ann Rutledge, whom he loved. Tarbell wrote, "But though [Lincoln] had regained self-control, his grief was deep and bitter. Ann Rutledge was buried in Concord cemetery . . . To this lonely spot Lincoln frequently journeyed to weep over her grave. 'My heart is buried there,' he said to one of his friends." Lincoln's feelings about Rutledge mattered to the historiography of the future president, the subtext being that Mary Todd, the eventual Mrs. Lincoln, never could attain first place in her husband's heart.

Tarbell's account of Lincoln's early life ends lyrically, demonstrating her mixture of realism and hope: "Such was Abraham Lincoln at twenty-six, when the tragic death of Ann Rutledge made all that he had attained, all that he had planned, seem fruitless and empty." But, she added, Lincoln refused to give up: "He rallied his forces and returned to his law, his surveying, his politics. He brought to his work a new power, that insight and patience which only a great sorrow can give."

As Tarbell's research effort shifted from Lincoln's early life to his political career, she redoubled her efforts to achieve verisimilitude. "I was particularly interested in the setting of the Lincoln-Douglas debates, which

I followed in their order," she recalled. "But it was not until I reached Galesburg, Illinois, where on October 7, 1858, the fifth debate was staged, that I found the stirring and picturesque material I sought in order to picture the scene." It was during this legendary moment in the U.S. Senate race that Lincoln honed his anti-slavery arguments.

The debate occurred on the campus of Knox College, McClure's alma mater. By the mid-1890s, Tarbell had developed her own helpful contact there—John H. Finley, her former assistant at *The Chautauquan*, who had risen to the college presidency. In January 1895, Tarbell arrived at Knox to gather Lincoln material. She stayed at Finley's home. He helped her locate obscure newspaper accounts of the debate and connected her to area residents who had witnessed it. She and McClure then worked with artist William R. Leigh to recreate the scene from the eyewitness accounts.

An even more daunting challenge was finding the "lost speech" reportedly given by Lincoln on May 29, 1856, in Bloomington, Illinois, where he had supposedly made his most strident criticism of slavery. Apparently he did not prepare a text, and journalists in the audience were so spellbound they forgot to take notes. By the time Tarbell began her research, some Lincoln scholars doubted whether the speech had ever been delivered.

Tarbell contacted journalists who might have been following Illinois politics during the mid-1850s, but her early attempts proved fruitless. Then she heard a vague remembrance that Henry Clay Whitney, a Massachusetts lawyer on the campaign trail with Lincoln, claimed to have taken notes of the speech. Not even sure if Whitney would still be living, Tarbell searched for him. She found him in Beachmont, Massachusetts. To her amazement, he produced yellowed notes that seemed to capture Lincoln's words from that day nearly forty years before. Tarbell returned to her Illinois sources, who said that the version recorded in the yellowed notes sounded much like the lost speech. When Joseph Medill, the editor of the *Chicago Tribune*, told Tarbell that the version approximated what he recalled hearing in 1856, she felt confident enough to include the anecdote in the magazine serialization.

As the Lincoln material flowed in, McClure began promoting Tarbell as more than a mere staff writer. He capitalized on her publishing successes by identifying her as the face and soul of the magazine. In the March 1898 issue, he published a prominent photograph of her, writing in the caption that "no name is more familiar to readers of *McClure's Magazine* than that of Ida M. Tarbell." He said that Tarbell's life of Napoleon "was by far the most successful feature the magazine had had up to that time. Rarely, indeed, in all the course of magazine publication has there been a success equal to it." But the Lincoln series surpassed it. Every day, McClure said, he received letters from readers asking when Tarbell would delve into Lincoln's later life.

Tarbell's contacts with sources during the Lincoln research unexpectedly led to a couple of mostly unrelated feature packages for McClure. Each turned out to be a coup. The first centered on Carl Schurz, born in Germany. He entered the United States in 1852 as a twenty-three-year-old political exile, settled in Wisconsin, and became a journalist, a lawyer, and a campaigner for Lincoln. After winning the presidency, Lincoln rewarded Schurz with a ministerial appointment to Spain. Schurz returned to the United States after a year, however, to fight in the Civil War, and he lobbied Lincoln to issue a proclamation unambiguously ending slavery.

The more Tarbell and McClure learned about Schurz, the more they wanted to publish his reminiscences in the magazine. Schurz said no, but changed his mind when McClure offered "a handsome sum" of money. Working with Schurz on the serialized memoir turned out to be fulfilling, Tarbell said: "He was gay, companionable, full of anecdotes, frank in comment. I remember him best at his summer home at Lake George, where it was necessary for me to go two or three times to settle some editorial point." After Schurz's death in 1906, McClure's book publishing subsidiary issued a three-volume memoir covering 1829 to 1869 in the subject's own words. Working with Tarbell, two outside scholars summarized the remainder of Schurz's eventful life to complete the memoir.

The second feature focused on Charles A. Dana, the editor of the *New York Sun* and Lincoln's eyes at the front during the Civil War. Tarbell pursued an in-depth interview with Dana for months, emphasizing that "no one in the administration had better opportunity of judging Lincoln, particularly in relation to the conduct of war, and none was a better judge of character." Dana agreed, after much coaxing, to publish his Civil War reminiscences in *McClure's Magazine* if Tarbell would dig out fresh information from archives first, then develop a plan for interviewing him that would supplement the documents. Tarbell approached J. Leslie Perry, in charge of the federal government's Civil War records. Apparently miffed at being asked to cooperate with a woman, Perry constructed roadblocks to the documents. Tarbell, normally calm—at least outwardly—in the face of gender discrimination, sought an accommodation rather than storming out. Eventually she wore down Perry, convincing him that she was not a shallow, flighty female.

Tarbell took notes as the revelations flowed from Dana's memory. She did her best to craft the language in his voice. Associate editor John S. Phillips, after skimming a draft, told McClure, "I have read all of Miss Tarbell's Dana. It contains lots of bully stuff. Some of the campaign descriptions will have to be cut down, but it has unusual freshness and an air of veracity."

McClure himself read most of Tarbell's manuscripts three times. If during the third reading he found that any sentence failed to hold his attention, he asked for a rewrite. He wanted factual accuracy, contextual accuracy, new information, and moral uplift simultaneously—a lot to expect. Tarbell possessed equally high standards. At one point, she wrote to Phillips after he and McClure suggested substantial changes in an early draft, "I had a sneaking notion myself that it was pretty poor and I think the greatest difficulty is that it is so scrappy. I attempted to get too much stuff in, which I could not knit together."

The Lincoln research naturally led Tarbell to thoughts about the Civil War. She could not resist trying to make sense of the aftermath. Employing an unusual research technique, she sent letters, apparently hundreds of them, to former Confederate soldiers, painstakingly locating their addresses through word of mouth and archival materials in Washington, D.C. Tarbell's letter said, in part, "I have been deeply interested in the condition . . . which the disbanding Confederates found themselves [in] at the close of the war, and in their struggles to start in life and to build up the South again." Tarbell told the recipients of the letter that "my whole object is to call attention more forcibly than has ever been done to the fine heroism of the Southerner in building up the South after the war." The letter-writing technique worked well, as she received dozens of illuminating, candid responses.

With the Schurz, Dana, and Civil War aftermath projects under way and the Lincoln stories being requested by readers who had missed the original episodes in the magazine, McClure told Tarbell that he planned to publish the serial as a two-volume book, titled simply *The Life of Abraham Lincoln*. Dedicating the book to her father, Tarbell organized it into acts. The first act, encompassing eleven chapters, opens with the earliest documented appearance of the Lincolns in Massachusetts and ends in 1842, as Lincoln marries and is elected to Congress. Act two, consisting of ten chapters, stops with Lincoln's election to the presidency. The third act covers Lincoln's presidency and assassination. "No attempt has been made [here] to cover the history of Lincoln's times save as necessary in tracing the development of his mind and in illustrating his moral qualities," Tarbell told readers modestly. Instead, she explained, "It is Lincoln the man, as seen by his fellows and revealed by his own acts and words, that the author has tried to picture."

Tarbell closed the biography by commenting on the posthumous adoration of Lincoln: "The first and inevitable result of the emotion which swept over the earth at Lincoln's death was to enroll him among martyrs and heroes. Men forgot that they had despised him, jeered at him, doubted him." Hindsight yielded something new to Lincoln's detractors, Tarbell said. "They saw now, with the vision which an awful and sudden disaster so often gives, the simple, noble outlines on which he had worked." The long-ago critics realized that Lincoln "had sunk every partisan and personal consideration, every non-essential, in the tasks which he had set for himself—to prevent the extension of slavery, to save the Union." The new view led too far in the other direction, with Lincoln being called "a prophet . . . a man raised up by God for a special work."

Not so, Tarbell concluded. "He is the simple, steady, resolute, unselfish man whose supreme ambition was to find out the truth of the questions which confronted him in life, and whose highest satisfaction was in following the truth he discovered."

Tarbell's Lincoln opus reached bookstores and libraries in the first year of the new century. Historian Don E. Fehrenbacher commented that it "combined respectable scholarship with great popular appeal. Its publication in 1900 serves to mark the beginning of a new period in Lincoln literature." While there was consensus that the book made an enormous impact, historians were split on their evaluations of the message. Albert J. Beveridge, a U.S. senator who wrote a Lincoln biography, invented the verb "to Tarbellize," meaning to elevate Lincoln while sanitizing his faults. "The dear girl's efforts to fumigate are pathetic," Beveridge said. Historian Samuel E. Morrison agreed, telling Beveridge that Tarbell and her followers were no more than "sentimental sob sisters." Tarbell's advocates outnumbered her critics, however, both in the world of Lincoln scholars and in bookstores.

Tarbell published books, magazine articles, and newspaper editorials about Lincoln for the remainder of her life. She would always be linked to his name in the minds of millions. Her next subject was a different sort of self-made man, John D. Rockefeller. But where she had glossed over Lincoln's faults, Tarbell went to great lengths to pull back the curtain on Standard Oil and the machinations of its founder. The era of heroic biography was fading. The new century would bring new hopes for the nation, new leaders, and a new kind of journalist: the muckraker.

The Exposé Mentality

I nvestigative reporting did not come naturally to S. S. McClure or other magazine publishers at the beginning of the twentieth century. Nobody had even invented a term for the concept. But however they verbalized the concept of ferreting out waste, fraud, and abuse to afflict the comfortable and comfort the afflicted, publishers understood intuitively that complications might arise. It would be expensive to conduct that sort of journalism because of travel costs. It would quite likely attract lawsuits that would be costly to defend, and the finished pieces would require extensive, skilled editing. But as magazine and newspaper publishers began to understand their power, indeed their responsibility, to explain an increasingly complex, often unfair, and sometimes corrupt society, in-depth journalism began to bloom despite the hazards.

Journalists, especially Tarbell and McClure, played significant roles during what historians eventually labeled the Progressive Era, a roiling, traumatic period starting approximately in 1890 and lasting until the outbreak of World War I. Journalists, politicians (including President Theodore Roosevelt), judges, and private-sector good-government groups hoped to alter the national ethos to minimize inequalities among individuals. Part of their agenda involved government regulation aimed at trusts, such as Standard Oil, and trust owners, such as John D. Rockefeller.

Many who benefited from the status quo, including Rockefeller, opposed the reformist tenets of the Progressive Era. Many others—including the disenfranchised, the illiterate, and the non-English-speaking immigrants—knew little or nothing about the movement allegedly sweeping the nation. As journalist-philosopher Walter Lippmann observed about the emergence of a new sort of journalism, "It began to apply the standards of public life to certain parts of the business world. Now when [businessmen] are muckraked, what puzzles them beyond words is that anyone should presume to meddle with their business." Lippmann, in his book *Drift and Mastery*, predicted that businessmen would learn "that it is no longer altogether their business. The law may not have realized this, but the fact is being accomplished, and it's a fact grounded deeper than statutes."

Toward the end of the Progressive Era, President Woodrow Wilson summarized what he had observed. Historian Steven J. Diner used part of Wilson's summary to open the insightful book *A Very Different Age: Americans of the Progressive Era*. Speaking in 1912, Wilson said,

> We have come upon a very different age from any that preceded us. We have come upon an age when we do not do business in the way we used to do business, when we do not carry on any of the operations of manufacture, sale, transportation or communication as men used to carry them on. There is a sense in which in our day the individual has been submerged. In most parts of the country men work, not for themselves, not as partners in the old way in which they used to work, but generally as employees—in a higher or lower grade—of great corporations. There was a time when corporations played a very minor part in our business affairs, but now they play the chief part, and most men are the servants of the corporations.

Standard Oil and other trusts created new jobs and sold products that improved the quality of life of the purchasers. Those improvements came with a cost, however—chasms of wealth between owners and employees; large-scale labor-management strife; the struggle between white-collar workers and blue-collar workers for their perceived fair share of income and status; the separation of licensed professionals such as lawyers and physicians from laborers; frayed family bonds owing to factory and office work schedules; environmental degradation; the decline of small-scale farming; increasing stranger-on-stranger crime; and the sped-up pace of day-to-day living.

McClure stood in the vanguard of those documenting the societal shifts. Recognizing the unrest and the yearning of the exploited for clamps on corporate greed, he fashioned a magazine filled with explanatory and investigative journalism as well as fiction and other entertainments. For example, in the August 1900 edition, McClure published an article about the nation's criminal underclass. The byline said Josiah Flynt, but the writer's real name was Josiah Willard. As much as any writer, Willard set the stage for muckraking journalism. Born in 1869 to a Chicago newspaper editor and his wife, Willard came from a family accustomed to joining the public discourse. Frances Willard, the temperance leader and feminist, was his aunt. Despite his privileged upbringing, Willard gravitated toward the unsavory at an early age. His underworld friends called him Cigarette. He smoked and drank heavily and used drugs, and he peppered his language with street jargon unknown to many of his readers—"pinch" for arrest, "fix" for bribe, "graft" for corruption. By age twenty-five, Willard was publishing articles about the homeless and other dispossessed persons. In 1899 he collected this work into a book with the revealing title *Tramping with Tramps: Studies and Sketches of Vagabond Life.*

McClure, Tarbell, and the rest of the *McClure's Magazine* staff had started on a journalistic mission, hoping to expose corruption while offering a profound sense of revelation about underreported communities. McClure introduced the August 1900 article by Willard and Francis Walton (the pen name of Alfred Hodder) with the explanation that his writers, while documenting the lives of lawbreakers, did not want to break the law, "but to understand as thoroughly as possible the motives and methods of that great part of the community which they describe as 'The Under-World.'" The stories could be considered "philosophical studies, about a class concerning which the great mass of people know nothing, except that they are lawbreakers . . . The stories are intended to point to a moral as well as to adorn a tale."

From a different background from Willard, Tarbell did not seek a role as the inventor of modern-day investigative reporting. Nothing about that role seemed inevitable. It never would have occurred, either, except for an overriding reality: Throughout work on her retrospectives of Bonaparte and Lincoln, Tarbell never lost sight of John D. Rockefeller and Standard Oil. As thoroughly as she had come to know the lives and times of her subjects, she felt out of touch with current events. Before she could consider turning her undivided attention to the Standard Oil trust and Rockefeller, she needed to catch up with contemporary politics and commerce. The presidential administration of Republican William McKinley presented the opportunity.

McKinley had lived in Poland, Ohio, the same town where Tarbell taught school after graduating from college. While a U.S. congressman, from 1877 until 1891, McKinley gained national attention for his support of high tariffs on imported goods desired by domestic industries worried about being undercut by foreign competitors. Then, during four years as Ohio's governor, the pro-business McKinley proposed maintaining a gold standard as the foundation of the national economy, a philosophy complementing high tariffs and bound to divide voters with feelings about the nation's most debated issue. When McKinley sought the presidency in 1896 against William Jennings Bryan, a Democrat and a populist, it proved an epic clash.

Wary of Bryan's populism and feeling good about McKinley's politics, in large measure because of McKinley's pro-corporate campaign manager, Mark Hanna, Rockefeller contributed about $250,000 to the

Republican candidate. An enormous contribution for that era, the quarter million dollars amounted to approximately half the total raised by Bryan from all sources. Normally reticent about commenting on politics, Rockefeller said of his support for McKinley, "I can see nothing else for us to do, to serve the country and our honor."

Such unusual political activism underscored the importance of the issues at stake for corporate America, not to mention individual citizens. Unlike most journalists and the average reader, who found tariffs too complicated to understand fully, Tarbell grasped the profound ways in which tariffs affected workers, consumers, and taxpayers. She knew that the issues needed to be articulated clearly for working men and women, so she began collecting material with a *McClure's Magazine* article in mind. Soon she expanded her study to the handling of tariff issues within the White House and Congress. She cultivated sources within the McKinley administration, including General Nelson A. Miles. When the *Maine*, an American vessel, blew up in the harbor of Havana, Cuba, on February 16, 1898, Tarbell met with Miles, who trusted her enough to provide inside information about the McKinley adminstration's strategy during what became known as the Spanish-American War.

The war had come as no surprise to those observing corporate chieftains wanting new sources of raw materials and new markets for their products. Politicians eagerly waged war too, given their vision of the United States as the rightful ruler of the globe. Loss of life seemed a small price to pay for believers in America's manifest destiny. With expansion west of the Mississippi River pretty much exhausted, with Indian tribes subjugated and their land appropriated without due process, nearby foreign territories provided a tempting target for a country eager to expand. Furthermore, many argued, war might stimulate the damaged American economy and perhaps open new markets for the products of United States–based corporations.

The Spanish-American War tested Tarbell's resources as a writer and an editor. A pacifist, Tarbell opposed the war, but she attempted to make sense of the conflict—as well as the warring instinct of nations—for herself and for readers. She helped chronicle U.S. expansionism for *McClure's Magazine* as both writer and editor. McClure asked her to take charge of so much coverage, in both her roles, that she began to despair of being able to immerse herself in any project as deeply as she had for the Napoleon and Lincoln biographies.

In her editor role, Tarbell absorbed lessons about effective narrative from established writers such as Edwin Markham, Theodore Dreiser, Stephen Crane, Sarah Orne Jewett, Hamlin Garland, William Dean Howells, James Parton, and Charles A. Dana. From her editing desk, she watched McClure reposition the magazine from a leisurely companion to a scoop-driven public affairs periodical. It soon became evident that McClure was fostering an environment for revelatory journalism that would allow Tarbell to begin her inquiry into the corporate trusts. "There was a continuous flow of war articles," Tarbell recalled. "*McClure's* suddenly was a part of active, public life. Having tasted blood, it could no longer be content with being merely attractive, readable."

The magazine staff at the turn of the century included an array of talent, perhaps the best lineup in the history of journalism. Ray Stannard Baker came to the attention of McClure while still a newspaper reporter, when he queried the magazine about chronicling the career of General Lafayette C. Baker. The general had helped capture Lincoln's assassin, John Wilkes Booth. Tarbell assigned the story to Baker, starting a professional relationship that lasted the rest of their lives. Baker turned out to be a superb reporter and a team player at the magazine. No assignment seemed to faze him. "He was the least talkative of us all," Tarbell recalled, "observant rather than garrulous, the best listener in the group, save Mr. Phillips. He had a joyous laugh which was more revealing of his healthy inner self than anything else about him."

Lincoln Steffens earned attention as a reporter and editor on New York City newspapers. He freelanced for McClure at first, then accepted a position as staff writer. Steffens's reputation impressed Tarbell, though she never warmed to him personally. Handsome, self-confident, with a strong academic background and two years of observing life overseas, Steffens "began his professional career unencumbered by journalistic shibboleths and with an immense curiosity as to what was going on about him," Tarbell commented. She marveled at his drive to reduce government corruption, which culminated in a classic series for the magazine exposing municipal graft at the same time that Tarbell was exposing Rockefeller and Standard Oil. "Incredibly outspoken, taking rascality for granted, apparently never shocked or angry or violent, [Steffens] coolly determined to demonstrate to men and women of good will and honest purpose what they were up against and warn them," Tarbell recalled.

Steffens, like Tarbell, personified what the new *McClure's Magazine* was becoming—not so much an intellectual bastion akin to the *Atlantic Monthly*, but rather a hybrid of an earnest schoolroom with its didactic articles and a department store offering a variety of topics. McClure became one of the first publishers to market his authors as brands, displaying bylines prominently and publishing their photographs. That Tarbell, Steffens, and Baker are so well known today is due in part to McClure's ability to distinguish them as individual reporters.

Viola Roseboro received none of the fame achieved by Tarbell, Steffens, and Baker. Within the office, however, she was a formidable presence, handling unsolicited submissions and copyediting texts. Before she applied for a job at the magazine, she had known McClure casually through her acting career and her sporadic attempts at freelancing. Like Tarbell, she struck McClure as possessing an innate purity of mind. Roseboro was a single woman who, like Tarbell, dedicated herself to productive activity at work every day. A seriousness of purpose—committing journalism to making the world a better place—linked the two women. Their differences in style sometimes masked their similarities in substance. Unlike Tarbell, Roseboro smoked cigarettes, treated freelance writers ruthlessly, and talked incessantly with a level of profanity that shocked her coworkers. Writer Will Irwin compared Roseboro's conversational skills to those of Samuel Johnson, the British literary figure, "and the comparison is not strained. It inclined toward dogmatism, but anyone with an indulgent heart felt that this was a small price to pay for so much wisdom." Irwin added that "in our family, we quote Viola Roseboro fully as often as we do Shakespeare."

Roseboro's biographer Jane Kirkland Graham speculated that Roseboro and Tarbell loved men with all the passion of modern women, but their love affairs, in their own opinion, were of no lasting importance. Exchanging ideas with men (and women), however, mattered deeply. For Roseboro and Tarbell, love "was only a key to unlock masculine minds— the thought exchanged was the important thing." Physical pleasure seemed to have no place in their lives, despite their desire for affection.

No matter how much Tarbell and Roseboro communed, McClure dominated the office atmosphere. He was energetic, untamed, and impossible to ignore. He would inspire heroic feats of journalism and then demand more. Although the same age as Tarbell, he sometimes adopted the tone of a father or an older brother with her. When Tarbell seemed physically weakened by an undiagnosed disorder during one stretch in 1899, McClure ordered her to stay away from the office, then wrote, "I always feel sorry when you go away; there are so many things I have not said to you. I did not think you looked very strong and vigorous. It is necessary for us all to get strong." Tarbell replied the next day, part archly and part affectionately, "I suppose that if I had stayed a week in New York there would still be a good many things that were left unsaid. One of the satisfactions of the S. S. McClure Company in fact is that the last word is never said, and I hope never will be."

If McClure sometimes played the role of father or older brother, Tarbell reciprocated by playing the role of McClure's sober older sister. McClure never fell out of love with his wife, but he found monogamy difficult to sustain. When he began a dalliance with the poet Florence Wilkinson, Tarbell, along with John Phillips, attempted to end the affair and keep the magazine on course while its owner was distracted. If Tarbell's meddling upset McClure, he was not bitter. Even as Tarbell was trying to break up the affair, McClure wrote to her of her value to the magazine, adding, "I have always cared for you in a special manner, as much as a man can care for a woman without loving her."

Amid the office camaraderie and drama, Tarbell contemplated how to advance her plan for meaningful investigations beyond the high-profile Napoleon and Lincoln projects, given her daily burdens of work. Her intensive study of the Lincoln presidency led her inexorably to seek an in-depth understanding of post–Civil War America. She squeezed historical research into stolen moments away from the editing desk. That study in turn gave her the confidence to define the most pressing issues for the readership at the start of a new century.

The biggest story, without question, concerned the role of gigantic corporations in industry after industry. She saw greed; she saw indifference to the plight of the common worker. The fallout from the big trusts such as Standard Oil seemed antithetical to democracy. "Were they not potentially a more subtle form of slavery, more dangerous because less obvious?" Tarbell reflected. She had long felt that she harbored not just the skills but also the ambition to make an impact with her research and writing. Given the national and global reach of Standard Oil, she felt the perfect time had arrived for an in-depth examination of multinational trusts, centering on John D. Rockefeller's creation.

More than any other piece of scholarship or journalism, what helped guide Tarbell's thinking was the book *Wealth Against Commonwealth*, by Henry Demarest Lloyd. The book reached Tarbell in Paris in 1894. Lloyd, the son of a poorly compensated Reformed Dutch Church minister, joined the intellectual elite when a patron of his father's paid his tuition to Columbia College in New York City. After earning a law degree and working as a free-trade advocate, he joined the *Chicago Tribune* staff, where he began writing critically about trusts as early as 1878. Lloyd joined the wealthy class by marrying the daughter of the *Tribune's* publisher. But money did not diminish his resentment of the trusts. The more he learned, the more he felt American capitalism encouraged greed, and like Tarbell, he decided to use journalism to change what he could.

Lloyd's 1881 article, "The Story of a Great Monopoly," published in the *Atlantic Monthly*, took aim at all monopolies but used Standard Oil as a prominent case study. Discussing Rockefeller's alleged bribing of politicians with Standard Oil money, Lloyd quipped that the oil trust had "done everything with the Pennsylvania legislature except refine it." He closed the *Atlantic Monthly* article on a sarcastic but ominous note by stating that "America has the proud satisfaction of having furnished the world with the greatest, wisest and meanest monopoly known to history."

In 1887, Lloyd, before expanding his article into a book, watched

Rockefeller testify before the newly created Interstate Commerce Commission. Afterward, he headed his notes "Fanatic Standard Oil," writing about Rockefeller that he is "a czar of plutocracy, a worshipper of his own money power over mankind . . . He will stop when he is stopped—not before . . . Think cold, ruthless."

Lloyd wrote as much from his heart as from his head. He did nothing to contact Standard Oil sources while composing his book-length indictment. Partly because of that omission, the book is filled with factual errors. *Wealth Against Commonwealth* is an elliptical book written in simultaneously flowery and white-hot prose. Lloyd rarely names names (Rockefeller's name appears just once), but he excoriates trust magnates in general. Commentators assumed that he had omitted names of individuals either to avoid libel or to practice civility. Instead, he omitted them—despite his belief in the legal and moral guilt of corporate directors—because he worried that specific names would divert attention from the systemic indictment. It seems like an unwise choice, at least in retrospect. Without concrete targets, Lloyd's book lacked punch. "The public seems to be utterly stagnant, but their enemy is not," Lloyd complained. If his book had been published later, it might have cast a permanent shadow over Standard Oil's practices. But the Progressive Era had not flowered fully; the preachings of William Jennings Bryan and Theodore Roosevelt, among others, about the negatives of industrial trusts had not caught on yet.

Lloyd's restraint about naming names allowed Rockefeller to dismiss the book. Decades later, Rockefeller told his authorized interviewer, William Inglis, that he had refused to dignify Lloyd's allegations by replying. Furthermore, he said, "a man cannot concentrate his faculties at the same time on two opposite things, and I was concentrated upon extending and developing and perfecting our business, rather than to stop by the wayside and squabble with slanderers."

Having digested Lloyd's indictment, Tarbell visited the ideas of other reform-minded authors. She located Charles Francis Adams, Jr.'s 1869 article in the *North American Review* advocating government regulation of quasi-monopolistic railroads. She sought to understand rural suspicion of corporate power as chronicled in D. C. Cloud's 1872 book *Monopolies and the People.* She examined arguments for unhampered competition—a level playing field—put forth by Thomas A. Bland in his 1881 book *The Reign of Monopoly.* Probably most influential of all were Henry George's *Progress and Poverty* (1880) and Edward Bellamy's *Looking Backward,* published toward the end of the decade, in 1888.

Through Henry George, Tarbell began to understand that the kind of capital produced by Rockefeller should never be valued more highly than the capital produced by individual laborers, including those cultivating the land. "God gave man the land, but man has to use his hand and brain in its cultivation before he can feed and clothe and shelter himself," she wrote while explicating George's philosophy. "It is the partnership of the two—land and labor—which produces wealth." Given that labor created capital, how had it come to be that capital, represented by the likes of Rockefeller and Standard Oil, held itself superior to labor? Tarbell wondered. Improper behavior, she concluded. "Labor has been made dependent on capital by capital's theft of the land which God gave to all." Land use would be taxed in George's plan, with the proceeds of that tax paying for government services. No other tax would be necessary—thus George's creation of the "single tax" model.

Bellamy, like other Progressive Era writers, used allegory and satire to criticize the trusts. The hero of *Looking Backward* is Julian West, a Boston gentleman who falls asleep at home in 1887 and awakens in the year 2000. By then the United States citizenry has overthrown corporate tyranny in much the way an earlier generation had overthrown political tyranny imposed by England. In Bellamy's novel, the country's commerce serves the mass good rather than enriching a small number of tycoons and their managers. *Looking Backward* encouraged Tarbell to consider the larger implications of the capitalist structure, the government's role in it, the ethical obligations of individuals who wielded power, and the fates of those who did not.

Tarbell also learned a great deal about trusts from the 1888 campaign for the U.S. presidency. The Republicans, through their candidate, Benjamin Harrison, wanted to unseat incumbent Democrat Grover Cleveland, the first of his political party to occupy the White House since James Buchanan in 1856. Rockefeller, Carnegie, and other wealthy business owners traditionally supported the Republicans. Contributions from individual industrialists and their corporations to elected politicians were common during the final decades of the nineteenth century and into the twentieth century. Carnegie, and to a lesser extent Rockefeller, became targets of the Democrats, who wanted to portray Harrison and the Republican Party as beholden to the founders of the trusts. Carnegie publicly and loudly denied the existence of an iron and steel trust, while Rockefeller, who always took a circumspect view of the press, tried to remain in the background. On the dramatic election day, Cleveland won the popular vote, but the Republicans prevailed as Harrison won the electoral vote and thus entered the White House.

The Republican victory in a campaign where antitrust sentiment had become an issue focused McClure's mind. By 1890 he began to assign articles and offer material from his syndicate about the trusts. The Sherman Antitrust Act had been approved by Congress and signed into law, unenthusiastically, by President Harrison, raising consciousness about how far government could and should go in regulating monopolistic practices. McClure distributed a symposium of opinion titled "After the Trusts: Are They Legal and Who Derives Benefit?" One of the symposium's participants was lawyer Samuel C. T. Dodd, Standard Oil's general counsel. Dodd had published academic papers under titles such as "Aggregated Capital: Its History and Influence." Over and over in his writings, he found reasons to justify and even praise trusts.

The passage of the Sherman Antitrust Act meant little in practice during the 1890s. Congress allocated only small sums to the Justice Department for enforcement. When Grover Cleveland regained the White House in 1892, he did not place enforcement of the Sherman Antitrust Act high on his agenda. The law's intent seemed vague, and government legal advisers told Cleveland that the loopholes would make effective action against Standard Oil or any other trust a long shot. Rockefeller and his colleagues began shifting toward a legal model called a holding company, raising new difficulties for federal prosecutors, given the Sherman Act phrasing. Then, with the election of Republican McKinley to the White House in 1896, it seemed that the Sherman Act would become no more than a footnote as the new century arrived, given the new president's anathema toward trust-busting.

A few state governments whose legislators and governors needed the support of farmers and small-town entrepreneurs—groups suspicious of the trusts—moved forward (gingerly, given federal preeminence) to fill the antitrust breach. As early as 1889, David K. Watson, Ohio's Republican attorney general, had begun worrying about the hegemony of trusts and abuses by Standard Oil in particular. When Watson realized that the corporate headquarters in Cleveland had become something of a shell, with actual control exercised from New York City, he filed fraud charges against Standard Oil with the Ohio Supreme Court. Rockefeller pressured Republican Party officials to tell Watson to relent. The attorney general, however, refused to back down. In 1892, the Ohio Supreme Court found that the New York trustees indeed controlled Standard Oil, in violation of state law against absentee ownership.

Standard Oil's counsel Dodd told a journalist that the ruling would have little impact on the trust, which would simply adjust its operations, as it had done in the past after legal challenges. Rockefeller and Dodd assigned staff to study the corporation laws of each state, to determine which might offer the most favorable atmosphere for the trust arrangement. After the Ohio Supreme Court's adverse ruling, Standard Oil shifted its headquarters, at least in name, to New Jersey. Standard Oil (New Jersey) became a dominant unit among the twenty intertwined corporations that developed as a reaction to the Ohio court mandate. Standard Oil and Rockefeller could not and would not be contained by a state government's legal challenge.

In 1897, Frank Monnett, Watson's Republican successor as Ohio attorney general, charged that the Standard Oil trust continued to defy state law and that the reorganization in New Jersey served merely as a sham. He obtained an order for Rockefeller to testify, though he accommodated the tycoon by allowing the testimony to take place in New York City. During five hours on the witness stand, Rockefeller managed to say nothing of substance. His lawyers objected frequently to the questions.

When Rockefeller did answer, he often said that details had escaped his memory. The *New York World* commented the next day, "The virtue of forgetting, which is one of the most valuable virtues that a monopolist can have under cross-examination, is possessed by Mr. Rockefeller in its highest degree."

Quite a bit of Monnett's evidence and some of his funding came from George Rice, a veteran oilman four years older than Rockefeller. Rice had become an oil producer in northwest Pennsylvania during the 1860s, then moved to Marietta, Ohio, where he expanded into the refinery business. He refused to merge with Standard Oil and styled himself a Rockefeller antagonist. For decades Rice had pushed federal and state prosecutors to hold Standard Oil to account. At least once he confronted Rockefeller publicly—on October 12, 1898, in the New Amsterdam Hotel in New York City. Present because of an oil industry gathering, Rockefeller approached his avowed enemy. "How are you, George?" Rockefeller said, according to those present. "We are getting to be gray-haired men now, aren't we? Don't you wish you had taken my advice years ago?" Rice refused to shake the hand put forward by Rockefeller, then replied, "Perhaps it would have been better for me if I had. You have certainly ruined my business, as you said you would." Rockefeller denied that allegation, but Rice retorted, "But I say it is so. You know well that by the power of your great wealth you have ruined my business, and you cannot deny it." At that point Rockefeller walked away, saying to onlookers that Rice's allegation contained no truth.

U.S. Senator Joseph B. Foraker, whom Tarbell later revealed as being on the Standard Oil payroll, expressed his displeasure to Monnett that the attorney general had challenged Rockefeller. Monnett brushed off the warning. When Monnett sought renomination as attorney general from the Ohio Republican Party in 1899, he came away empty. Challenging Rockefeller and Standard Oil had quite likely cost him his career.

During the 1890s, Texas was the only state other than Ohio to seriously challenge Standard Oil on antitrust grounds. But soon after the start of the new century, another six states moved against Standard Oil, encouraged by an invigorated press and a seeming surge in adoption of the Progressive platform by the citizenry. The antitrust activity led to little meaningful change, however. In his book *Antitrust and the Oil Monopoly: The Standard Oil Cases, 1890–1911*, scholar Bruce Bringhurst documented failed efforts to curtail the trust in Nebraska, Minnesota, Iowa, Arkansas, Kansas, and Mississippi, plus the Oklahoma territory.

Bringhurst said Standard Oil prevailed most of the time because of the huge amounts of money it could spend on "the nation's greatest lawyers," on elected politicians who pressured antitrust activists within their political parties, and on public relations experts who quietly launched campaigns to discredit prosecutors in their communities. Furthermore, he believed, at least some of the prosecutors filed antitrust actions for their public relations value. The cases "helped institutionalize the antitrust suit as the politician's recourse when corporate abuse offended too deeply the public's collective sense of propriety."

Rockefeller naturally resisted the antitrust wave, usually finding the reception he wanted among journalists and government officials. Sometimes, however, the press treated his outlook on trusts with skepticism, leading to ripples of opposition to his views in the larger society. A *New York Times* editorial about an unfriendly exchange between Rockefeller and members of a national industrial commission took the stance that trusts "should no longer be managed by a few directors or head men behind closed doors, that its millions of capital may no longer be diminished, withheld or increased without informing the shareholders—and the public—of the business facts that have warranted the policy pursued." The newspaper had prominently covered the controversial tycoon's testimony, given his normal refusal to cooperate with any government entity. The front-page headline of January 11, 1900, said, "Rockefeller on Trusts/Standard Oil President Gives Expression to His Views/Believes in Control by Law/He Asserts That Combinations Are Necessary and Points Out Their Dangers and Advantages."

Given all the coverage and all the controversy, the *McClure's Magazine* staff decided that they must figure out how to present the trust issue in a memorable manner. "About that time the talk about the trusts had become general—it was an important subject," McClure recalled. "The feeling of the common people had a sort of menace in it; they took a threatening attitude toward the trusts, and without much knowledge." The office discussions led to the inexorable conclusion that the magazine should concentrate on one trust, presenting, McClure said, "its history, its effects and its tendencies." Standard Oil and Rockefeller were obvious targets, but they seemed so formidable that the magazine staff hesitated. At one point Tarbell suggested that they examine how the sugar trust gained control of prices and gouged consumers. McClure thought that sugar seemed trivial compared to other products controlled by trusts.

In a previous attempt to explain the beef trust, McClure had sent reporter Arthur Warren to the World's Fair in Chicago to write about Philip Armour and his meat company. Warren's report, appearing during the magazine's first year, carried the mild headline "Philip D. Armour: His Manner of Life, His Immense Enterprises in Trade and Philanthropy." Revisiting the Armour story seemed sensible; President Theodore Roosevelt had singled out the beef trust for attention by charging its principals with restraint of trade. But Armour had died in 1901, making it difficult for the magazine staff to personify the story for its audience.

The U.S. Steel Corporation had become huge and dominant, but it lacked the visibility already attained by Standard Oil with most *McClure's Magazine* readers. The reasons for the differing interest revolved around the nature of the products. Standard Oil purchased materials from thousands of suppliers, and the petroleum products that resulted ended up in millions of homes through wholesalers, retailers, and jobbers. U.S. Steel dealt with far fewer suppliers, and during its early decades individual homeowners purchased few of its products.

As the decisionmaking process unfolded, Tarbell sought a variety of opinions about which trust to investigate. She corresponded with people outside the New York City newsroom, like John Finley, who attended a national conference about trusts called by the Chicago-based reformer Jane Addams and then discussed with Tarbell what he had learned. She was also exchanging letters with Alfred Maurice Low, a British-born economist turned journalist living in Washington, D.C. "Can an investigation of trusts be made of sufficient interest to the readers of a popular magazine?" Low asked, trying to challenge her intellectually while angling for a *McClure's Magazine* assignment. "Can it also definitively, absolutely and unassailably and for the first time settle the question of whether the trust is a good or bad thing?" Could such an investigation appeal, Low wondered, "to the masses as well as that smaller, but not inconsequential, class, the political economist and the student of sociological problems?" He asserted optimistically, "I think it can, because the question is full of intense human interest."

Throughout the staff's deliberations, Tarbell referred to the experiences her father and brother had had with Rockefeller and Standard Oil. The more she spoke up during the staff meetings, the more it became clear to her colleagues that Rockefeller and his Standard Oil trust "had been a strong thread weaving itself into the pattern" of her life. She uniquely could bring the requisite passion and skills to the project. Nobody had published a thoroughly researched, journalistically responsible, compellingly composed explanation of how Rockefeller and Standard Oil had achieved such influence and wealth. The staff agreed that Tarbell should be the first.

She drafted an outline for a series about the nation's trust problem, using Standard Oil as the connecting link. In September 1901, she sailed to Europe to present the outline to McClure, who was living on the continent with his wife for part of each year. Tarbell met McClure in Lausanne. He looked over the outline but refused to render a quick verdict. Instead, he dragged her along to Greece with his family for a working holiday. On the way east from Lausanne, he decided that he and Hattie needed a cure in the ancient watering place of Salsomaggiore. There, Tarbell recounted, "in the interval of mud baths and steam soaks . . . we finally came to a decision. I was to go back to New York and see what I could make of the outline I had been expounding. Greece was to be abandoned."

Tarbell retained notes of her discussion with McClure on a piece of yellow stationery from the Hotel des Thermes in Salsomaggiore. The notes, archived with the rest of her papers at Allegheny College, reveal that the goal of the Standard Oil trust project was to give readers "a clear and succinct notion of the processes by which a particular industry passes from the control of the many to that of the few." Furthermore, McClure told Tarbell, Rockefeller's prominence within the Standard Oil trust "would lend itself almost to the simplicity of biographical treatment." Harking back to an earlier success at the magazine, McClure ruminated, "There is no question that he is the Napoleon among business men."

McClure approved a three-part, 25,000-word series. Neither he nor Tarbell could have guessed how inadequate that length would prove to be.

〡〡

Researching the Behemoth

The new century arrived on January 1, 1900, with much pomp across the nation. The round number of the new century, the twentieth, gave it a certain gravitas, a sense that great changes were to come for the United States of America. Indeed, with the country expanding its imperial holdings abroad and undergoing a near-miraculous industrial boom, commentators began using the phrase "the American century."

Ida Tarbell reached age forty-three in 1900. Although she could not have known it, she had lived half her life. Nevertheless, she sensed that her life was pivoting as the century began. In fact, the two halves of Tarbell's life, each lived in a different century, would mirror the profound shifts that the nation itself experienced.

The final decades of the nineteenth century, which had spawned the Standard Oil Company and other trusts, had ended. The trusts remained, however, dominating industry after industry, apparently above, or at least outside, the law. The early years of the new century would yield an important new factor—the saturation of an increasingly literate citizenry with magazines willing to question the status quo. The seemingly quixotic project upon which Tarbell had embarked—to investigate the

Ida Tarbell rarely relaxed, and often she felt guilty for putting her work aside. Her second home, in rural Connecticut, which she shared with her sister, provided her a peaceful retreat for writing and research away from the demands of New York City. *Ida M. Tarbell Collection, Pelletier Library, Allegheny College*

Though Tarbell remained humble in public and private, other journalists were quick to lionize her. *Courtesy of the Pennsylvania Historical and Museum Commission, Drake Well Museum, Titusville*

Even after she became famous, Tarbell (left) never neglected her family. Her father's death in 1905 depressed her, but her beloved mother lived another decade, and her sister, Sarah, proved a constant companion. Although Sarah managed her own career as an artist, she devoted herself diligently to keeping her older sister's life in order.

Ida M. Tarbell Collection, Pelletier Library, Allegheny College

As public outrage against Standard Oil grew, the trust began to disguise some of its business dealings through captive companies. One of those companies placed its headquarters in Missouri. During the first decade of the twentieth century, Missouri officials unmasked the arrangement, which led to this editorial cartoon. *Courtesy of the Pennsylvania Historical and Museum Commission, Drake Well Museum, Titusville*

The dismantling of the Standard Oil monopoly by the Supreme Court was seen as a great triumph of the Progressives, yet the thirty-three spin-off companies served to expand Rockefeller's wealth (and the federal government's responsibilities) exponentially, as this 1911 editorial cartoon suggests. *Courtesy of the Pennsylvania Historical and Museum Commission, Drake Well Museum, Titusville*

Ida Tarbell's exposé hurt Standard Oil's reputation, but the trust continued to dominate the oil industry and enrich its executives as well as its shareholders. On February 3, 1909, Luther Daniels Bradley's commentary in the *Chicago Daily News* suggested that Standard Oil was continuing to expand by quietly subsuming related businesses. *Courtesy of the Library of Congress*

As pressure mounted against Rockefeller and Standard Oil, Rockefeller did not shy away from public life. In fact, he hired public relations consultants in an attempt to reestablish a positive image. This standing portrait, made around 1910, conveys an imposing aura. *Photographer unknown; Courtesy of the Library of Congress/RMP Archive*

The New York headquarters of Standard Oil made the address 26 Broadway known internationally. Tarbell conducted key interviews in the building, though not with Rockefeller himself. The building still stands in Lower Manhattan. *Copyright © Irving Underhill, N.Y. / Courtesy of the Library of Congress*

This photograph from about 1909 shows the west front of Rockefeller's estate Kykuit, in the Hudson River Valley. Rockefeller was not an ostentatious man, but his son, John Jr., who also lived there with his wife, Abby, was fond of luxury. *Courtesy of the Library of Congress*

John D. Rockefeller's wife, Laura Celestia (Cettie) Spellman, preferred the privacy of her family homes to high society. Like her husband, whom she married in 1864, Cettie found Kykuit overly ostentatious in many ways. Although she did not play an active role in the management of Standard Oil, she served as a trusted confidante for her husband until her death in 1915. The couple is shown here in the summer of 1911, just months after the Supreme Court ruling that disbanded Standard Oil. *Courtesy of the Library of Congress*

Rockefeller, who believed that his Baptist faith accounted for much of his success, strolled on Fifth Avenue with his only son, John Jr., on Palm Sunday 1915. *American Press Association/Courtesy of the Library of Congress/ RMP Archive*

As their fame waned, S. S. McClure, novelist Willa Cather, and journalists Ida Tarbell and Will Irwin, all of *McClure's Magazine*, met on a park bench in 1925. © *Bettmann/ Corbis*

Ida Tarbell lived half of her eighty-seven years in the nineteenth century and half in the twentieth century. This portrait, taken about six years before her death, appeared in many of her 1944 obituaries. *Ida M. Tarbell Collection, Pelletier Library, Allegheny College*

In this 1909 portrait, John D. Rockefeller conveys the relentless determination and intelligence that made him one of the great business leaders of the United States and the world. He would never outlive the stigma of Tarbell's famous report, however, despite years of dedication to his family, his faith, and his philanthropic work. He died at age ninety-eight in 1937. *Courtesy of the Library of Congress*

world's most dominant economic organization—would come to define the new century like few other struggles. It became, indeed, an American epic.

And yet the personification of that dominant economic organization seemed at first glance to have removed himself from his position of influence. Rockefeller had reportedly retired from day-to-day management of Standard Oil in 1897 because of health concerns. By 1900, he was sixty-one years old and was worried about dying. Obsessed with longevity—he wanted to reach age one hundred—he had taken up bicycling and golf for recreation and continued to supervise expansion of his estate in Upstate New York. Rockefeller pursued each hobby with the single-mindedness he had previously shown in learning about oil refining. To improve his golf score, he hired a professional teacher, employed a photographer to assemble a stop-time sequence of his backswing and down swing, recorded all his scores in a booklet, and even retained a young man to say "Keep your head down" to him before each stroke.

The evidence is overwhelming that after his supposed retirement, Rockefeller rarely stopped thinking about Standard Oil. He continued to hold nearly 30 percent of Standard Oil's stock, more than any other individual, and he was kept informed about corporate decisions, sometimes directly, sometimes through his youngest child, John D. Rockefeller, Jr., who worked diligently at the corporate headquarters.

Rockefeller had a lot at stake. His personal wealth and the staggering breadth of the family fortune at the turn of the century can be understood only in terms of comparison. In 1901, the average income for the American working man was $10 per week, lower for women. Rockefeller was receiving about $3 million from Standard Oil each year in stock dividends alone. The influence of his wealth transcended oil. He had spread his capital throughout the economy, investing in railroad companies, real estate firms, agriculture, steel factories, steamship lines, and banks and financial houses, among other businesses.

Given Rockefeller's wealth and perceived ruthlessness, Tarbell's relatives, friends, and work colleagues who sensed the scope of the *McClure's Magazine* project worried about her safety. "Don't do it, Ida, they will ruin the magazine," warned her elderly, ailing father, who had felt Rockefeller's retribution in the past. She shrugged off such warnings and found it puzzling when she received compliments for her courage. "Courage implies a suspicion of danger . . . ," she commented later. "We were undertaking what we regarded as a legitimate piece of historical work. We were neither apologists nor critics, only journalists intent on discovering what had gone into the making of this most perfect of all monopolies. What had we to be afraid of?"

Tarbell had experienced Rockefeller's influence. Her father had spoken out against Standard Oil's operations during its formative years. Her brother, known as W. W. Tarbell in the business world, served as an executive of Pure Oil Company, an independent producer and marketer. Pure Oil, having acquired assets incrementally in the shadow of Standard Oil, owned producing wells in Oklahoma, Illinois, and eastern states, as well as pipelines and trunk lines in several regions. To bolster its market position, Pure affiliated with independent refiners in locales such as Titusville. Will Tarbell looked for business connections overseas too, despite efforts by Standard Oil to seal off business there.

Ida's family connections to the oil business could have opened her to allegations of bias in her reporting and writing about Standard Oil, but her colleagues did not doubt her motives. They understood her fairminded nature and her research skills. They understood that coming of age in the oil region and having family in the oil industry only fueled her passion to conduct an exhaustive inquiry, not to settle personal or philosophical scores. Moreover, the McClure's Magazine staff had dedicated itself to progressive journalism.

During the early months of Tarbell's research, the antitrust cause received a boost grounded in tragedy. On September 6, 1901, an assassin who considered himself an anarchist shot President McKinley, who died eight days later. Vice President Theodore Roosevelt took up residence in the White House, ready to cooperate with journalists, reformminded politicians, and state attorneys general. Despite his privileged upbringing, Roosevelt could be counted on to speak candidly about the dangers of corporate concentration. As governor of New York State, he

had alienated business executives by accepting their campaign contributions, then enacting taxes and regulations they opposed. Roosevelt did
not uniformly revile the trusts; he distinguished between good trusts
that kept the public interest in mind and those that gouged the citizenry.
He tended to point to Standard Oil as the epitome of the abusive trust,
and to Rockefeller as its personification. As one Rockefeller biographer
put it, Roosevelt "had a glint in his eye for Standard Oil. He was a big-
game hunter, and Standard Oil was big game. In a speech he said that the
nation had to grapple with the problem of fortunes in big business." The
speech included the line "Of course, no amount of charities in spending
such fortunes can compensate for the misconduct in acquiring them."
Jules Abels commented archly, "Every hearer knew whom he meant."

Encouraged by Roosevelt's outspokenness about the dangers of trusts,
especially Standard Oil, state regulators around the country began inquiries into the dominance of industrial leaders. Court cases against trusts
proliferated. As the judicial activity unfolded, the industry expanded to
Kansas, Oklahoma, and California, as new oil reserves yielded to increasingly sophisticated technology. The geographic dispersion of wells gave
reformers hope that Standard Oil's control would weaken as a matter of
course. Rockefeller and his lieutenants found it difficult to change with
the times. They viewed government intervention of any sort as unwarranted, and they considered Standard Oil's business activities to be above
and beyond government control.

Unlike previous Standard Oil critics, who wrote with passion but used
facts selectively, Tarbell intended to dig up new material. Congressional committees and state legislatures had held hearings and published
reports about Standard Oil for decades. Tarbell expected the mining of
such documents to yield material for a rich narrative account. "This mass
of testimony—most, if not all, of it taken under oath—contained the different charters and agreements under which the Standard Oil trust had
operated, many contracts and agreements with railroads, with refineries, with pipelines," she recalled. Furthermore, she found, the testimony
"contained the experiences in business from 1872 to 1900 of multitudes
of individuals. These experiences had exactly the quality of the personal

reminiscences of actors in great events, with the additional value that they were given on the witness stand." Some of that sworn testimony came from Rockefeller himself. So Tarbell had access to his words conveying the public version of his thinking.

Beginning to feel overwhelmed by the research, Tarbell received permission to hire an assistant. Looking for someone who would match her own intelligence, drive, and work ethic, she solicited recommendations from three newspaper editors in Cleveland, where Standard Oil conducted much of its business. She gave each candidate a research test by mail from New York City, then traveled to Cleveland to interview the most promising. John McAlpine Siddall proved the best of the lot. A former editor at *The Chautauquan*, he was serving as secretary to the Cleveland Board of Education.

Fearful that Rockefeller's agents would intercept their correspondence, Tarbell and Siddall decided to communicate vaguely or in coded phrases. Occasionally the letters conveyed veiled excitement, as when Tarbell wrote to Siddall, "Yesterday I took my proofs and went to Philadelphia, where I spent the whole evening . . . with my brother and the man who gave me the documents. I wish you were here to see them before I have to give them up. They are very remarkable."

Lawsuits filed in courthouses around the nation yielded documents never before used by journalists. Although the paperwork undergirding legislation and the court files from litigants are often available, most journalists in those days did not seek them. Tarbell's Standard Oil research demonstrated how documents could be used to substitute for otherwise inaccessible human sources. Tarbell and Siddall also searched newspaper files, especially in Cleveland, for published articles that described Rockefeller's philanthropies, business deals, and family activities. They tracked down church records of Rockefeller's charitable contributions. They asked Standard Oil competitors for revealing correspondence with Rockefeller.

Setting the protocols for a new kind of journalism, Tarbell and Siddall gathered as much information as possible before approaching Standard Oil officials. "Someone once asked me why I did not go first to the heads of the company for my information," Tarbell told an interviewer. "This person did not know overmuch of humanity, I think, else he would have realized instantly that the Standard Oil Company would have shut the door of their closet on the skeleton. But after one had discovered the skeleton and scrutinized him at a very close range, why then shut the door? That is the reason I did not go to the magnates in the beginning."

Tarbell's initial attempts at conversations with Standard Oil executives proved fruitless. She began to encounter the problems of trying to penetrate a corporate culture. "I had been met with that formulated chatter used by those who have accepted a creed, a situation, a system, to baffle the investigator trying to find out what it means." Finally she found her entry point in the unlikely person of Henry Rogers, a man of high rank in the Standard Oil trust. A former independent oil producer who had fought the Rockefeller juggernaut until finally capitulating, Rogers possessed a strong curiosity that drew him to Tarbell. But their face-to-face meetings at Standard Oil headquarters perhaps never would have occurred without a pair of fortuitous circumstances.

First, Rogers had lived in Rouseville while Tarbell was a young girl there and had known of Franklin Sumner Tarbell. "At the very moment I was beginning to run the hills above Rouseville, he was running a small refinery on the creek and living on a hillside just below ours, separated only by a narrow ravine, along each side of which ran a path," Tarbell noted.

Second, Rogers, a patron of the arts, had become friendly with the celebrity author Samuel Clemens. After Rogers heard rumors that Tarbell was investigating, he wrote to Clemens on December 26, 1901. Worried that she would obtain all her information from Standard Oil's enemies, Rogers hoped she would approach sources at the trust: "I do not know whether you can be of any service in the matter, but it would be a kindness to Mr. McClure as well as myself if you could suggest to him that some care should be taken to verify statements which may be made through his magazine, whether affecting corporations or individuals." Within a week, Clemens had met with August F. Jaccaci, the art director at *McClure's Magazine*. On January 2, 1902, Clemens wrote to Rogers that Jaccaci "said Miss Tarbell would be only too glad to have both sides, and I told him she could have free access to the Standard Oil's archives." Shortly after, Tarbell and Rogers began meeting at Standard Oil headquarters.

Also through the coincidence of geography, Tarbell gained insight into the mind of another Standard Oil executive, John D. Archbold, who had moved to Titusville in 1864 at age fifteen, separating from his family to make a living in the oil fields. He married Annie M. Mills, the daughter of the proprietor of Titusville's finest hotel. Coming of age in Titusville, Tarbell had admired the Mills family members for their refined tastes and considered Archbold himself to be a paragon of good sense and manners. In business, however, Archbold came across as a flamboyant and aggressive entrepreneur. Rockefeller first took notice of him while at an oil region hotel where Archbold had registered earlier in the day. In the registry, he had written "John D. Archbold, four dollars a barrel." As Rockefeller recalled, "He was a young and enthusiastic fellow, so full of his subject that he added his slogan . . . after his signature on the register so that no one might misunderstand his convictions."

It is uncertain whether Tarbell and Archbold discussed her research before publication. The transcript of a 1934 interview with Tarbell in the papers of historian Allan Nevins at Columbia University suggests that she never approached Archbold for substantive information about Standard Oil. "I would not get straight goods from Archbold . . . ," she said. "He took the attitude that the Standard could do no wrong. In view of his success, he considered that the company was so great an element in the industrial life of the nation that they were exempt from criticism."

When Tarbell and Archbold both ended up in New York City because of their vocations, she assumed that they would cross paths as a matter of course, coming from the same region of Pennsylvania. For years that did not occur, to her surprise. It was only when Tarbell's Standard Oil investigation became public knowledge that she received a dinner invitation from Archbold's wife. With trepidation, she decided to accept, and one evening found herself at his "fine brownstone house uptown." She ate a "superior" meal. But Tarbell realized during that evening, with finality, that she neither liked nor trusted Archbold, so did not accept any more social invitations from his wife.

On the other hand, Tarbell liked and trusted Rogers. They met frequently both at his home and at Standard Oil headquarters. Though he cooperated with Tarbell, Rogers was circumspect. She recalled how "the alert, handsome, businesslike little chaps who received me at the entrance to Rogers' suite piloted me unerringly by a route where nobody saw me and I saw nobody into the same small room opening on to a court, and it seemed never the same route." Worried about being compromised, Tarbell would not accept even the glass of milk offered by Rogers at the meetings unless she could pay for it. She and Rogers agreed that she would show him drafts of her manuscript when she thought the timing appropriate. He would offer comments, but Tarbell reserved the right to accept or reject them.

Rogers seems to have engaged with Tarbell for several reasons. They came from the same region of Pennsylvania; he enjoyed interacting with her at an intellectual level, and he might have been trying to exercise control over the narrative she would write. Whatever his reasons, he agreed, month after month, to meet again. Some sessions proceeded smoothly. At other sessions, Rogers was confrontational or evasive. News of the meetings reached a small number of Standard Oil advocates and critics, including Henry Demarest Lloyd, whose *Wealth Against Commonwealth* had captured Tarbell's attention nearly a decade earlier. She had been hoping that Lloyd would supply documents from his vast collection; according to Lloyd's papers at the State Historical Society of Wisconsin, Tarbell introduced herself to him by letter on March 28, 1902. She felt optimistic about obtaining Lloyd's cooperation, but when he learned about the meetings with Rogers, Lloyd wondered if she had been compromised journalistically. Only after a face-to-face meeting at his Rhode Island summer home did Lloyd set his worries about her independence to rest. He later shared his thinking and a limited amount of his material with her.

In hindsight, Tarbell decided that Rogers continued the sessions "because of his interest in my presentation of a particular episode in their history. It was a case in which Mr. Rogers and John Archbold, along with all of the members of the board of a subsidiary . . . the Vacuum Oil Company of Rochester, New York, had been indicted for conspiring to destroy an independent refinery in Buffalo." Rogers believed himself wronged by the grand jury, so wanted Tarbell to hear his version. After she read the confidential grand jury proceedings Rogers shared with her, Tarbell told him that she believed in his innocence—although others aligned with Standard Oil seemed guilty.

As their meetings continued, Rogers began to realize how infrequently Tarbell could be persuaded to view matters his way. He angrily halted the meetings when he discovered that she had been researching allegations that Standard Oil had developed an espionage network to gain corporate intelligence about rivals—allegations that he had insisted were unsubstantiated.

Tarbell unexpectedly obtained access to Henry M. Flagler, Rockefeller's longtime business partner—off the record. Rockefeller would have been appalled had he known what Flagler said about his character. Flagler told Tarbell, according to the journalist's notes, that Rockefeller "is the biggest little man and littlest big man he ever knew, that he would give one hundred thousand dollars one minute to charity and turn around and haggle over the price of a ton of coal . . . He would do me out of a dollar today—that is, if he could do it honestly."

Starting with court testimony and other statements from independent oil producers over a thirty-year period and bolstered by information from Standard Oil insiders, Tarbell pieced together a corporate espionage saga perhaps greater than anything previously perpetrated by a government. As she studied the material, she noticed complaints from Standard Oil competitors about mysterious interference with oil shipments. Train cars would be inexplicably sidetracked while buyers awaiting the shipment received last-minute pressure to cancel orders. She began to suspect that railroad freight clerks might be reporting the shipments to Standard Oil.

"I did not take the matter seriously at first," Tarbell said. "The general suspicion of Standard dealings by independents had to be taken into consideration, I told myself. Then, too, I was willing to admit that a certain amount of attention to what your competitor is doing is considered legitimate business practice." But as the documented problems continued to multiply, she found the espionage theory difficult to rule out. Eventually she received unimpeachable proof of a conspiracy. A teenage clerk working in a Standard Oil office began reading the documents he had been given to burn. On one of those documents, he noticed the name of an independent oil refiner who had served as his Sunday school teacher. Both surprised at the content of the documents and shocked at the involvement of his Sunday school teacher, the clerk delivered the papers to the independent refiner, who contacted Tarbell because of his admiration for her reporting in *McClure's Magazine*.

Tarbell so valued thoroughness that she probably would have continued to research full-time for at least several years before writing the opening installment for the magazine. McClure, however, with proof of Standard Oil's espionage in hand, wanted the first installment quickly, with others to follow month by month. His excitement building, he placed an announcement prominently in the magazine, even before he knew the full extent of Tarbell's discoveries: "The leading feature for the ensuing year is Miss Tarbell's history of the Standard Oil Company. This series of articles will furnish an object lesson in the paramount public question of today—the question of trusts. Here we have a vivid illustration of how a trust is made, of what it costs to replace competition by a single-headed combination." McClure explained how Tarbell would tell "the amazing story of the attempt in 1872 of a few men, aided by the leading officials of the Standard Oil Company and the railroad kings of the day—Vanderbilt, Gould and Scott—to seize the oil industry, an attempt frustrated by a popular uprising in the Oil Regions." McClure promised that Tarbell would document "how later the Standard was able to secure special freight rates which enabled it to become the most nearly perfect monopoly of the nineteenth century. It rehearses the tragedies which the rise of the Standard necessitated." This account of Standard Oil and Rockefeller constituted "a great human drama," McClure said, "the story of the conflict of the two great commercial principles of the day—competition and combination.

Miss Tarbell . . . tells this history . . . without partisan passion and entirely from documents."

McClure's preview was no exaggeration. But not even McClure, the ringleader of the muckrakers, could have predicted just how important Tarbell's narrative would be.

‖‖

CHAPTER THIRTEEN

Exposed

In a speech about trusts at Brown University, John D. Rockefeller, Jr., once said, "The American Beauty Rose can be produced in its splendor and fragrance only by sacrificing the early buds which grow up around it." In the November 1902 issue of *McClure's Magazine*, Ida Tarbell used those exact words to launch her investigation of Standard Oil's rise and the role John D. Rockefeller, Sr., had played. She captured Rockefeller's influence when she accompanied the rose quotation with another epigraph, from Ralph Waldo Emerson's essay on self-reliance: "An institution is the lengthened shadow of one man."

It quickly became evident that neither Standard Oil and Rockefeller nor any powerful American institution had ever encountered a journalist like Tarbell. She exhibited passion grounded in her childhood around oil wells, intellectual curiosity about what made Rockefeller who he had become, lack of concern for personal safety when challenging power, an ability to dig out facts unlike that of any journalist before her, and a narrative storytelling skill that captivated readers. To understand the quality of her writing and the epic nature of the investigation, it is worth reading the opening paragraphs in their entirety:

One of the busiest corners of the globe at the opening of the year 1872 was a strip of northwestern Pennsylvania, not over fifty miles long, known the world over as the Oil Regions. Twelve years before this strip of land had been but little better than a wilderness; its chief inhabitants the lumberman, who every season cut great swaths of primeval pine and hemlock from its hills, and in the spring floated them down the Allegheny River to Pittsburgh.

The great tides of Western emigration had shunned the spot for years as too rugged and unfriendly for settlement, and yet in twelve years this region avoided by men had been transformed into a bustling trade center, where towns elbowed each other for place, into which three great trunk railroads had built branches, and every foot of whose soil was fought for by capitalists. It was the discovery and development of a new raw product, petroleum, which had made this change from wilderness to marketplace . . .

What had been done [to find oil] was, in [the independents'] judgment, only a beginning. Life ran swift and ruddy and joyous in these men. They were still young, most of them under forty, and they looked forward with all the eagerness of the young who have just learned their powers, to years of struggle and development. They would solve all these perplexing problems of overproduction, of railroad discrimination, of speculation. They would meet their own needs. They would bring the oil refining to the region where it belonged. They would make their towns the most beautiful in the world. There was nothing too good for them, nothing they did not hope and share.

But suddenly, at the very heyday of this confidence, a big hand reached out from nobody knew where, to steal their conquest and throttle their future. The suddenness and the blackness of the assault on their business stirred to the bottom their manhood and their sense of fair play, and the whole region arose in a revolt which is scarcely paralleled in the commercial history of the United States.

Tarbell proceeded to explain the history of the oil region in Pennsylvania—how oil had settled under the earth's crust through centuries of

geologic time, how various generations back to Indian tribes had realized its uses, how scientific advances during the 1850s had made mass
extraction more than a dream. She then tackled her protagonist head-
on, recounting how Rockefeller ended up in Cleveland and became
involved in the oil industry. She took great care to demonstrate how he
had extinguished competition not only in Cleveland but also in Pittsburgh and Philadelphia, and how his astuteness had led to unimagined
growth of what at first appeared to be a modest business enterprise.
Rockefeller, however, had remained restless as the 1870s opened: "He
was a brooding, cautious, secretive man, seeing all the possible dangers as well as the possible opportunities in things, and he studied, as a
player at chess, all the possible combinations which might imperil his
supremacy."

Tarbell demonstrated how Rockefeller had played a significant role
in forming a low-profile entity with a nondescript name, the South
Improvement Company, to buy competing oil refineries at below book
value, simultaneously secretly negotiating anti-competitive, unpublished shipping rates with the major railroads. She then used fore-
shadowing to explain an unexpected crack in the Rockefeller scheme
during 1872.

> A little more time and the great scheme would be an accomplished
> fact. And then there fell in its path two of those never-to-be-foreseen
> human elements which so often block great maneuvers. The first
> was born of a man's anger. The man had learned of the [railroad
> rebate] scheme. He wanted to go into it, but the directors [of Rock-
> efeller's enterprises] were suspicious of him. He had been concerned
> in speculative enterprises and in dealings with the Erie [rail]road
> which had injured these directors in other ways. They didn't want
> him to have any of the advantages of their great enterprise. When
> convinced that he could not share in the deal, he took his revenge by
> telling people in the Oil Regions what was going on.
>
> At first the Oil Regions refused to believe, but in a few days
> another slip born of human weakness came in to prove the rumor

true. The schedule of rates agreed upon by the South Improvement Company and the railroads had been sent to the freight agent of the Lake Shore Railroad, but no order had been given to put them in force. The freight agent had a son on his death bed. Distracted by sorrow, he left his office in charge of subordinates, but neglected to tell them that the new schedules on his desk were a secret compact, whose effectiveness depended upon their being held until all was complete.

On February 26, those subordinates, failing to understand the consequences of their actions, started enforcing the rates. When the oilmen trying to survive the Standard Oil onslaught heard that freight rates had been increased nearly 100 percent, they felt certain about the truth of the conspiracy rumors that had been spreading.

The independent oil producers and refiners refused at first to submit, but eventually they could no longer compete effectively against Rockefeller's trust. The serial told the story day by day and in some sections even hour by hour. Tarbell transported readers into the oil fields and the town meetings called by angry independents. She described the sedate corporate boardrooms where the trust's directors formulated plans to stifle competition and manipulate oil prices. The *McClure's* audience read about unruly congressional and state legislative hearings, the courtrooms where judges and juries considered lawsuits filed by state attorneys general and independent oilmen. Above all, they began to see the apparent immunity of Rockefeller and his trust to normal market forces and government regulation.

Tarbell admired the capitalist system, but only if those participating in it agreed to act honorably or otherwise allow a referee to enforce a level playing field. Her expert analysis extended to a critique of how Rockefeller often paid homage to capitalism yet subverted it when it suited him: "If, as he claimed, the oil business belonged to him, and if, as he announced, he was prepared to refine all the oil that men would consume, it followed as a corollary that the markets of the world belonged to him. In spite of his bold pretensions and his perfect organization, a few obstinate oil refiners still lived and persisted in doing business. They were a fly in his ointment, a stick in his wonderful wheel. He must get them out; otherwise the Great Purpose would be unrealized."

Tarbell did not advocate banning all trusts, nor did she rail against monopoly gained legally and ethically. She grounded her journalistic indictment of Standard Oil and Rockefeller in unfair competition, with the railroad rebates serving as what contemporary investigative reporters would call the smoking gun. She demonstrated how the railroad rebates that Rockefeller insisted upon could not be excused by the thinking that everybody else did it: "Everybody did not do it. In the nature of the offense everybody could not do it. The strong wrested from the railroads the privilege of preying upon the weak, and the railroads never dared give the privilege save under the promise of secrecy."

Much of the exposé cast a shadow on the probity of Standard Oil and Rockefeller. Some of the text is neutral. A significant portion is laudatory. Not everything Standard Oil accomplished during Rockefeller's reign was illegal or immoral. Tarbell understood the genius of his vision and many of his practices. She did not identify personally with Rockefeller or his goals, but she could appreciate his talents. In a segment titled "The Legitimate Greatness of the Standard Oil Company," she wrote: "While there can be no doubt that the determining factor in the success of the Standard Oil Company in securing a practical monopoly of the oil industry has been the special privileges it has enjoyed since the beginning of its career, it is equally true that those privileges alone will not account for its success. Something besides illegal advantage has gone into the making of the Standard Oil Trust. Had it possessed only the qualities which the general public has always attributed to it, its overthrow would have come before this. But this huge bulk, blackened by commercial sin, has always been strong in all great business qualities—in energy, in intelligence, in dauntlessness."

The way business is conducted should concern all Americans, Tarbell wrote. "We are a commercial people. We cannot boast of our arts, our crafts, our cultivation; our boast is in the wealth we produce. As a consequence, business success is sanctified and, practically, any methods which achieve it are justified by a larger and larger class. All sorts of subterfuges and sophistries and slurring over of facts are employed to explain aggregations of capital whose determining factor has been like that of the Standard Oil company—special privileges obtained by persistent secret effort in opposition to the spirit of the law." To accept unethical conduct in the corporate realm poisons all of society, Tarbell said. "Very often people who admit the facts, who are willing to see that Mr. Rockefeller has employed force and fraud to secure his ends, justify him by declaring, 'It's business.' That is, 'it's business' has come to be a legitimate excuse for hard dealing, sly tricks, special privileges . . . If the point is pushed, frequently the defender of the practice falls back on the Christian doctrine of charity, and points out that we are erring mortals and must allow for each other's weaknesses!—an excuse which, if carried to its legitimate conclusion, would leave our business men weeping on one another's shoulders over human frailty, while they picked one another's pockets."

Even as the serialization unfolded in *McClure's Magazine*, Tarbell and her research assistant, John Siddall, continued to uncover new information. On April 28, 1903, after six issues of the magazine's investigation had appeared in print, Siddall wrote to Tarbell, "I have always supposed that Mr. Rockefeller's father died years and years ago, and I am startled almost beyond expression to learn, as I have through the telephone within the last five minutes, that the old man is living . . . I can't for the life of me explain how we happened to miss this important fact." Furthermore, Rockefeller's estranged brother Franklin began supplying information from his Cleveland office as the serialization revealed new details month by month. Frank felt he had been unfairly cut off from the Standard Oil fortune and viewed his oldest brother as condescending.

Tarbell often disclosed her sources to her readers, an uncommon practice at the time but a precursor to the best investigative reporting of the late twentieth and early twenty-first centuries. She did it mostly so that readers could evaluate the reliability of her information. Most remarkably, she continued her transparent sourcing despite Rockefeller's ability to retaliate. More than once she withstood pressure in publishing her findings. At one point she uncovered a document suggesting that Mark Hanna, a confidant of President McKinley's, had intervened with Ohio prosecutors to halt a case against Rockefeller. When Tarbell shared the document with David K. Watson, an Ohio lawyer who had proved a good source, he persuaded her that disclosure might hasten the death of Hanna, already in ill health. Tarbell delayed publication, at Watson's request, but soon regretted her promise. She recalled that Watson "got me where he could make a plea to me on the ground of my obligation to him, and I have a sense of defeat that I have not had in any other single incident in the conduct of this work."

As the magazine serialization unfolded during 1903, Rockefeller reportedly shared his thoughts with the publisher of *Wilshire's Magazine* when they met by chance at a Santa Barbara, California, hotel-resort. In the May 1903 issue of the magazine, Rockefeller is quoted as saying that Tarbell was publishing information "without foundation. The idea of the Standard forcing anyone to sell his refinery to us is absurd. The refiners wanted to sell to us and nobody has sold and worked with us but has made money and is glad he did so." The article commented that Rockefeller "thought of having an answer made to the *McClure* articles," but explained "you know it has always been the policy of the Standard to keep silent under attack and let our acts speak for themselves, and I suppose it is the best policy for us to continue upon that line, don't you, Mister Wilshire?"

Privately, Rockefeller shared his feelings about Tarbell's exposé over the decades. He reportedly told acquaintance Hiram Brown, "Things have changed since you and I were boys. The world is full of socialists and anarchists. Whenever a man succeeds remarkably in any particular line of business, they jump on him and cry him down." He reportedly commented at another time, "Not a word about that misguided woman" and sometimes referred to Tarbell as "Miss Tar Barrel."

Looking back, it seems surprising that McClure never emphasized that the writing came from the mind and pen of a woman. During her Standard Oil investigation, Tarbell mentioned in one letter, "The whole office goes on Thursday to the publishers' dinner—that is, everybody but myself. It is the first time since I came into the office that the fact of petticoats has stood in my way, and I am half inclined to resent it." She escaped such irritations by working from her Manhattan apartment. At one point during the project she rented a vacation cabin in Turnersville, New York, near the Catskills. There in Greene County she arranged to ride a horse for recreation and took in a collie with five puppies for companionship, but otherwise she worked steadily on her writing.

Praise for her Standard Oil exposé arrived steadily during the early months of serialization. Responding to early praise from Henry Demarest Lloyd, Tarbell said, "It is a great satisfaction to me to know that you think the work I am doing is effective. I have been trying hard to give both sides of the matter and have felt very often that naturally I was having no sympathy from either. However, I propose to stick to my purpose; it is a case, in my opinion, where all that is necessary is to tell the facts."

McClure understood that the magazine and its articles were changing American politics and business. The January 1903 issue of the magazine carried three historic pieces: part three of Tarbell's exposé, Ray Stannard Baker's investigation of labor-management unrest in Pennsylvania's anthracite fields, and Lincoln Steffens's anatomy of municipal government corruption. McClure could not contain his justifiable pride. The three stories constituted "an arraignment of American character," particularly "the American contempt of law," he said. He blamed more than one class: "Capitalists, working men, politicians, citizens—all breaking the law, or letting it be broken." McClure was the first publisher to inspire and coordinate the investigations of the muckrakers. He was one of the few journalists who believed, from the beginning, that the separate efforts of the chroniclers added up to a coherent and damning portrait of American society.

In the introduction to the January 1903 issue, McClure wrote that

Miss Tarbell has our capitalists conspiring among themselves, deliberately, shrewdly, upon legal advice, to break the law so far as it restrained them, and to misuse it to restrain others who were in their way. Mr. Baker shows labor, the ancient enemy of capital and the chief complaint of the trusts' unlawful acts, itself committing and excusing crimes. And in "The Shame of Minneapolis" we see the administration of a city employing criminals to commit crimes for the profit of the elected officials, while the citizens . . . stood by complacent and not alarmed.

Capitalists, working men, politicians, citizens—all breaking the law, or letting it be broken. Who is left to uphold it? The lawyers? Some of the best lawyers in the country are hired, not to go to court to defend cases, but to advise corporations and business firms how they can get around the law without too great a risk of punishment. The judges? Too many of them so respect the laws that for some "error" or quibble they restore to office and liberty men convicted on evidence overwhelmingly convincing to common sense. The churches? We know of one, an ancient and wealthy establishment, which had to be compelled by a Tammany holdover health officer to put its tenements in sanitary condition. The colleges? They do not understand.

There is no one left: none but all of us . . . The public is the people. We forget that we all are the people; that while each of us in his group can shove off on the rest the bill of today, the debt is only postponed. The rest of us are passing it on back to us. We have to pay in the end, every one of us. And in the end the sum total of the debt will be our liberty.

McClure believed that he, his reporters, and his magazine were providing the evidence that would enable the citizenry to eradicate, or defray, the pervasive and insidious efforts of the trusts. Tarbell expressed quiet pride about her role, but she was exhausted. For the first time in her career, she began to feel worn down by the long hours and the attacks on her integrity by the defenders of corporate hegemony.

By 1905, with the serialization complete and the expanded book version appearing on bestseller lists around the country, Tarbell craved a change of topic. She recalled longing to "escape into the safe retreat of a library where I could study people long dead, and if they did things of which I did not approve, it would all be between me and the books." She would be liberated from "harrowing human beings confronting me, tearing me between contempt and pity, admiration and anger, baffling me with their futile and misdirected power or their equally futile and misdirected weakness."

Tarbell thought she had finished delving into the activities and character of John D. Rockefeller. She did not then realize how closely their lives would be intertwined for the next several years.

CHAPTER FOURTEEN

||||||||||||||||||||||||||||||||||||||||||||||||||||||||||||||||||||||||||||||||||||||||||||||||||||

A Question of Character

Perhaps the greatest catalyst for Ida Tarbell's foray into Rockefeller's personal life—a foray going beyond the influence of Standard Oil—was the strong impression he made on her the only time she saw him in person. That occurred on October 11, 1903, at the Euclid Avenue Baptist Church and Sunday school in Cleveland.

Four months earlier, while gathering material for the Standard Oil exposé, John Siddall had visited the church without announcing himself. Hiram Brown, a Cleveland resident and longtime Rockefeller friend, had talked to him about Rockefeller's church-going schedule. After watching Rockefeller at the pulpit from a front-row seat, Siddall composed a report for Tarbell that said, "My whole impression is that [Rockefeller] began this sort of [church participation] as a part of the oil business and that way back somewhere he got an impression that the devil would get him if he didn't watch out . . . His religion, I should say, is chiefly a sort of ignorant superstition." Even after Siddall learned that Rockefeller sometimes quietly gave contributions to destitute members of the congregation, he could not dispel his doubts.

Later that year, Siddall and magazine sketch artist George Varian accompanied Tarbell on her unannounced visit to the church. She felt "a little mean about it . . . It was taking him unaware." After two hours of observation, she left the church unobtrusively.

Rockefeller emanated power when he spoke to the congregation as a deacon and as a guest preacher. Tarbell was never able to forget that strength, combined with what she considered his uneasy manner in a house of worship. She noted where he positioned himself when not at the lectern: "They say in Cleveland Mr. Rockefeller always sits with his back to the wall when it is possible. So many things can happen behind one's back in any assembly." Rockefeller seemed as uneasy as the children in the Sunday school room, she noted. "Throughout the church service which followed, this same terrible restlessness agitated him. He sat bent forward in his pew, for a moment, his eyes intent on the speaker, then with a start he looked to his right, searching the faces he could see, craning his neck to look backward. Then his eyes would turn again to the speaker, but not stay there."

Fellow churchgoers told Tarbell he had demonstrated such apparent uneasiness for many years. Tarbell found herself surmising, "Fear, fear of the oft-repeated threats of the multitude of sufferers from the wheels of the cars of progress he has rolled across the country . . . It does not matter what it is. It is pitiful, so pitiful, that one cannot watch John Rockefeller sit through a church service and never cease to feel that he is one of the saddest objects in the world."

After seeing Rockefeller in person, Tarbell could not shake the image of his prominent bald head, made that way by a condition known as generalized alopecia, which can make an entire body hairless. She devoted significant thought to Rockefeller's stark physical appearance, wondering if it might somehow be viewed as a punishment for his misdeeds. "Concentration, craftiness, cruelty and something indefinably repulsive are in the [pictures] . . . Brought face to face with Mr. Rockefeller unexpectedly," Tarbell said, "and not knowing him, the writer's immediate thought was 'This is the oldest man in the world—a living mummy.'" At the time, Rockefeller was sixty-six.

Elderly, but not weak, Tarbell thought: "There is no sense of feebleness with the sense of age; indeed, there is one of terrific power. The disease which in the last three or four years has swept Mr. Rockefeller's head bare of hair, stripped away even eyelashes and eyebrows, has revealed all the strength of his great head." After noting Rockefeller's "powerful shoulders and a neck like that of a bull," Tarbell focused on his face. "Eyes more useful for a man of Mr. Rockefeller's practices could hardly be conceived. They are small and intent and steady, and they are as expressionless as a wall. They see everything and reveal nothing." Next came Rockefeller's mouth. "It is only a slit—the lips are quite lost, as if by eternal grinding together of the teeth, teeth set on something he would have," Tarbell commented. "It is at once the cruelest feature of his face . . . and the most pathetic, for the hard, close-set line slants downward at the corners, giving a look of age and sadness." Tarbell drew a moral from her analysis of Rockefeller's face: "Mr. Rockefeller may have made himself the richest man in the world, but he has paid. Nothing but paying ever ploughs such lines in a man's face, ever sets his lips to such a melancholy angle."

With all those images in her brain, Tarbell could not let go of the Rockefeller saga quite yet. In early 1905, as her Standard Oil exposé became a bestseller and an instant classic in book form, she decided to write a personality profile of Rockefeller for *McClure's Magazine*.

Rarely in the torrent of words that formed the book had Tarbell lost sight of Rockefeller's role in the creation, growth, and domination of the trust. A section in volume two of the Standard Oil exposé demonstrated that oil consumers tended to look upon "Mr. Rockefeller with superstitious awe. Their notion of him was very like that which the English common people had for Napoleon in the first part of the nineteenth century, which the peasants of Brittany have even today for the English—a dread power, cruel, omniscient, always ready to spring." Nobody else associated with the world's most powerful trust could inspire such fear, Tarbell says. "It is worth noting that while all of the members of the Standard Oil Company followed Mr. Rockefeller's policy of saying nothing, there was no such popular dread of any other one of them." To her credit, rarely did Tarbell portray Rockefeller as personally evil. She set out the facts of his actions, delved into his thoughts as best she could without his cooperation, and let readers reach their own conclusions. Now she would do something different.

Decades later, reflecting in her memoir, Tarbell said, "I was not keen for it. It would have to be done like the books, from documents; that is, I had no inclination to use the extraordinary gossip which came to me from many sources." Insisting on verifiable information to the end, she emphasized, "If I were to do it, I wanted only that of which I felt I had sure proof, only those things which seemed to me to help explain the public life of this powerful, patient, secretive, calculating man of so peculiar and special a genius."

Throughout 1904 and 1905, Tarbell reviewed documents already collected for the corporate history and accumulated new material. "The more intimately I went into my subject, the more hateful it became to me," she commented. "No achievement on earth could justify those methods, I felt. I had a great desire to end my task, hear no more of it. No doubt part of my revulsion was due to a fagged brain."

Just as she put the finishing touches on the Rockefeller character sketch, Tarbell's father became ill and died. Eventually she made peace with her father's passing and continued to draw on his memory when she needed inspiration. In 1905, however, while struggling for the right words to describe Rockefeller, she felt like she was sinking in a "dark sea of loss." She pushed ahead, though, knowing her colleagues at the magazine were counting on her.

Two years after Tarbell observed Rockefeller in church, in July 1905, McClure introduced what would become the most searing, controversial, and influential Rockefeller profile published during his lifetime. Commenting on the timing of publication, he said, "It is not too much to say that he is the founder of a School of Business which is on trial today by the people . . . The growing influence of this school is evident to the most casual observer. The menace it carries with it to individual opportunity and commercial integrity is no longer seriously debated."

McClure explained why the profile spilled over into Rockefeller's religious practice and charitable donations. After all, McClure said, Rockefeller "is not only the founder and the chief beneficiary of this powerful commercial system, he is our present most liberal supporter of Christian Education, Christian Charity, the Christian Church. His contributions cannot but be a powerful defense of his business school." McClure, and Tarbell, firmly believed that "the works of a man's life stand together. They cannot be separated. It is the intimate and intricate relation of the Rockefeller Business Code with the Rockefeller Religious Code that makes it imperative the public study the man and his influence."

Given her own doubts about finding the mental energy to complete the character sketch, as well as the divided opinions about its fairness, Tarbell felt compelled to justify it beyond what McClure wrote. Although beginning to see that her exposé of Standard Oil might someday lead to the breakup of the trust, she believed her work would remain incomplete unless the man controlling the trust could be unmasked. Tarbell told readers of *McClure's Magazine* that "a man who possesses this kind of influence cannot be allowed to live in the dark. The public not only has the right to know what sort of man he is; it is the duty of the public to know." How else, she wondered, "can the public discharge the most solemn obligation it owes to itself and to the future to keep the springs of its higher life clean?"

She set up the character sketch by establishing Rockefeller's sterling reputation among the masses, among historians, and among so many journalists other than herself: " 'The most important man in the world' a great and serious newspaper passionately devoted to democracy calls him, and unquestionably this is the popular measure of him." In a discerning passage about the nature of celebrity, she wrote, "His importance lies not so much in the fact that he is the richest individual in the world . . . it lies in the fact that his wealth, and the power springing from it, appeal to the most universal and powerful passion in this country—the passion for money." Tarbell understood the perverse attraction: "How did he get it, the eager youth asks, and asking, strives to imitate him as nearly as ability and patience permit. Thus he has become an inspirer of American ideals, and his methods have been crystallized into a great national commercial code."

Even those harboring reservations about Rockefeller felt compelled to restrain themselves if they wanted to benefit from his largesse, Tarbell explained: "All over the land those who direct great educational, charitable and religious institutions are asking, 'Can we not get something from him?' Receiving his bequests, they become at least the tacit supporters of the thing for which he stands."

Tarbell did her utmost to demonstrate how the child is often the predictable precursor of the adult. She portrayed Rockefeller's paternal grandfather and father as mixtures of ne'er-do-wells and con men. Even his mother, sainted in his mind, won faint praise at best from Tarbell. While impressed with Rockefeller's youthful persistence at achieving financial independence, she conveyed a quiet horror as she parsed his fascination for accumulating money: "It was combine, save, watch. A sort of mania for saving seemed to possess him. It was over this he brooded from morning to night, and it was the realization of this alone which awakened in his face, already grave with incessant reflections, a sign of joy." It seemed that the admirable desire to make an honest profit turned gradually into a mania for profit no matter how gained, Tarbell came to believe: "It is quite probable that Mr. Rockefeller, natural trader that he was, learned early in his career that unless one has some special and exclusive advantage over rivals in business, native ability, thrift, energy—however great they may be—are never sufficient to put an end to competition."

According to Tarbell, by the late 1860s Rockefeller realized "that he had no legitimate superiority over those competing with him in Cleveland which would enable him to be anything more than one of the big men in his line." As a result, he sought an advantage through unfair means: "It lay in transportation, in getting his carrying done cheaper than his neighbors could. It was a very seductive idea to a man with a passion for wealth."

If the maxim is true that a biography reveals as much about the biographer as it does about the subject, then the character sketch of Rockefeller affords the reader a look into Tarbell's psyche with every paragraph. For instance, Tarbell wrestled with traditional religion versus secular belief most of her life, so it is interesting how she presents the details of Rockefeller's vast charitable contributions, then turns his philanthropy against him: "It is evident that his giving is governed by some theory of the percent[age] due to the Lord, though it is evident that he never has gone as high as ten percent! Whatever the percentage he has decided on he distributes cautiously and reverentially . . . The spirit in which he gives is one of plain, hard duty." Tarbell came to believe that Rockefeller was purchasing peace of mind for the hereafter, commenting, "He himself has stated his theory—'According as you put something in, the greater will be your dividends of salvation!'"

Tarbell examined whether the money donated by Rockefeller to worthwhile causes should be considered tainted. She suggested that Rockefeller could have contributed more to society by playing fair in business than by doling out ill-gained money to needy institutions and individuals: "The principles of the religion he professes are so antagonistic to the principles of the business he practices that the very world which emulates him has been turned into hypocrites and cynics under his tutelage." In her judgment, "Not only has his charity been tainted by the hypocrisy of his life, the church itself has been polluted and many a man has turned away from its doors because of the servile support it gives to the men of whom Mr. Rockefeller is the most eminent type."

Worrying about the degradation of society, Tarbell said, "Our national life is on every side distinctly poorer, uglier, meaner for the kind of influence he exercises . . . No price is too great to pay for winning. In commerce 'the interest of the business' justifies breaking the law, bribing legislators, defrauding a competitor of his rights."

Tarbell wondered whether the cleansing effects of her Standard Oil exposé could successfully wipe away the "commercial Machiavellism" of Rockefeller. At times she felt optimistic: "Since the world began her progress has been in proportion to her knowledge and her judgment of the men who symbolized the influence of a period. History is but a museum of dissected heroes, warriors, kings, philosophers, their records stripped bare, their influence traced to their flowering." She hoped that her exposé would help its readers render a verdict on her subject, that "Rockefeller, much as he dislikes the light, cannot escape the fate of his own greatness. All his vast wealth spent in one supreme effort to evade the judgment of men would be but wasted, for a man can never escape the judgment of the society which has bred him."

What can only be interpreted as an uncharitable and perhaps unwarranted analysis of Rockefeller's sincerity was suddenly softened as she pointed out his positive qualities as a loving husband and father, a faithful churchgoer, a man who avoided carousing and ostentation. Tarbell's ambivalence occasionally became dizzying. At one point she praised Rockefeller for his relative frugality: "Family and servants are trained to strictest economy. There is no more gas burned than is needed, no unnecessary heating . . . This frugality certainly is a welcome contrast to the wanton lavishness which on every side of us corrupts taste and destroys the sense of values." Then, without pause, she turned Rockefeller's frugality against him: "One would be inclined to like Mr. Rockefeller the better for his plain living if somehow one did not feel that here was something more than frugality, that here was parsimony . . . made a virtue."

Tarbell further turned Rockefeller's dislike of ostentation into an indictment by criticizing the appearances of his three family homes— Forest Hill, outside of Cleveland; Pocantico Hills, near Tarrytown, New York; and the New York City townhouse. She called Forest Hill "a monument of cheap ugliness," and described all three buildings as "unpretending even to the point of being conspicuous" given Rockefeller's means to build something attractive. Her praise for the grounds surrounding the buildings was sincere, however. Rockefeller, Tarbell said, "has the love of noble land. At Forest Hill the park of over four hundred acres is one of great loveliness—rolling wooded hills, shady ravines, fine fields with splendid trees—the whole cared for with more than intelligence. There is something like affection gone into the making of this beautiful spot."

Rockefeller devoted part of the grounds to a golf course, so he could play the game day after day, month after month. Tarbell portrayed his golfing as both positive and negative, reaching for a conclusion that seemed speculative at best, and certainly uncharacteristically nasty: "So long as golf occupie[s] him as it does, there is little to fear that Mr. Rockefeller will trouble himself to complete his ownership of the Nation . . .

Taking it all in all, however, there is little doubt that Mr. Rockefeller's chief reason for playing golf is that he may live longer in order to make more money."

In paragraph after paragraph, Tarbell attempted to unlock what she saw as the duality of Rockefeller's personality. Because she posed her analysis of his psyche in the form of questions, she seemed to leave open the possibility that perhaps she would accept a positive evaluation of Rockefeller's life if she were to uncover additional evidence. A careful reading of her public and private writings, however, suggests that she had formed a permanent opinion of Rockefeller's dual nature by 1905.

The good Rockefeller, as envisioned by the public before Tarbell's exposé, seemed like an ideal husband, father, and grandfather, a "quiet, modest church-going gentleman, devoted to Sunday school picnics, golf and wheeling . . . whose chief occupation, outside of business, is giving away as much money as he can." Rockefeller deserved praise for such qualities, Tarbell conceded. But, she asked, "how harmonize it with the Mr. Rockefeller the business world knows, the man with a mask and a steel grip, forever peering into hidden places for money, always more money, planning in secret to wrest it even from friends, never forgetting, never resting, never satisfied?" She wondered, "Is the amiable Mr. Rockefeller a foil for the man before whom the public writhes? Does Mr. Rockefeller know that, when he patiently points out how gentle, charitable and devoted he is, and asks how can it be that a man who is all this can do a business wrong, more people will hesitate and keep silent than before any other face he could present?"

Tarbell did not want to seem immodest. She noted, "It is supposing a great knowledge of human nature . . . to explain Mr. Rockefeller, but that it is a plausible explanation cannot be denied." Yet her intensive study of Rockefeller might qualify her as the Great Explainer. Maybe Rockefeller's dual personality could be understood by the maxim that the means justify the ends. Or maybe, Tarbell suggested, Rockefeller possessed a dual nature that would "puzzle" any psychologist, no matter how astute. Perhaps he was "a man whose soul is built like a ship in air-tight compartments . . . one devoted to business, one to religion and charity, one to simple living and one to nobody knows what. But between those compartments there are no doors . . . It is an uncanny explanation, but it may be the true one."

The consequences of Rockefeller's actions could fairly be termed unpleasant, Tarbell maintained. Rockefeller "has done more than any other person to fasten on this country the most serious interference with free individual development which it suffers, an interference which, today, the whole country is stuggling vainly to strike off—which it is doubtful will be cured, so deep-seated and subtle is it—except by revolutionary means." Rockefeller, according to Tarbell's evidence, "has introduced into business a spy system of the most odious character. He has turned commerce from a peaceful pursuit to war, and honeycombed it with cruel and corrupt practice, turned competition from honorable emulation to cutthroat struggle."

Tarbell's typically careful reporting gave the Rockefeller character sketch authority. But her judgmental tone, added to the substance behind the judgments, precipitated debate across the nation. Receiving feedback about her mean-spirited profile, Tarbell, so generous to family and friends, tried to prevent the negativity from wounding her. Corresponding with *McClure's Magazine* reader Fannie Hardy Eckstorm, she revealed on August 8, 1905, that she had found the assignment "repugnant . . . to me personally . . . Most of my friends seem to think that I am getting some kind of satisfaction out of the sordid business." Not so, she said. "It was just one of those things that had to be done; there seemed to be no way for me to get around it. I trust that it has not been useless."

McClure and his business partner, John S. Phillips, discussed whether to reprint the character sketch as a book. They decided against a book version, even though Phillips, for one, thought of Tarbell as a dispenser of "divine pity," a quality "deeper and stronger than benevolence." A New York City correspondent for the *Chicago Record-Herald* reported that the McClure-Phillips firm "wishes to be known only as an enemy of Mr. Rockefeller's methods, not of Mr. Rockefeller himself."

As the magazine profile resonated during the summer and fall, about four hundred community leaders in Cleveland organized a visit to the

Forest Hill estate to show their appreciation for Rockefeller's benefactions and to excoriate Tarbell's portrait. Rockefeller greeted every guest and presented an emotional, brief speech. He refrained from mentioning Tarbell's name or the mean words she had published. His only reaction reached the public indirectly, through Virgil P. Kline, one of his Cleveland lawyers. Kline disputed one portion of the lengthy character sketch, concerning allegations that Rockefeller had treated his boyhood friend James Corrigan unfairly in their financial dealings. Corrigan had eventually sued Rockefeller. Kline emphasized that arbitrators and judges had ruled in Rockefeller's favor against Corrigan.

Much to Tarbell's dismay, Rockefeller continued his silence even after the book version reached bestseller status. "I wanted an answer from Mr. Rockefeller," Tarbell recalled. "What I got was neither direct nor, from my point of view, serious. It consisted of wide and what must have been a rather expensive anonymous distribution of various critical comments."

After the character sketch appeared in print, Standard Oil hired a public relations executive, one of the first employed by any U.S. corporation. Joseph I. C. Clarke, a former New York City newspaper editor, coddled journalists, granted access to Rockefeller, and began to help cultivate an image of him as an engaging elderly gentleman. Clarke encouraged features describing a grandfatherly Rockefeller spending Christmas within the warmth of an adoring family. Rockefeller also agreed to cooperate with Leonard Woolsey Bacon, a minister, on a Standard Oil history meant to rebut Tarbell, though Rockefeller, always reticent about revealing company operations, expressed reservations. Bacon began the project in 1906 but the next year became too ill to continue. Nobody at Standard Oil took the initiative to replace him, and the official history never appeared.

Elbert Hubbard almost surely would have accepted the assignment if offered. From the mid-1890s until his death in 1915, Hubbard helped define the practice of public relations, in addition to founding a publishing house called Roycroft Press and organizing a writers' colony in East Aurora, New York. Hubbard encouraged Rockefeller to reply to Tarbell's findings, commenting, "She shot from cover, and she shot to kill. Such literary bushwackers should be answered shot for shot. Sniping the commercial caravan may be legitimate, but to my mind the Tarbell-Steffens-Russell-Roosevelt-Sinclair method of inky warfare is quite as unethical as the alleged tentacled-octopi policy which they attack."

Writing in *Public Relations Journal*, Charles F. Hamilton told how Hubbard tried to diminish the impact of Tarbell's Standard Oil exposé by publishing a pamphlet extolling the trust. A source told Tarbell that Standard Oil had paid for five million copies of Hubbard's broadside and distributed them to schoolteachers, preachers, journalists, and other opinion leaders across the United States. "Hardly were they received in many cases before they were sent to me with angry or approving comments," Tarbell noted, dismissing Hubbard with the adjective "entertaining."

Perhaps the most widely distributed rebuttal came, at least ostensibly, from Gilbert Holland Montague, a twenty-two-year-old Harvard University student who started by writing a senior thesis. Published in book form in 1903, before Tarbell's serialization had ended, *The Rise and Progress of the Standard Oil Company* benefited from the counsel of S.C.T. Dodd, the trust's in-house lawyer. Standard Oil paid to disseminate the book to libraries, news organizations, churches, schools, and other venues throughout the country. Tarbell commented that Montague's book "separated business and ethics in a way that must have been a comfort at 26 Broadway."

Criticisms of Tarbell by Rockefeller partisans came and went. So did obviously partisan attacks, such as an article in the Oil City, Pennsylvania, *Derrick* newspaper under the headline "Hysterical Woman Versus Historical Fact/How Miss Tarbell Distorted a Legitimate Business Deal." Despite the efforts of the public relations practitioners, the anti-Tarbell actions never amounted to more than a feeble attempt to spin the story. Ultimately, as Ron Chernow commented, Rockefeller never spoke out publicly against Tarbell because "he couldn't dispute just a few of Tarbell's assertions without admitting the truth of many others, and a hard core of truth did lie behind the scattered errors." Another Rockefeller biographer, Jules Abels, noted, "It is ironic that conquest by book happened to John D. Rockefeller, who, though an admirer and patron of higher education, was himself a most unbookish person who must have been astounded when the pen proved mightier than the Almighty Dollar."

Because Tarbell's two-part profile of Rockefeller proved so provocative, analysis of it, of its writer, and of its subject never faded completely. Four decades later, Allan Nevins praised Tarbell's history of Standard Oil, for the most part, but excoriated her for the profile. He devoted considerable space to his analysis of her motives for "the shrill abuse of Rockefeller." First, Nevins said, Rockefeller's decision not to set the record straight concerning allegedly false anecdotes fed the hatred of him and seemed to confirm the truth of the lies. Second, the sheer size and dominance of Standard Oil made it a target. Third, "Rockefeller was pictured as a despotic head of his organization, responsible for its every act, when he was simply the chief of a group of powerful men, each largely supreme in his own sphere." Fourth, Rockefeller's critics wrongly doubted the sincerity of his philanthropy, so felt morally justified in attacking him for hypocrisy.

President Theodore Roosevelt, portraying himself as a trust-buster, participated in criticism of Rockefeller and Standard Oil, but Tarbell felt the president's sting too. Generally friendly with reform-minded reporters and editors, Roosevelt seemed out of sorts in the spring of 1906, especially during a speech presented April 14 during a cornerstone-laying ceremony at the House of Representatives. The audience included Supreme Court justices, foreign diplomats, and members of Congress. It is quite likely that Roosevelt delivered the speech in part because of his anger at "The Treason of the Senate," a freshly published series of articles by David Graham Phillips in *Cosmopolitan* magazine. William Randolph Hearst owned the magazine and was not reluctant to use it to further his desire to become president on a Democratic Party ticket. In 1906, Hearst, already elected to the House of Representatives, was hoping to win the governorship of New York State, presumably as a steppingstone to the White House. Roosevelt disliked Hearst as a politician and worried about him bumping the Republican Party from the White House. Roosevelt also disliked Hearst as a publisher—of the nearly two dozen politicians exposed by Phillips, almost all were Republicans.

In the widely disseminated April speech, Roosevelt indicted a type of journalist who, he said, "never does anything else, who never thinks or speaks or writes, save of his feats with the muckrake, speedily becom[ing] not a help to society, not an incitement to good, but one of the most potent forces for evil." Roosevelt did not deny the need for journalists to expose corruption. "There should be relentless exposure of and attack upon every evil man, whether politician or businessman, every evil practice, whether in politics, in business or in social life," Roosevelt said. He was concerned, however, that too many journalists failed to achieve accuracy, and that some knowingly printed lies.

On March 17, Roosevelt had presented an off-the-record version of this speech at the Gridiron Club in Washington, D.C. Ray Stannard Baker worried about the impact of Roosevelt's remarks on progressive journalism. Replying to Baker before going public with the speech, Roosevelt offered assurances that he had Hearst's publications, not *McClure's Magazine*, in mind. Baker had misunderstood some of the March version, Roosevelt said. "I want to let in light and air, but I do not want to let in sewer gas. If a room is fetid and the windows are bolted I am perfectly content to knock out the windows, but I would not knock a hole in the drain pipe." Referring to writers for a "yellow newspaper" or a "yellow magazine," Roosevelt said that they should not make "a ferocious attack on good men or even attacks [on] bad men with exaggeration or for things they have not done." Such journalists should be considered "a potent enemy of those of us who are really striving in good faith to expose bad men and drive them from power."

After Roosevelt coined the term "muckraking," it stuck to Tarbell, even if he had not been aiming at her. She argued with him, telling him "that we on *McClure's* were concerned only with facts, not with stirring up revolt." The label disturbed her so much for a while that she vowed to abandon her new style of investigative reporting. Roosevelt's speech "helped fix my resolution to have done for good and all with the subject that had brought it on me."

Tarbell could not pull away from her investigative reporting, however. The Standard Oil exposé, bolstered by the Rockefeller character sketch, spawned reform efforts within the U.S. Congress, state legislatures, the White House, and governors' mansions. It led to precedent-shattering court rulings as well as populist movements outside government institutions. A critical mass of Progressive voters began to coalesce. The reformers needed Tarbell, and she could not resist.

||||||||||||||||||||||||||||||||||||||||||||||||||||||||||||||||||||||||||||||||||||||||||||||||||||||||

Aftermath of an Exposé

Ida Tarbell thought she had finished exposing the machinations of the Standard Oil Company and John D. Rockefeller. She calculated that perhaps the U.S. government or state governments would find useful information in her book, information that might lead to antitrust proceedings that would curb corporate practices harmful to the general public. Maybe even enough citizens would band together on election day to insist that politicians deal meaningfully with corporate domination of American life. She did not dream, however, that in fewer than five years the Supreme Court would issue an antitrust ruling that would change everything, a ruling grounded in her reporting.

After Tarbell finished her character study of Rockefeller in August 1905, she planned to throw herself into understanding other contemporary controversies. Reporting and writing were her raison d'être; she knew that she would want to publish, if her health allowed, until she died. She looked eagerly toward new investigations into the use of import and export tariffs to finance government operations while protecting American industries, the poisonous relations between labor and management in all sectors of American commercial life, and the subordinate role of women in a nation seeking to improve the lot of all citizens during the

Progressive Era. She had edited the work of other journalists on those topics and had touched on them in her own writing.

The next month, however, Tarbell's byline in the pages of *McClure's Magazine* appeared above a story on a familiar topic. The headline read "Kansas and the Standard Oil Company: A Narrative of Today." Accustomed to boosts in circulation when Tarbell wrote about Rockefeller, McClure had encouraged her to chronicle the story of President Roosevelt's newly aggressive attacks on the trusts; events in Kansas were becoming part of that saga.

The Standard Oil Company controlled pipelines throughout Kansas and dominated the railroads serving the western territory. The nervous independent oil producers turned to Tarbell, hoping to avoid the fate of their predecessors in Pennsylvania and Ohio. As proposals to rein in Standard Oil moved through the Kansas legislature, the oil producers became convinced that lobbyists for the trust were using underhanded tactics to sway the vote. Unsure whether they could trust Congress or the federal regulatory agencies to protect them, they felt confident of Tarbell's steadfastness. They hoped she could explain how their situation looked similar to the situation in the northwestern Pennsylvania oil fields, how it looked different, and what, if anything, they could do to stave off subjugation.

Tarbell found that Standard Oil was doing to independent producers in Kansas what it had started doing thirty-five years earlier in Pennsylvania. Her documentation of illegal or unethical conduct in Kansas, as always painstakingly gathered, was accompanied by invective against Rockefeller and the entire corporate machine. She set up her compelling account by posing the question "What could Kansas do?" After all, nothing had halted Standard Oil before 1905. "For thirty years they had been passing laws aimed at its head and there it was, playing calmly the same old game it had played all these years. What could Kansas do to the Standard Oil Company?" Tarbell saw the dilemma of the Kansas oil drillers as symptomatic of corporate dominance across the economy. "What can a few hundred cattle-raisers do today, if convinced the packers are getting an unfair percentage of the profits? What can a lumberman of

Missouri do today, if he wishes to find an independent market? What can a Colorado coal owner do, if he is outside the Colorado Fuel and Iron Company? What can scattered tobacco growers, iron miners, copper miners, do? What, but yield to the rulings of the trusts which, through the complacency, the cowardliness and the greed of the railroads have corralled these various industries."

Despite the confidence she exhibited in this piece, her private correspondence reveals that she was uncomfortable in her role as sage. Her words were helping to shape public opinion and yielding remarkable results, but Tarbell never shed her modesty: "It was not long before I was being taken for something more serious than a mere journalist. Conservative Standard Oil sympathizers regarded me as a spy and not infrequently denounced me as an enemy to society. Independent oilmen and radical editors, who were in the majority, called me a prophet." She could not adjust to her own satisfaction: "It brought fantastic situations where I was utterly unfit to play to part. A woman of twenty-five, fresh, full of zest, only interested in what was happening to her, would have reveled in the experience. But here I was—fifty, fagged, wanting to be let alone while I collected trustworthy information for my articles—dragged to the front as an apostle."

Later, Ralph W. Hidy and Muriel E. Hidy, business historians who were granted complete access to the Standard Oil archives while writing a book, concluded that agitation over developments in Kansas "transformed a local conflict into a national political issue. Unprecedented were the planning, breadth and vigor of the campaign against the oil 'Octopus.' It was attacked in newspapers and periodicals, in legislatures and in courts, both federal and state." Standard Oil and Rockefeller fueled the controversy, to their detriment, by refusing to respond frankly to the evidence. They mostly ignored journalists, except for those perceived as favorable to the company, and handled legal and regulatory challenges from government agencies in much the same manner. Even when Standard Oil officials tried to disseminate accurate information to Kansas oilmen, the suspicion built up against the "Octopus" caused that information to be discounted.

While some Standard Oil executives began to grasp the value of responding to negative allegations, Rockefeller himself refused to budge. He had become a fugitive from lawsuit-related subpoenas, structuring his life to avoid process servers by refusing to travel to certain states. He could have told a stirring counterstory—about his vigorous health despite the rumors of grave illness, about his gradual withdrawal from Standard Oil decisionmaking, about the breadth and sincerity of his charitable donations, about his role as paterfamilias. By stonewalling government investigators and reporters, he caused those positive public relations messages to be buried. Perceptions of Rockefeller himself among the citizens changed as state and federal investigations expanded, based in part on Tarbell's findings. Rarely did those investigations yield information to reduce antagonism aimed at the trust.

In Missouri, Herbert Spencer Hadley became attorney general in 1905. He approached Tarbell with his suspicions that improper Standard Oil activities had infiltrated his jurisdiction. Hadley also sought out small refiners struggling to remain in business, ascertaining that some oil marketers in St. Louis who were advertising their independence from Standard Oil were actually captive corporations of the trust. After reading Hadley's legal briefs, Tarbell wrote that he had drafted "the cleanest and completest presentation of a case for conspiracy in restraint of trade that I have ever seen."

Scholar Hazel Tutt Long has pointed out that until Hadley's investigation, "Standard Oil had practically everything its own way, in spite of the agitation and discontent in Kansas and the publication of Ida M. Tarbell's account of the Standard Oil trust. But the outlook changed when the attorney general of Missouri brought to light that ninety-five percent of the state's oil business was controlled by the Standard Oil Company of Indiana with Waters-Pierce and other subsidiaries." Hadley filed suit in the Missouri Supreme Court, asking the judges to revoke licenses that had allowed Standard Oil to operate in the state. Rockefeller managed to escape Hadley's reach, even though the attorney general held subpoena power and directed process servers to deliver papers that would force him to testify or end up in contempt of court. Reports leaked that Rockefeller had left the United States to avoid testifying or had worn a wig to disguise his appearance, or both.

Litigators in Pennsylvania also wanted to question Rockefeller in person. A letter in the Rockefeller Center Archive dated March 15, 1906, shows that the fugitive worried about meeting his son at a Brown University event, or even sending a greeting. "If the location from which I wrote was not given it would cause comment. If the letter was dated from 26 Broadway, that would cause comment, especially in connection with the statement that I had not been in my office for many years," he wrote to his son.

Eventually Rockefeller managed to avoid most of the public appearances and direct testimony he so feared. In an unpublished account, Hadley explained his decision to drop his quest to depose Rockefeller personally: "As it was a lawsuit that I was conducting and not a general investigation, I had no disposition or desire to continue what would have been a sensational hunt, but so far as the litigation was concerned, an unprofitable pursuit of the richest man in America." But that was Hadley's only concession. Evidence he had gathered convinced him that Standard Oil had divided the state in half for commercial purposes. Standard Oil of Indiana controlled supply north of the Missouri River, and its partner, Waters-Pierce, controlled the south. "The division was so arbitrary that if a customer lived near the distributing depot, but with the dividing line between, he was forced to travel to the nearest station on his side to get oil," Long's scholarship concluded. In a series of rulings, the Missouri Supreme Court supported Hadley's antitrust effort.

In a federal lawsuit against Standard Oil of Indiana regarding railroad rebates connected to its Illinois operations, the judge ordered U.S. marshals to track down Rockefeller and deliver him to the Chicago courtroom. At first Rockefeller defied the subpoena by hiding at the home of his daughter Alta in Pittsfield, Massachusetts, but perhaps to avoid the spectacle of a public arrest, he eventually took a train to Chicago to appear in court on July 6, 1907.

As he passed through a mob to reach the courtroom, the sixty-eight-year-old legend seemed alert. After being sworn in as a witness, however, Rockefeller seemed like somebody suffering from memory loss in old age. Eyewitnesses wrote that he adopted a confused demeanor to deflect questions while avoiding a perjury charge. A month later, when Rockefeller learned that Judge Kenesaw Mountain Landis had imposed a nearly $30 million fine against Standard Oil, he was playing golf with a Cleveland *Plain Dealer* reporter. The judge "will be dead a long time before this fine is paid," Rockefeller told the journalist before finishing the round of golf. Eventually Standard Oil's lawyers persuaded an appellate court to cancel the fine. A retrial led to exoneration for Standard Oil, angering government officials all the way to President Roosevelt, who said that federal lawyers would charge the trust again for accepting illegal railroad rebates.

The retrial left Rockefeller feeling vindicated, and his forgetful behavior kept him out of jail. Standard Oil, however, could not avoid the hefty lawyers' fees, court-imposed fines, and negative press. It had taken sixteen years since passage of the Sherman Antitrust Act for trust-busting to reach the stage of serious initiative. For years federal prosecutors inclined to use the law had faced daunting obstacles in their attacks on monopolists. Trusts had hired defense lawyers practiced in evasion, delay, and appeals. Even if prosecutors prevailed in court, judges lacked an effective enforcement mechanism; at the beginning of the twentieth century, no federal agency existed to levy and collect fines. The law had not evolved so that individual corporate officers and directors such as Rockefeller could be punished meaningfully for violations attributed to the company. Far away from agency headquarters and courtrooms, trusts used their wealth to make strategic political campaign contributions, place politicians on their payrolls, lower prices temporarily to defuse consumer outcries, and threaten to close factories or otherwise reduce employment unless threats of antitrust actions disappeared.

With the mood of both the public and legislators finally turning against the trusts, prosecutors began to craft antitrust filings that relied on the reporting of Tarbell and other journalists. President Roosevelt encouraged the prosecutors' efforts. Standard Oil executives and other business leaders had contributed large sums to his presidential campaign, but their generosity failed to moderate his antitrust zeal. Within the executive branch, a newly aggressive Bureau of Corporations (later the Federal Trade Commission), supported by Roosevelt, supplied ammunition to the White House.

The Roosevelt administration served notice to Standard Oil that it hoped to dismantle the corporation. On November 15, 1906, U.S. Attorney General Charles Bonaparte, a Roosevelt appointee, filed an antitrust action against Standard Oil in a St. Louis federal court. He chose that jurisdiction because the judges there had issued antitrust rulings to the government's liking. In the end, the Roosevelt administration filed about two dozen antitrust cases against a variety of industrial giants. The Standard Oil case, however, produced the most outcry at the time and is the best remembered today.

Bonaparte's complaint named Standard Oil Company of New Jersey, seventy related corporations and partnerships, John D. Rockefeller, William Rockefeller, Henry M. Flagler, Henry H. Rogers, John D. Archbold, Oliver H. Payne, and Charles M. Pratt. It tracked Tarbell's exposé, following her evidence by enumerating instances of Standard Oil's conspiring with railroads for preferential treatment, manipulating wholesale and retail prices, spying on competitors, and establishing subsidiaries under false pretenses. Even the judges evaluating the government's case found it difficult to digest all the evidence. As the chief justice of the Supreme Court wrote nearly six years later, "The record is inordinately voluminous, consisting of twenty-three volumes of printed matter, aggregating about twelve thousand pages, containing a vast amount of confusing and conflicting testimony relating to innumerable, complex and varied business transactions, extending over a period of nearly forty years."

Tarbell revisited the Standard Oil melodrama in *The American Magazine* in 1907 and 1908, under the headline "Roosevelt Versus Rockefeller." By then *McClure's Magazine* had declined in quality because of financial difficulties, its owner's intervals of inattention because of his international travels, and his own and his wife's precarious health. Tarbell and some of her colleagues migrated to *The American Magazine*, with John S. Phillips handling the financial end of the deal.

An editor's note accompanying Tarbell's three-part Standard Oil series said, "One of the chief problems of the present day is restoring to business that freedom of opportunity which democracy presupposes. It is a problem in which *The American Magazine* is particularly interested and for which it expects to labor continuously. The importance of the present struggle of the government to break the monopolistic power of interstate corporations is so great, its present suit against the Standard Oil Company illustrates so admirably all the features in the problem of freeing commerce, that we have asked Miss Tarbell to postpone the publication of her notable studies of the Tariff and give to our readers her reasons for believing the great suit justifiable. These articles will bring Miss Tarbell's work on the Standard Oil Company up to date."

The conduct of Standard Oil in Kansas had confirmed to Roosevelt, his attorney general, and many clear-minded observers that the company operated in a predatory manner against the public interest. One of the most dogged investigators with the federal government was James R. Garfield, the son of a president, who had served as commissioner of the Bureau of Corporations in the Commerce and Labor Department. He was instrumental in confirming Tarbell's allegations about shipping rates.

Garfield's efforts embarrassed Standard Oil but did not halt its practices. When government authorities cracked down on rate discrimination by railroads under Standard Oil's sway, the trust shifted its transportation and profit centers to the pipelines it controlled. When authorities attempted to regulate pipelines, Standard Oil rejiggered the configurations so that technically no specific pipeline crossed state lines and thus they were qualified for an exemption from federal rules. Violating the spirit of the rules constituted something other than model citizenship but did not qualify for prosecution. Government legislation and regulation simply could not provide a completely level playing field for independents hoping to thrive in a near-monopolistic atmosphere.

Tarbell explained clearly how federal prosecutors hoped to prove that Standard Oil should be dismantled. The legal briefs, the underlying documents, and the testimony needed to persuade judges that "the Standard Oil Company used the railroads illegally; that it controlled the great pipeline system for gathering and carrying crude oil . . . that it organized and reorganized the multitude of companies of which it is made up to evade the laws . . . that it did all of these things in secret, by connivance and by bribery, and for the purpose of limiting the trade of its rivals." After all, she noted, "The Standard Oil Company is an integral part of the commerce of this nation. It is the most magnificent example of efficient organization on a large scale that has ever been worked out in any country. It is a thing of which we ought to be able to be proud." Instead, she said, the trust's illegal behavior "shames us in every country of the globe. It has become a synonym for commercial depravity. We have seen European countries legislating against it, far-away Burma refusing it a footing because of its methods, Chinamen seeking independent products because of its hard dealing."

At Standard Oil, the new generation of executives who decided policy as Rockefeller pulled back seemed as incredulous as the old man at the hatred the trust inspired. After all, Standard Oil products had improved the quality of life across the United States and increasingly around the globe. Besides, trusts had become a way of life. The Standard Oil way of doing business had not arisen in a void. The company had simply adapted its organizational structure to the rapid industrialization of commerce, which made big-scale business possible and efficient. Its executives believed they had done nothing illegal; they had worked within the frame of American business, creating new wealth and uplifting the glory of the national economy. Speaking sarcastically, John Archbold told a dinner audience, "For nearly forty-four years of my short life, I have been engaged in somewhat strenuous effort to restrain trade and commerce in petroleum and its products, in the United States, the District of Columbia, and in foreign countries. I make this confession, friends, as a confidential matter to you, and in the strong conviction and belief that you will not give me away to the Bureau of Corporations."

The worldview of Archbold, Rockefeller, and their colleagues diverged wildly from those calling themselves Progressives. The American political landscape seemed sorely divided. The Progressives, reformers from numerous callings (including journalism), found political corruption, inhumane work conditions, exploitation of individual consumers, and inequalities of income just about everywhere they looked—including the trust known as Standard Oil. They called into question the basis of American capitalism, which had been almost entirely laissez-faire since the dawn of the Republic.

The contest for the soul of capitalism played out most definitively in the judicial branch of government. In 1909, a four-judge federal circuit court panel ruled for the government and against Standard Oil's appeal. The Supreme Court would become involved next. That same year, Rockefeller, the focal point of so much litigation, published his memoir, *Random Reminiscences of Men and Events*. Some of it had already appeared serially in the periodical *World's Work*. In hindsight, a description of the memoir by Jules Abels seems apt: "Stung by the Tarbell book, Rockefeller deserted his policy of silence . . . [and wrote] a general defense containing some rationalizations and a good deal of soft soap."

Rockefeller never mentioned Tarbell by name. He did, however, provide his views about practices Tarbell exposed, including why railroad rebates made good business sense for Standard Oil and the consuming public. Rockefeller, who wrote the book in his own words, without assistance from a ghostwriter, employed language strategically, as if composing a legal brief. In answer to damaging allegations, he argued, "We did not ruthlessly go after the trade of our competitors and attempt to ruin it by cutting prices or setting up a spy system." It is uncontested that Standard Oil did cut prices and set up a spy system, so the sentence revolved around the ambiguous word "ruthlessly." Over and over, Rockefeller assumed a defensive posture throughout the 200-page book, using two devices: emphasizing the collegial nature of decisionmaking within Standard Oil during the formative decades, and distancing himself from the day-to-day management of Standard Oil starting in the mid-1890s, saying that he had begun his retirement at age fifty-five.

At the request of a Chicago newspaper editor, Tarbell reviewed the book. She deemed a portion of Rockefeller's life "admirable," noting especially his devotion to nature conservation. But, she added, "There is the other Mr. Rockefeller," the one who would bend and break the rules to dominate in business, harming consumers in the process. After comparing Rockefeller to "a conquering Hun," Tarbell cleverly qualified that statement: "No, he's not a Hun—the destructive force of him is too intelligent. He is more like Bernard Shaw's Napoleon—great, because for himself he suspended the ordinary laws of conventionality and morality while keeping them in operation for other people. He is a mastodon of mental machinery. And would you ask a steam plow for pity? Would you look for scruples in an electric dynamo?"

The dynamo had no intention of pulling back, not because of negative book reviews, litigation, or any other irritation. During the first decade of the 1900s, Standard Oil carved out significant territories in California, drilling, marketing, and distributing oil and its byproducts along the West Coast as well as shipping commodities across the Pacific Ocean to Asian consumers. The first Texas well arrived in 1901, near Beaumont. Although Rockefeller and his colleagues had written off Texas geologically before then, the company moved quickly to expand its markets there. Even when Standard Oil failed to dominate the Texas market, fear of its predations governed decisionmaking in the executive offices of its competitors. In some markets, Standard Oil's share of business fell. In dollars, however, the income kept climbing, and Rockefeller's already unimaginable wealth grew too.

As Standard Oil continued operating as a trust, as its critics continued pointing out the dangers of such big businesses, everybody kept watch on the justices of the Supreme Court. When would they issue their decision in the federal government's lawsuit against Standard Oil, and what would it say?

In 1911, after years of deliberation about trust controversies, the justices spoke. Because justices are frequently unpredictable, it would be mistaken to say that their ruling in the Standard Oil case seemed inevitable. Be that as it may, the Court upheld the legal authority of the four-judge circuit court panel. In a nearly inaudible voice, Chief Justice Edward White read the decision from the bench: Standard Oil must divest its subsidiaries. The ruling effectively ended the existence of the trust and its quasi-monopolistic practices.

The chief justice, writing for the court, commented, "We think no disinterested mind can survey the period in question without being inevitably driven to the conclusion that the very genius for commercial development and organization, which it would seem was manifested from the beginning, soon begat an interest and purpose to exclude others." The desire to dominate the industry, the chief justice said, "was frequently manifested by actions and dealings wholly inconsistent with the theory that they were made with the single conception of advancing the development of business power by usual methods, but which, on the contrary, necessarily involved the intent to drive others from the field and exclude them from their right to trade and thus accomplish the mastery which was the end in view."

Justice John Marshall Harlan, who died five months after the ruling, dissented in part because he worried that the majority opinion left loopholes for Standard Oil to continue its unsavory practices. As early as 1890, Harlan reminded his fellow justices, the citizenry had experienced "a deep feeling of unrest" over a kind of slavery that had nothing to do with race and plantations. Harlan termed it "the slavery that would result from aggregations of capital in the hands of a few individuals and corporations controlling, for their own profit and advantage exclusively, the entire business of the country, including the production and sale of the necessaries of life." Hence, a sweeping antitrust law had come into being. The dangers addressed by the law had not disappeared, Harlan emphasized.

The outcome of the Supreme Court's ruling had been suspected, so reactions around the globe were muted. From London, the *New York Times* correspondent wrote, "The Supreme Court decision in the Standard Oil case created surprisingly little interest or flurry in financial circles here as the result had been generally anticipated. Dealings in stocks for some time past have been on the bear side, and in the hands of Continental and Wall Street houses. Brokers, therefore, did not remain in the financial district over night as in times of crises." But numerous trustbusters certainly did not consider the victory total at the time. The Court's ruling seemed to allow restraint of trade by powerful trusts up to a point; the justices seemed to say that trusts could act reasonably without violating the public interest.

Although portions of the Supreme Court ruling seemed unduly harsh to Rockefeller and his colleagues, Standard Oil had prepared itself for the eventuality and took painless steps to comply with the ruling, which suggested that previous corporate reorganizations had amounted to shams—window dressing to avoid further prosecution by government entities and further civil litigation by competitors and investors. The largest of the units from before the ruling, Standard Oil of New Jersey, retained its identity and eventually became known as Exxon. Standard Oil of New York evolved into Mobil. Standard Oil of Ohio became Sohio, and so on. Although each entity had to disband its overlapping management, they generally avoided immediate competition by respecting one another's geographic markets.

Analyzing the court-ordered breakup, author Jules Abels demonstrates in his book *The Rockefeller Billions* that "salutary changes" occurred within Standard Oil because of the dissolution. First, he notes, "A fresh wind blew through the company, since the decree was a signal for the withdrawal of many old personalities and the coming to the fore of a host of young faces, given their chance years before they expected it. Then, too, there was far too much centralization in the old company—every authorization for more than five thousand dollars had to be approved by New York . . . Another change for the better was the demise of the Rockefeller-Archbold practice of secrecy in corporate affairs and the exclusive reliance on plowing back of profits for capital needs."

Competition within the oil industry did not increase meaningfully for a long time, however. Financier J. P. Morgan summarized the dilemma when he reportedly asked rhetorically, "How in hell is any court going to compel a man to compete with himself?" As Abels noted, "Bonds of friendship continued, and by tacit understandings the different companies preserved and respected spheres of influence where one or the other company continued to dominate. Each of the Standard units had been set up with specific functions, and they continued to do business in the same way."

Furthermore, neither Rockefeller nor other Standard Oil executives suffered meaningful punishment for their decades of evasion. The Supreme Court decision actually multiplied Rockefeller's wealth. Because he held approximately 25 percent of Standard Oil stock before the atomization of the corporate structure, he received that percentage of stock in Standard Oil of New Jersey in addition to cash from each of the thirty-three spinoffs formed in response to the Supreme Court mandate. Anticipating a boom in automotive travel, investors eagerly bought into the new companies. As the stock prices rose, Rockefeller's net worth tripled, then quintupled, making him almost certainly the first billionaire in America's existence. Four years after the Supreme Court had seemingly given Roosevelt what he wanted, the former president noted acidly the presumably unintended consequences, "No wonder that Wall Street's prayer now is 'Oh Merciful Providence, give us another dissolution.'"

In other words, the impacts of the Supreme Court ruling were far-reaching but slow-moving. In 1923, twelve years after the ruling, Tarbell wrote, "The price we pay for gasoline is the price fixed by the Standard Oil Company. Although the components of this company were segregated by the U.S. government in 1911 with the expectation that thereafter there would be open competition, its control over the production and price of oil is as great as ever." As late as 1925, Tarbell mentioned that she was waiting to update her Standard Oil exposé "until the effect on the oil industry of the dissolution suit of 1911 should have been fairly demonstrated."

Rockefeller commented on Tarbell too as he aged. During interviews with William O. Inglis, a New York City journalist hired to memoralize his life, Rockefeller finally revealed some of his private emotions about Tarbell and his career.

Inglis first approached Rockefeller through Ivy Lee, a public relations consultant on retainer to the Rockefeller family. Inglis requested a round of golf with the aging tycoon, hoping to persuade him to cooperate on a biographical account to be published in the *New York Evening World*. Afterward, Inglis wrote a story about the round of golf, portraying Rockefeller as an enjoyable companion on the course and a warm human being, quite the opposite of his public image. Lee wrote to Rockefeller that Inglis's story "is the kind of thing that gets the people to know you, and I cannot but feel that the more they know you . . . the better will the public understand and sympathize with what you are trying to do."

Regular conversations between Inglis and Rockefeller began during 1917; Inglis was paid with Rockefeller money for his time. He took short-hand notes, then transcribed the interviews on a typewriter. At first he despaired of recording anything useful. Rockefeller told him that "we shall not take up anything controversial. A great deal of mud has been thrown at me in the past. Much of it has dried and fallen off since then. To take up those questions now would only revive bitter controversy." Rockefeller even withheld the truth about his father, telling Inglis that his only "disappointment" had been when William Rockefeller refused to pay for his college education.

But over the years, Rockefeller relented somewhat about the ban on controversial matters. Decades later, after studying the Rockefeller-Inglis conversations, Ron Chernow commented, "In responding to Tarbell, Rockefeller alternated between biting criticism and his express desire to avoid unpleasantness." Rockefeller believed that Tarbell made "a pretense of fairness," but "like some women, she distorts facts, states as facts what she must know is untrue, and utterly disregards reason." Inglis read passages from Tarbell's exposé aloud to the elderly Rockefeller. As he absorbed Tarbell's words, Rockefeller softened his attitude. "I'm amazed at her writing, all the time!" he exclaimed. "There's so much in it favorable to the Standard Oil company, what with all her prejudices."

When Inglis finally completed the manuscript of the biography in 1923, everybody who read it—even Rockefeller's son and Ivy Lee—deemed it unpublishable because of its unvarnished laudatory nature. The transcripts remained available to researchers, with permission from the Rockefeller family. Tarbell, however, did nothing with the material. She felt that her masterpiece had said what needed to be said.

For the Rest of Their Lives

If Ida M. Tarbell had never written her magazine serialization of Standard Oil's history and the articles that followed, John D. Rockefeller might be revered today rather than reviled by so many. Because of Tarbell's exposé, however, the most admired and feared individual in America during his lifetime ended up consigned forever to an infamous group of popular villains.

For his part, Rockefeller found it impossible to grasp the personal impact of Tarbell's disclosures. The negative portions of her work would surely be viewed as wrongheaded, he thought. After all, he sincerely believed that his Baptist God would never have so richly rewarded the kind of man she portrayed. Rockefeller seemed especially surprised that because of his negative reputation, potential and actual recipients of his philanthropy began to question acceptance of his "tainted" money. During the serialization of Tarbell's Standard Oil exposé, an editor at the *Omaha World-Herald* contacted her to ask her opinion about whether the University of Nebraska should accept Rockefeller money. The newspaper published her reply. "If the acceptance of the gift . . . brings with it tacit recognition of the commercial principles which he has employed with more conspicuous success than any other man in the country; if it closes the mouth of any man in Nebraska to the corruptive influence of those principles, no greater calamity could befall the university," she said. Tarbell wrote that human nature suggested "the receiver of the gift becomes sooner or later the apologist of the donor and his methods. Where there is a possibility of such a result, jealous regard for the moral atmosphere of the institution makes refusal of the gift an imperative duty."

From mid-1905, after Tarbell's devastating character study of Rockefeller, until his death thirty-two years later, the billionaire gave priority to spending his unprecedented fortune wisely. Believing that worthy men and women are bound to receive worldly blessings through God's grace, Rockefeller wanted to avoid promoting dependency among the unworthy through his philanthropy. As a result, he supported causes such as universities and medical research institutes, which he felt might equip the weak with the mental and physical tools to succeed on their own. In selecting his causes, he worked closely with his son, John Jr., and with Frederick T. Gates, who had trained as a minister. Before becoming a paid Rockefeller adviser in 1891, Gates had raised money for various Baptist educational institutions, including perhaps the grandest of all, the University of Chicago. He had little experience in the world of finance, but because of his thoroughness as well as his pleasant demeanor, he persuaded insiders to reveal undisclosed details, which enabled him to sniff out financial shenanigans that Rockefeller sometimes overlooked in the businesses of others.

Even though Rockefeller became the University of Chicago's financial angel, he did not seek immortality there by asking the school to carry his name. Nor did he usually interfere in campus policymaking. In his profit-making ventures, Rockefeller found it difficult to delegate authority. In his philanthropic ventures, for reasons perhaps only he knew, he usually did so easily. He understood that his detractors might judge his philanthropy to be a salve for real or imagined sins, so he chose recipients who could not easily be perceived as promoting his own interests, and he maintained a low profile as much as his renown would allow, unlike fellow multimillionaire industrialist Andrew Carnegie, who widely publicized his innumerable donations of vast sums.

Indeed, Carnegie's strategy worked from a public relations perspective. Though a tyrant in the business world, he is remembered largely for his philanthropy. More than 3,000 public libraries built with Carnegie money created appreciation in town after town. Rockefeller, who outlived Carnegie by eighteen years, kept making generous donations, many of them appreciated not only by the direct beneficiaries but also by the public at large. Still, he is not remembered as a philanthropist in the same way as Carnegie—perhaps because Carnegie's detractors tended to appear after his death. While alive, Carnegie did not experience an exposé by Ida Tarbell or any comparable muckraker. Rockefeller's generous philanthropy could not redeem his reputation. He will forever remain one of the most important individuals in the history of the United States. But because of Tarbell, he will always be viewed as a pioneer who violated the public trust to reach the pinnacle of power.

As for Tarbell, she lived seven years beyond Rockefeller, thirty-three years after the Supreme Court ruling that validated her exposé. Her reputation as the first great modern investigative journalist remains undisturbed.

Her legacy as a female pioneer has been clouded, however, by her personal philosophies. Tarbell became an enigma to twentieth-century scholars of feminism, who found her views a challenge to explain while lauding her accomplishments. A feminist by example but not by ideology, Tarbell is not easily pigeonholed. She questioned the logic of women's suffrage. She published ideologically ambiguous stories about the roles of women at home and in the workplace. Her thinking about gender, collected in the books *The Business of Being a Woman* and *The Ways of Woman*, ignited passionate discussions in the academy and the popular press. Deeply reported and painstakingly composed, Tarbell's writings about gender and the workplace are both thought-provoking and unexpected.

"Is Woman's Suffrage a Failure?" reads the headline in the October 1924 edition of *Good Housekeeping*, above a long feature by Tarbell. Perhaps more than anything else she published about gender, this article demonstrates Tarbell's thinking and suggests how difficult she is to categorize. Four years after women secured the right to cast ballots, she cautioned those disappointed at the slowness of change in the political landscape to be patient. "As one who has ever been lukewarm toward suffrage and who regarded the argument that quick and drastic remedial results were sure to come from it as mischievous and dishonest, I want to say that I believe something has happened—something rather more in the time than I at least thought probable—and that something is spreading," Tarbell wrote. Journeying across the United States to gather examples for the story, she had found women more interested in issues outside the home than they had been before. "Everywhere the women I met as individuals and as groups—many of them formerly anti-suffragists—invariably soon turned the conversation to law enforcement, the [Teapot Dome] oil scandal, the regulation of industry, the League of Nations, [presidential hopefuls] Coolidge, Smith, McAdoo."

During her research, Tarbell had drawn encouragement from the increased number of women holding political offices during the 1920s—eight in the Pennsylvania legislature, for example. After lauding the development and explaining the accomplishments of those women, she inserted an aside apparently aimed at the ardent feminists who had complained about her views: "One of the anomalies of this situation is that there are women who do not take this result as a matter of course! Not a few old-style professional suffrage agitators seem actually to resent women coming noiselessly into public office and going about their business as any other public servants do and not as women politicians vindicating their sex!"

Tarbell addressed whether a woman should aspire to the White House, something she believed should come to pass. After all, queens had ruled nations as well as or better than kings: "Consider Catherine of Russia, Louise of Prussia, Maria Theresa of Austria, Elizabeth of England, Catherine de Medici of France. And it was of Marie Antoinette that Mirabeau said she was the only man the king had about him." She said she could think of "a half-dozen women in these United States that I believe would do better in the presidency than at least three or four incumbents since Lincoln, and nothing would be better for the country at this moment than to substitute this same half dozen for a half-dozen senators I could name!"

Tarbell counted among her friends a number of feminist leaders. During World War I, for example, she accepted an appointment from President Woodrow Wilson to serve on the eleven-member Council of National Defense Woman's Committee. Although suffrage questions fell outside the council's mandate, Tarbell knew that eight of the female members favored giving women the vote. Still, she developed friendships with women like Anna H. Shaw, president of the National American Woman Suffrage Association. "It is not to be wondered that Dr. Anna suspected me, had a certain resentment at my being a member of her committee," Tarbell recalled. "In spite of all this, as the months went on she and I became better and better friends. She was so able, so zealous, so utterly given to her cause . . . I found her a most warm-hearted . . . person, as well as delightfully salty in her bristling against men."

Tarbell's gentleness in her private relationships contrasted with her reputation for ferocity when exposing Rockefeller and the trusts. Mary Glenn Newell, a secretary at the Council of National Defense Woman's Committee, attested eloquently to her warm charisma. Just before Tarbell arrived at the committee office, Newell had decided to quit what she considered an unpleasant job. But Tarbell's kind eyes and politeness as she asked Newell to take dictation produced an instant liking: "I did not know until after you had finished dictating that you were the great Ida M. Tarbell," Newell said, adding that only her own mother had influenced her as much. In correspondence with Tarbell, Newell reminded her about the day news arrived at the committee that Esther Tarbell had died in Titusville. Ida was scheduled to attend a wedding in Washington, D.C. After learning that she could not catch a train to Titusville until the evening, she made her appearance at the wedding, saying nothing about her mother's death so as not to cast a pall over the ceremony. "That to me was supreme unselfishness," Newell commented.

Tarbell's public service, while conscientious, took second place to her journalism. She wrote as if her life depended on it. To some extent it did, because she earned her livelihood almost entirely from publishing in magazines and advances from book publishers. The extent and quality of her investigations after her Rockefeller exposé are astounding. Writing more and more from her rural homestead in Easton, Connecticut, rather than from her New York City apartment, she finally delved into tariff controversies, examined labor-management relations in workplaces across the nation, and sought to explain the misunderstood role of women in the life of the nation.

An excerpt from one of her many tariff stories suggests how skillfully Tarbell made an important but arcane topic interesting to a wide audience: "The city of Pittsburgh is the greatest monument in this country to the practice of High Protection. For fifty years it has been the stronghold of the doctrine. For fifty years it has reaped, as no other center in the United States, the benefits of prohibitive duties." Iron, steel, tin, and plate glass formed the backbone of the Pittsburgh economy. "All of these articles have for years had the American market practically to themselves. All of these articles have for years been exported and sold at [lower] prices than the American consumer can buy them," she explained. Legislators promised that tariffs would protect low-income American workers from lost jobs and degraded living conditions, she wrote. But the results turned out differently. Instead, tariff policy "produced enormous fortunes. So many, so conspicuous are they that a recognized American type in Europe and the United States is the 'Pittsburgh millionaire.'" Not only did the Pittsburgh millionaires exploit laborers, but they also used tariff protection to gouge consumers.

As an example of price gouging, Tarbell used shoes. Given modern shoe manufacturing machinery, prices paid by American consumers should have decreased. That did not happen, though, because of tariff politics. First a tariff was laid on hides in 1897. Until then, South American hides had been available and affordable to shoe dealers. "But the cattle growers of the West raised a cry that they should have more money for their hides, that Congress should pass a law which would compel the people to give it to them . . . The effect was immediately to raise the price of shoe leather." Prices rose further when the cost of linen thread used in shoe manufacturing increased. "Why had thread advanced?" Tarbell asked. "It is a pretty study of combined tariff and trust manipulation."

Having concluded from her research that Senator Nelson W. Aldrich, a Rhode Island Republican, served the trusts most slavishly of all on tariff matters, Tarbell toured factories in his state. She reported how breathing the hot, dirty air in the factories made efficient work difficult. She wrote about how the noise from the machinery became unbearable, causing hearing loss. Buckets for drinking water contained floating contaminants. The toilets stank. Work-related illnesses, including bronchitis, pneumonia, and tuberculosis, disabled laborers. Perhaps coincidentally, as Tarbell was quick to mention, Aldrich's daughter had married Rockefeller's son nine years earlier. "This, then, is high protection's most perfect work," Tarbell summed up. "A state [Rhode Island] of half-a-million people turning out an annual product worth $187 million, the laborers in the chief industry underpaid, unstable and bent with disease, the average employers rich, self-satisfied and as indifferent to social obligations as so many robber barons."

Tarbell's expertise about tariffs caught the attention of President Wilson, who asked the journalist to serve on the newly formed Tariff Commission, offering her an annual salary of $7500, which was more than she earned from her writing in lean years. Tarbell resisted, telling Wilson that the commission would be sabotaged by trusts and their free-spending lobbyists. The commission's research, "however sound, would stand no chance in Congress when a wool or iron and steel or sugar lobby appeared."

As Tarbell visited workplaces for two decades after her Rockefeller–Standard Oil exposé, the linkages between tariffs and labor-management relations became more and more obvious to her. Corporate owners sometimes suspected her of harboring sympathies toward laborers. Laborers sometimes suspected her of harboring sympathies toward management. Both sides were mistaken; she was seeking the facts that served as the foundation of the investigative reporting she invented.

Some of her best reporting on labor-management relations appeared in the book *New Ideals in Business: An Account of Their Practice and Their Effects Upon Men and Profits*. Tarbell, fervent about workplace reform, wanted to promote cooperation not only by exposing on-the-job strife but also by chronicling exemplary situations, hoping to teach via narrative journalism. Presentation of potentially difficult information obtained through investigative reporting became more understandable and memorable to readers when presented in narrative fashion. Tarbell was a pioneer in the craft of character-driven narrative, as in her 1912 magazine feature about the death of a twenty-six-year-old heiress turned workplace reformer. It opened like this:

> When we attempt to set down the social symptoms of our day, we must include the Revolt of the Young Rich. All over the land it is going on—a questioning of the fortunes laid in their hands, a resentment at the chance for a life-fight of their own taken away, a rising passion of pain and indignation at meaningless inequalities and sufferings. They are not taking it out in talk, at least not all of them. An increasing number are offering themselves in humility as learners. Such a one was a young girl, Carola Woerishoffer by name, who four years ago suddenly appeared among the social workers of New York City. She had come "to learn and help," she said.
>
> A few months ago she was suddenly killed like a soldier at his post in the discharge of her self-imposed task of learning and helping. Brief as was Carola Woerishoffer's term of service, it has left an impression whose significance, those who now sit bewildered by the seeming meaningless of her death, will surely in time more and more fully realize.

Throughout the profile, Tarbell folded in anecdotes about the working conditions of the laborers Woerishoffer had tried to assist. Here is Tarbell's account of what Woerishoffer learned after volunteering to work in laundries to document conditions there: "As she was determined to shirk nothing, she was regularly at her tub or mangle or feeding machine at 7:30 A.M. and whenever work demanded it she stayed on into the night. There were no provisions for seating in the long work period; frequently the rooms were practically unventilated, always more or less stifling from steam and damp. In some places she found neglect and uncleanliness adding to the disagreeable features inevitable in the industry. She worked days over unguarded machines where the girls told her cynically, 'You didn't get burned today or yesterday, but you sure will some time. Everybody does.'"

Tarbell's late-in-life biographies of U.S. Steel Corporation magnate Elbert Gary and General Electric Company magnate Owen D. Young underscored their reformist treatment of employees. Some reviewers expressed disappointment that she failed to eviscerate Gary and Young the way she had Rockefeller. Tarbell, who had anticipated the criticism, calmly insisted that she wrote what the evidence showed. She also never halted her research into the inspiring accomplishments and character of Abraham Lincoln. For her 1924 book, *In the Footsteps of the Lincolns*, she shunted aside the physical discomfort caused by Parkinson's disease while traveling thousands of miles.

When not traveling to conduct research on Lincoln, Gary, or Young, Tarbell traveled to present paid lectures on the evils of war, the need for world peace, American politics, trusts, tariffs, labor-management relations, and the status of women. She spoke to audiences large and small in each of the forty-eight states. Audience members sometimes disagreed with her messages but ended up respecting the way she listened acutely to other points of view, answered every question directed to her on the stage, and replied to every letter reaching her back home.

A woman from Birmingham, Alabama, wrote to her after hearing the childless, unmarried Tarbell discuss how women in the workplace deserved equal responsibility and pay with men but should never stop cherishing the joys of motherhood and marriage. It is not easy to find happiness, Tarbell's correspondent wrote, as the mother of six children under age ten with an unemployed husband. Would Tarbell lend the family $200? Instead of ignoring the letter, Tarbell—who late in life openly expressed regret at never having children—replied that she could not afford the loan but on an upcoming visit to Birmingham would be willing to meet and perhaps arrange a referral to a friend involved in a local charity. The correspondent, surprised to receive a personal reply, wrote back, apologizing for her audacity and insisting that she did not want to impose on Tarbell's brief stay in Birmingham.

Always observing, always processing her observations into theories, Tarbell concluded presciently as early as World War I—long before the omnipresence of McDonald's and Wal-Mart—that towns across the United States had surrendered much of their individual character. She saw charming downtown hotels giving way to cookie-cutter motels. She noticed dress shops on Main Street emulating New York City boutiques. She expressed alarm at the standardized beauty parlors, where customers asked for hair styling as seen in East Coast magazine advertisements. Tarbell lectured that commercial standardization "is the surest way to destroy the initiative, to benumb the creative impulse above all else essential to the vitality and growth of democratic ideals."

Back home in New York City, she kept a full calendar. As president of the Pen and Brush Club for thirty years, Tarbell exercised influence over thousands of professional women. But when those accomplished women tried to honor her, she demurred. Addressing an open letter to her "beloved but misguided friends," she said that the proposed celebration "would send me to my grave . . . I am simply a hardworking—so I think—journalist. There is no reason for the public singling me out in the way you propose, not nearly so much reason as for many others . . . I don't think I could stand it to sit up in the middle of a table and have people make remarks at me."

Even as Parkinson's disease progressively crippled her efforts during the final two decades of her life, Tarbell continued to research, write, and publish. She needed to pay the rents for the Connecticut farmhouse and the Manhattan apartment; supplement the often meager income of her sister, an artist, who was her housemate in Connecticut; contribute to medical expenses for her retired oilman brother as he descended into mental illness; and assist her nieces and nephews with their college tuitions. Tarbell struggled through disease and unpredictable income, but she was not pitiable. Her mind stayed clear and her byline appeared often.

Unexpectedly for the reading public, she harked back to the Standard Oil trust and Rockefeller in 1936, when her book *The Nationalizing of Business, 1878–1898* appeared as the ninth volume in a series titled *A*

History of American Life. History professors Arthur M. Schlesinger and Dixon R. Fox, the general editors of the series, had chosen her as one of the authors. The 300-plus page book read smoothly; dozens of reviewers complimented Tarbell for her masterful explanations. In their editors' foreword, Schlesinger and Fox praised her lavishly. Behind the scenes, however, their correspondence suggested that the elderly Tarbell was slipping professionally. On February 11, 1936, Schlesinger wrote, "I have spent nearly four months in putting the manuscript of our seventy-eight-year-old author into shape. The result is nothing to crow about." Schlesinger mentioned "meandering and sometimes incoherent sentences" as well as "factual errors" and confusing citations. Fox replied on February 28, "If what you have done should be called editing, it certainly surpasses any editing that I have ever seen or heard of . . . I do not know whether to marvel most at your skill or at your patience."

Whether or not Tarbell was slipping as a journalist, she remained active and optimistic. S. S. McClure, in contrast, descended into despair. After Tarbell and her colleagues left his magazine staff in 1906, the periodical continued to offer interesting nonfiction and fiction for a while. But McClure could not find replacements with equal talent and passion. As the editorial quality declined, he learned that the business staff had managed its assets poorly. In 1911, McClure reluctantly sold the magazine. He expected to remain as editor, but the new owners pushed him out the next year. At age fifty-five, he had lost his job, his professional identity, and his bearings.

For a decade, McClure drifted. He was occasionally hired for newspaper editing, drafting chapters for an autobiography that appeared in 1914, speaking for a fee, but in 1921 he purchased the much-degraded *McClure's Magazine* from bankruptcy court. With a skeleton staff and precarious financing, he managed to issue a monthly magazine through the summer of 1924. But it never achieved acclaim editorially and never achieved stability on the business side. After the August 1924 issue, it folded. Given McClure's depressed state after he lost his magazine a second time, it seems cruel that he lived until age ninety-two.

Late in life, Rockefeller remained a stereotype of so much good and evil. Like most stereotypes, he appeared one-dimensional to outsiders. William H. Allen, who published a biography of Rockefeller in 1930, when his subject was ninety, commented that he is "one of the least known personalities of prominence in the world."

Following the court-ordered breakup of the Standard Oil trust, Rockefeller lived well, as perhaps the wealthiest individual in the United States. He enjoyed spending time with his children and grandchildren, although he outlived his wife by twenty-two years, a sad situation for a loving husband, and outlived three of his five children, a sad situation for any parent.

Rockefeller's spouse, children, and grandchildren provided joy but in the course of human nature caused complications, which were sometimes magnified rather than resolved because of his wealth. After his wife, Cettie, died in 1915, for example, Rockefeller wanted to transport her remains to Cleveland for burial. But Cleveland government authorities were pursuing him for back taxes totaling perhaps $2 million, contending that he had been a legal resident of the city in 1913 because of a relatively brief visit. Rockefeller had established legal residency in New York decades earlier and paid property taxes there. He considered the Cleveland tax bill outrageous. So he withheld his tax payment, but he worried that if he arrived in Cleveland to bury Cettie, he would be served with unwanted legal papers. He finally concocted a plan to sneak Cettie's remains into Cleveland and attend a quick burial ceremony before the authorities found out he was there.

Such sagas made Rockefeller seem less imposing, as sympathetic journalists and public relations masterminds combined to humanize the previously unemotional corporate predator. Feature stories told of Rockefeller enjoying his longtime pursuits—churchgoing, horseback riding, golfing, landscaping—while adding one other late in life: touring daily in a variety of chauffeured automobiles, usually with carefully chosen guests in the front and back seats. But no matter what he did or said, money was always central to his image. He found a way to make that work to his advantage in old age. When in public, he handed out shiny nickels to children and shiny dimes to adults. Sometimes he accompanied the gift with a brief lesson. He would tell children, for example, that the nickel could become the start of a personal fortune.

Unlike Tarbell, whose influence never waned because she continued doing what she had done for so long—exposing wrongdoing and explaining a complex society in print—Rockefeller lost influence in the corporate realm. His son and a new generation of executives ran Standard Oil. Instead, Rockefeller's influence showed up largely in the philanthropic realm. Until 1901, he had given gifts to deserving individuals and institutions either on an ad hoc basis or through already existing mechanisms of the Baptist church. But as he increasingly stepped away from day-to-day Standard Oil decisionmaking to focus on large-scale philanthropy, he created the Rockefeller Institute for Medical Research, in 1901, and the General Education Board, in 1902. The institute allocated money that Rockefeller hoped would lead to cures for a variety of diseases, such as polio, meningitis, and syphilis. The original intention of the board was to bolster education for blacks in the American South. The result turned out differently, as the vast percentage of the giving went to whites. Still, many southern high schools in low-income areas owe their beginnings to Rockefeller money.

In 1909, Rockefeller took the first steps to create a new philanthropic entity called the Rockefeller Foundation. The structure of the foundation shielded family money from inheritance taxes imposed by the government, but it served as more than a tax evasion mechanism. Public health in the United States and other nations, especially China, became the focus, and education of physicians and laboratory researchers emerged as a secondary effort.

It seemed that everybody who commented on Rockefeller's philanthropy during his final decades issued a variation of several themes: the amount of money was beyond imagination; some of it had been placed wise and altruistically; some of it had been placed unwisely and with a self-interested agenda. Allen, the Rockefeller biographer, wrote in his 1930 book, "The good his giving has done would fill volumes, as has the harm it has done."

Rockefeller looked inward to the extent that he paid attention, sometimes obsessively, to his health. He stated long before reaching old age that he planned to live to one hundred. At age eighty-two, he played golf with his physician and friend, Hamilton E. Biggar. On the golf course one day, the two men planned a golf date eighteen years in the future. Rockefeller had started napping regularly at age thirty-four, believing that the relaxation would reduce stress and thus prolong his life. Retiring to bed early, he also arose early. He never used tobacco or drank alcohol, ate moderately at every meal, played a numbers game with family members after dinner to aid digestion, and exercised daily. He died at age ninety-eight, though.

When he died, in 1937, Tarbell's exposé of his beloved Standard Oil Company and of his own morality figured prominently in the obituaries. The *New York Times* devoted space to Rockefeller's oft-repeated rebuttal, saying that he denied Tarbell's charges.

> He declared that there was a great difference between good trusts and bad trusts, between moral and immoral corporations. He insisted that Standard Oil was a good trust and that he had made his money honestly and honorably. In an age of waste and inefficiency, when the proper exploitation of natural resources was badly needed, he declared, industrial combinations were a necessity. He was proud of succeeding where others had failed in a highly hazardous industry, and was proud that there had never been any "water" in Standard Oil stock. Denying that he had coerced rivals into joining Standard Oil, he declared that they had been glad to join, and had often had so little faith in the oil business that they insisted on being paid in cash instead of taking Standard Oil stock when their companies were merged into his. Had they had the faith he had, they would have grown rich with him.

The obituary noted "the occasions on which Mr. Rockefeller answered the charges against him were very few." On one occasion, it reported, Rockefeller explained his silences by saying: "Sometimes things are said about us that are cruel and they hurt. But I am never a pessimist. I never despair. I believe in man and the brotherhood of man and am confident that everything will come out for the good of all in the end. I have decided to say nothing, hoping that after my death the truth will gradually come to the surface and that posterity will do strict justice."

Two years after Rockefeller's death, Tarbell published her own obituary, in a manner of speaking. Her autobiography, *All in the Day's Work*, received widespread review attention in 1939. In the *New York World Telegram*, reviewer Harry Hansen said, "Her autobiography shows the operation of the American conscience in her work." At age eighty-one, "Miss Tarbell might well be cynical . . . But she isn't. She still believes in doing the day's work with common sense and faith in a good outcome." As for the book that made so much difference, *The History of the Standard Oil Company*, although it was then infrequently purchased or borrowed from libraries, it remained a testament to how a determined author against unimaginable odds could accomplish her dream: making the world a better place. Hansen said that for general readers, the book served as "a foundation stone in American business history." For journalists, it remained "a milestone in intelligent reporting."

When Tarbell died in 1944, Rockefeller figured prominently in her obituaries. Even in death their names were linked inextricably.

BIBLIOGRAPHIC ESSAY AND SELECT BIBLIOGRAPHY

IDA MINERVA TARBELL

This book started out as a straightforward biography of Ida M. Tarbell. For ten years I traveled the nation seeking everything she wrote, everything written to her and about her. The quest stretched into the majority of the fifty states plus France and England. Two archives yielded the largest volume of information: Allegheny College in Meadville, Pennsylvania, and the Drake Well Museum, about half an hour away, in Titusville, Pennsylvania.

At Allegheny College, Tarbell's alma mater, I studied the original correspondence to and from Tarbell. At Pelletier Library I examined the books that Tarbell kept in her personal library; college annuals, newspapers, and magazines from her years as a student; and boxes filled with photographs. Jane Westenfeld, who doubled as a librarian on the main floor and the archivist on the second floor, shared her vast knowledge of the collection. Library director Connie C. Thorson and college historian Jonathan Helmreich helped too.

Throughout her life, Ida Tarbell corresponded frequently with members of her family—her parents, sister, brother, nieces, and nephew. She also corresponded often with work colleagues and friends and regularly answered letters from strangers. Much of her correspondence reflects a distinctive formality, but she sometimes shared her opinions and emotions. Her penmanship is flowery, which sometimes makes it difficult to read. Later in life, suffering from Parkinson's disease, she hired help to type her letters.

The Drake Well Museum collections are not specifically about Tarbell. The museum is, however, devoted to the early decades of the oil industry, and as a result there is abundant Tarbell material in its folders. Museum administrator Barbara T. Zolli, trained as an actress, sometimes leaves the premises dressed as Tarbell so she can perform her one-woman show to appreciative audiences. She assisted me over and over. Museum staff member Susan J. Beates used her encyclopedic knowledge to guide me through the collection when Zolli could not.

Others living in the Meadville-Titusville area who provided especially valuable information about Tarbell included amateur historian Margaret Anne (Margo) Mong; documentary filmmakers Lisa and Rich Gensheimer; newspaper editor Jon Sherman; and Barbara Gibson, who lived in what was once the Tarbell family home.

Tarbell's 1939 autobiography is admirable and invaluable. Although she did not disclose everything about her professional and personal life, the book is remarkably revealing for somebody raised in an era of reticence. Tarbell checked her memory often while composing the memoir by looking at documents and querying family members, work colleagues, and friends.

Tarbell died in 1944. When I began my research in the 1990s, almost nobody who knew her well still lived. Caroline Tarbell Tupper of Malibu, California, a grandniece, was an exception. She provided memories from her firsthand acquaintanceship with Ida Tarbell and shared memorabilia. Tarbell descendant Peter Price found uncatalogued material at his home in Rolla, Missouri; he and his wife, Mary Catherine, opened their home and also shared memorabilia. Francie Tarbell Fleek of Phoenixville, Pennsylvania, and Corban Goble, of Bowling Green, Kentucky, helped with genealogical questions.

In Easton, Connecticut, Verne Gay and Wendy Chaix allowed me to visit their home, which Tarbell owned as a getaway from New York City.

Robert C. Kochersberger, Jr., has not written a full-length biography of Tarbell, but he has researched specific periods of her life. In 1994, while an English professor at North Carolina State University, he published a selection of her journalism, accompanied by his commentary. I found the book, supplemented by conversations with him, enlightening.

Kathleen Brady wrote a Tarbell biography, which was published in 1984. I read it carefully at the time of its publication, then began, a decade later, to write a book with a different emphasis and new information.

Mary E. Tomkins wrote a book, published in 1974, stressing Tarbell's production as an author. I appreciate her interpretations of Tarbell's texts.

Because S. S. McClure served as such a catalyst in Tarbell's life and as the person who enabled her to investigate Rockefeller, I spent time at Indiana University studying the McClure papers. His autobiography and a biography by Peter Lyon filled important gaps. A privately published volume from 1925 helped capture the atmosphere at *McClure's Magazine*. It is *Albert A. Boyden, April 10, 1875–May 2, 1925: Reminiscences and Tributes by His Friends*. Boyden worked at the magazine on both the production and editorial sides.

I located Tarbell documents within repositories at the Library of Congress, National Archives, Catholic University of America, and Smithsonian Institution, in Washington, D.C.; Columbia University, Barnard College, New York Public Library, New York Historical Society, and the Pen and Brush Club, in New York City; Wagner College, Staten Island, New York; Cornell University, Ithaca, New York; Syracuse University, Syracuse, New York; Saint Lawrence University, Canton, New York; Chautauqua headquarters, Chautauqua, New York; Indiana University, Bloomington; Indiana Historical Society, Indianapolis; Chicago Historical Society and Newberry Library, Chicago, Illinois; Women's Christian Temperance Union, Evanston, Illinois; University of Illinois, Champaign-Urbana; Knox College, Galesburg, Illinois; University of California, Berkeley; Stanford University, Stanford, California; Huntington Library, San Marino, California; Johns Hopkins University, Baltimore, Maryland; Swarthmore College, Swarthmore, Pennsylvania; University of Pennsylvania, Philadelphia; Pennsylvania Historical and Museum Commission, Harrisburg;

Pennsylvania State University, State College; Erie County Historical Society, Erie, Pennsylvania; Crawford County Historical Society, Meadville, Pennsylvania; Princeton University, Princeton, New Jersey; University of Virginia, Charlottesville; Radcliffe College and Harvard University, Cambridge, Massachusetts; Smith College, Northampton, Massachusetts; Boston University, Boston, Massachusetts; Minnesota Historical Society, Saint Paul; University of Minnesota, Minneapolis; Yale University, New Haven, Connecticut; Ohio Historical Society, Columbus; University of Missouri, Columbia; Lincoln Farm Association, Hodgenville, Kentucky; Western Kentucky University, Bowling Green; Herbert Hoover Presidential Library, West Branch, Iowa; Brigham Young University, Provo, Utah; University of Michigan, Ann Arbor; State Historical Society of Wisconsin, Madison; University of Arizona, Tucson; University of Kansas, Lawrence; Louisiana State University, Baton Rouge.

County courthouses in several locales yielded relevant marriage records, wills, land deeds, and civil lawsuits. Records held by local cemeteries in several counties also proved helpful. Federal courthouses and Federal Records Centers contained litigation initiated by the United States government. Census records can be searched online, but I mostly searched for them in person at the National Archives.

JOHN DAVISON ROCKEFELLER

Rockefeller is far more famous than Tarbell and as a result has been mentioned far more often in books, newspapers, and magazines. But finding significant, useful information about him is far more difficult.

The main reason is obvious—Rockefeller did not write about himself and others every day for public consumption. Except for a few periods of his life and with a few people, he was not an avid letter writer. Within Standard Oil, to guard the control he exercised, he tended to keep his name off documents. Even the litigation files involving Standard Oil usually group Rockefeller together with other individual defendants, because state and federal prosecutors found it difficult to separate his decisionmaking from that of corporate underlings. Rockefeller was a master of deniability.

Rockefeller died in 1937. By the time I started my research, I could locate no one alive who had known him well.

The Rockefeller Archive Center in North Tarrytown, New York, is the obvious place for an author of a book like this to begin. Archivist Erwin Levold responded promptly to every request. As he noted, however, the material on the Rockefeller-Tarbell nexus was "not of great substance."

I have read the transcript of the interviews conducted by William O. Inglis. Rockefeller, age seventy-eight when the first interview occurred, allowed his emotions to show from time to time. But mostly he stuck to the simplistic and sometimes deceptive script he had formulated for his life. The same is true for his 1909 memoir.

As a result, newspaper and magazine accounts from the 1860s and 1870s, before Rockefeller achieved worldwide fame and became so guarded, proved especially valuable in establishing the facts and pointing toward the truth, despite their superficiality. Grace Goulder's research about Rockefeller's formative decades in Cleveland helped fill gaps.

Books by scholars of the oil industry often revealed more than Rockefeller biographies, which tend toward mythologizing. Daniel Yergin's oil industry history and Ron Chernow's Rockefeller biography rank as first in their classes. Other useful oil industry histories and Rockefeller biographies appear in the select bibliography.

SELECT BIBLIOGRAPHY

The books, articles, and archives I consulted on each contextual matter constitute a long list. Rather than place each of those items in the bibliography, I have chosen one or two or a few that proved the most informative. A more thorough bibliography is available from the author.

John D. Rockefeller, Standard Oil Company, the Oil Industry, and Antitrust Activities

Abels, Jules. *The Rockefeller Billions: The Story of the World's Most Stupendous Fortune.* Macmillan, 1965.

Akin, Edward N. Flagler: *Rockefeller Partner and Florida Baron.* University Press of Florida, 1992.

Allen, William H. *Rockefeller: Giant, Dwarf, Symbol*. Institute for Public Affairs, 1930.

Asbury, Herbert. *The Golden Flood: An Informal History of America's First Oil Field*. Knopf, 1942.

Black, Brian. *Petrolia: The Landscape of America's First Oil Boom*. Johns Hopkins University Press, 2000.

Bringhurst, Bruce. *Antitrust and the Oil Monopoly: The Standard Oil Cases*. Greenwood, 1979.

Carr, Albert Z. *John D. Rockefeller's Secret Weapon*. McGraw-Hill, 1962.

Chernow, Ron. *Titan: The Life of John D. Rockefeller, Sr*. Random House, 1998.

Clark, J. Stanley. *The Oil Century: From the Drake Well to the Conservation Era*. University of Oklahoma Press, 1958.

Coyne, Franklin E. *The Development of the Cooperage Industry in the United States, 1620–1940*. Lumber Buyers, 1940.

Destler, Chester M. *Roger Sherman and the Independent Oil Men*. Cornell University Press, 1967.

Ely, Richard T. *Monopolies and Trusts*. Macmillan, 1900.

Engelbrecht, Curt E. *Neighbor John: Intimate Glimpses of John D. Rockefeller*. Telegraphic Press, 1936.

Ernst, Joseph W., ed. *"Dear Father"/"Dear Son": Correspondence of John D. Rockefeller and John D. Rockefeller, Jr*. Rockefeller Center Archive/Fordham University Press, 1994.

Flynn, John T. *God's Gold: The Story of Rockefeller and His Times*. Harcourt, Brace, 1932.

Gale, Thomas. *The Wonder of the Nineteenth Century: Rock Oil in Pennsylvania and Elsewhere*. Self-published, 1860.

Giddens, Paul H. *The Birth of the Oil Industry*. Macmillan, 1938.

_____. *Standard Oil Company (Indiana): Oil Pioneer of the Middle West*. Appleton-Century-Crofts, 1955.

Goulder, Grace. *John D. Rockefeller: The Cleveland Years*. Western Reserve Historical Society, 1972.

Hardwicke, Robert E. *The Oilman's Barrel*. University of Oklahoma Press, 1958.

Hawke, David Freeman. *John D.: The Founding Father of the Rockefellers*. Harper & Row, 1980.

_____. comp. *John D. Rockefeller Interview 1917–1920*, Conducted by William O. Inglis. Meckler/Rockefeller Center Archive, 1984.

Hidy, Ralph W., and Muriel E. Hidy. *Pioneering in Big Business, 1882–1911: The History of the Standard Oil Company (New Jersey)*. Harper & Brothers, 1955.

Hubbard, Elbert. *The Standard Oil Company*. Roycroft Shop, 1910.

Kert, Bernice. *Abby Aldrich Rockefeller: The Woman in the Family*. Random House, 1992.

Knowles, Ruth Sheldon. *The Greatest Gamblers: The Epic of American Oil Exploration*. McGraw-Hill, 1959.

Latham, Earl, ed. *John D. Rockefeller: Robber Baron or Industrial Statesman?* Heath, 1949.

Lloyd, Henry Demarest. *Wealth Against Commonwealth*. Prentice-Hall, 1963 [Harper and Brothers, 1894].

Michener, Carolee K., ed. *Oil, Oil, Oil.* Venango County Historical Society, 1997.

Miller, Ernest C. *Oil Mania: Sketches from the Early Pennsylvania Oil Fields.* Dorrance, 1941.

Montague, Gilbert Holland. *The Rise and Progress of the Standard Oil Company.* Harper and Brothers, 1903.

_____. *Trusts of Today: Facts Relating to Their Promotion,* Financial Management and the Attempts at State Control. McClure, Phillips, 1904.

Moore, Austin Leigh. *John D. Archbold and the Early Development of the Standard Oil Company.* Columbia University Press, 1948.

Morris, Charles R. *The Tycoons: How Andrew Carnegie, John D. Rockefeller, Jay Gould, and J. P. Morgan Invented the American Supereconomy.* Times Books/Holt, 2005.

Nevins, Allan. *Study in Power: John D. Rockefeller, Industrialist and Philanthropist.* Scribner's, 1953.

Robbins, Philip Porter. "The Tarbell Papers and the History of the Standard Oil Company." Ph.D. dissertation, University of Pittsburgh, 1966.

Rockefeller, John D. *Random Reminiscences of Men and Events.* Doubleday, Page, 1909.

Strouse, Jean. *Morgan: American Financier.* Random House, 1999.

Tarbell, Ida M. *The History of the Standard Oil Company.* Macmillan, 1904.

_____. *The Nationalizing of Business, 1878–1898.* Macmillan, 1936.

Townshend, Henry H. *New Haven and the First Oil Well.* Yale University Press, 1934.

Williamson, Harold F., and Arnold R. Daum. The *American Petroleum Industry: The Age of Illumination, 1859–1899.* Northwestern University Press, 1959.

Winkler, John K. *John D.: A Portrait in Oils.* Vanguard, 1929.

Yergin, Daniel. *The Prize: The Epic Quest for Oil, Money, and Power.* Simon & Schuster, 1991.

Ida M. Tarbell and Investigative Journalism

Alden, Henry Mills. *Magazine Writing and the New Literature.* Harper and Brothers, 1908.

Aucoin, James L. *The Evolution of American Investigative Journalism.* University of Missouri Press, 2005.

Baker, Ray Stannard. *American Chronicle.* Scribner's, 1945.

Bannister, Robert C., Jr. *Ray Stannard Baker: The Mind and Thought of a Progressive.* Yale University Press, 1966.

Barry, Peter. "The Decline of Muckraking: A View from the Magazines." Ph.D. dissertation, Wayne State University, 1973.

Behrens, John C. *The Typewriter Guerrillas: Closeups of 20 Top Investigative Reporters.* Nelson-Hall, 1977.

Brady, Kathleen. *Ida Tarbell: Portrait of a Muckraker.* Seaview/Putnam, 1984.

Brasch, Walter M. *Forerunners of Revolution: Muckrakers and the American Social Conscience.* University Press of America, 1990.

Chalmers, David Mark. *The Social and Political Ideas of the Muckrakers*. Citadel, 1964.

Dicken-Garcia, Hazel. *Journalistic Standards in Nineteenth-Century America*. University of Wisconsin Press, 1989.

Digby-Junger, Richard. *The Journalist as Reformer: Henry Demarest Lloyd and Wealth Against Commonwealth*. Greenwood, 1996.

Downie, Leonard, Jr. *The New Muckrakers*. New American Library, 1976.

Dygert, James H. *The Investigative Journalist: Folk Heroes of a New Era*. Prentice-Hall, 1976.

Ettema, James S., and Theodore L. Glasser. *Custodians of Conscience: Investigative Journalism and Public Virtue*. Columbia University Press, 1998.

Fitzpatrick, Ellen F. *Muckraking: Three Landmark Articles*. Bedford/St. Martin's, 1994.

Francke, Warren T. "Investigative Exposure in the Nineteenth Century: The Journalistic Heritage of the Muckrakers." Ph.D. dissertation, University of Minnesota, 1974.

Graham, Jane Kirkland. *Viola [Roseboro], the Duchess of New Dorp*. Self-published, 1955.

Hartsock, John C. *A History of American Literary Journalism: The Emergence of a Modern Narrative Form*. University of Massachusetts Press, 2000.

Howe, Frederick C. *The Confessions of a Reformer*. Scribner's, 1925.

Hudson, Robert V. *The Writing Game: A Biography of Will Irwin*. Iowa State University Press, 1982.

Kaplan, Justin. *Lincoln Steffens*. Simon & Schuster, 1974.

Kennedy, Samuel V. III. *Samuel Hopkins Adams and the Business of Writing*. Syracuse University Press, 1999.

Kochersberger, Robert C., Jr. *More than a Muckraker: Ida Tarbell's Lifetime in Journalism*. University of Tennessee Press, 1994.

Kroeger, Brooke. *Nellie Bly: Daredevil*, Reporter, Feminist. Times Books, 1994.

Lee, Hermione. *Willa Cather: Double Lives*. Pantheon, 1989.

Lyon, Peter. *Success Story: The Life and Times of S. S. McClure*. Scribner's, 1963.

McClure, S. S. *My Autobiography*. Frederick A. Stokes, 1914.

Miraldi, Robert. *The Muckrakers: Evangelical Crusaders*. Praeger, 2000.

_____. *The Pen Is Mightier: The Muckraking Life of Charles Edward Russell*. Palgrave Macmillan, 2003.

Mott, Frank Luther. *A History of American Magazines, 1885–1905*. Harvard University Press, 1957

Mowry, George E. *The Era of Theodore Roosevelt, 1900–1912*. Harper & Brothers, 1958.

O'Mara, Roger J. *Ada [Peirce McCormick]: The Biography of a Woman Ahead of Her Time*. Little Chapel of All Nations, 1988.

Phillips, David Graham. *The Treason of the Senate* [Cosmopolitan serialization from 1906 reprinted in book form]. Quadrangle, 1964.

Pomper, Gerald M. *Ordinary Heroes and American Democracy*. Yale University Press, 2004.

Ponce de Leon, Charles L. *Self-Exposure: Human-Interest Journalism and the Emergence of Celebrity in America, 1890–1940*. University of North Carolina Press, 2002.

Riis, Jacob A. *How the Other Half Lives.* Scribner's, 1890.

Schneirov, Matthew. *The Dream of a New Social Order: Popular Magazines in America, 1893–1914.* Columbia University Press, 1994.

Schurz, Carl. *The Reminiscences of Carl Schurz.* McClure, 1907.

Semonche, John E. *Ray Stannard Baker: A Quest for Democracy in Modern America, 1870–1918.* University of North Carolina Press, 1969.

Shapiro, Bruce, ed. *Shaking the Foundations: 200 Years of Investigative Journalism in America.* Nation Books, 2003.

Sheifer, Isobel C. "Ida M. Tarbell and Morality in Big Business: An Analysis of a Progressive Mind." Ph.D. dissertation, New York University, 1967.

Steffens, Lincoln. *The Shame of the Cities.* McClure, Phillips, 1904.

Tarbell, Ida M. *All in the Day's Work.* Macmillan, 1939.

_____. *Madame Roland.* Scribner's, 1895.

Tomkins, Mary E. *Ida M. Tarbell.* Twayne, 1974.

Trubey, Lillian P. "The Public Speaking Career of Ida M. Tarbell." Ph.D. dissertation, University of Florida, 1972.

Wilson, Harold S. *McClure's Magazine and the Muckrakers.* Princeton University Press, 1970.

Americana

Braudy, Leo. *The Frenzy of Renown: Fame and Its History.* Oxford University Press, 1986.

DeVoto, Bernard. *The Year of Decision, 1846.* Little, Brown, 1942.

Fuller, Wayne E. *The American Mail: Enlarger of Common Life.* University of Chicago Press, 1972.

Huston, James L. *The Panic of 1857 and the Coming of the Civil War.* Louisiana State University Press, 1987.

Ierley, Merritt. *The Comforts of Home: The American House and the Evolution of Modern Convenience.* Clarkson Potter, 1999.

Kindleberger, Charles P. *Manias, Panics, and Crashes: A History of Financial Crises.* Basic Books, 1978.

Lacour-Gayet, Robert. *Everyday Life in the United States Before the Civil War, 1830–1860.* Ungar, 1969.

Ohmann, Richard. *Selling Culture: Magazines, Markets, and Class at the Turn of the Century.* Verso, 1996.

Peterson, Merrill D. *Lincoln in American Memory.* Oxford University Press, 1994.

Randel, William Pierce. *Centennial: American Life in 1876.* Chilton, 1969.

Richmond, Rebecca. *Chautauqua: An American Place.* Duell, Sloan and Pearce, 1943.

Schlereth, Thomas. *Victorian America: Transformations in Everyday Life, 1876–1915.* HarperCollins, 1991.

Stampp, Kenneth M. *America in 1857: A Nation on the Brink.* Oxford University Press, 1990.

Steel, Ronald. *Walter Lippmann and the American Century*. Atlantic Monthly/Little, Brown, 1980.

Tarbell, Ida M. *The Life of Abraham Lincoln*. McClure, Phillips, 1900.

Wall, Joseph Frazier. *Iowa: A History*. W. W. Norton, 1978.

Biography as a Craft

Alpern, Sara, Joyce Antler, Elisabeth Israels Perry, and Ingrid Winther Scobie, eds. *The Challenge of Feminist Biography*. University of Illinois Press, 1992.

Heilbrun, Carolyn. *Writing a Woman's Life*. W. W. Norton, 1988.

Thomas, Benjamin P. *Portrait for Posterity: Lincoln and His Biographers*. Rutgers University Press, 1971.

Weinberg, Steve. *Telling the Untold Story: How Investigative Journalists Are Changing the Craft of Biography*. University of Missouri Press, 1992.

Business Culture and Practice

Engelbourg, Saul. *Power and Morality: American Business Ethics, 1840–1914*. Greenwood, 1980.

Hiebert, Ray Eldon. *Courtier to the Crowd: The Story of Ivy Lee and the Development of Public Relations*. Iowa State University Press, 1966.

Josephson, Matthew. *The Robber Barons: The Great American Capitalists, 1861–1901*. Harcourt, Brace, 1934.

Marchand, Roland. *Creating the Corporate Soul: The Rise of Public Relations and Corporate Imagery in American Big Business*. University of California Press, 1998.

Tarbell, Ida M. *The Life of Elbert H. Gary: A Story of Steel*. D. Appleton, 1926.

_____. *New Ideals in Business: An Account of Their Practice and Their Effects upon Men and Profits*. Macmillan, 1916.

_____. *Owen D. Young: A New Type of Industrial Leader*. Macmillan, 1932.

Tye, Larry. *The Father of Spin: Edward L. Bernays and the Birth of Public Relations*. Crown, 1998.

Civil War

Ayers, Edward L. *In the Presence of Mine Enemies: The Civil War in the Heart of America, 1859–1863*. W. W. Norton, 2003.

Detzer, David. *Allegiance: Fort Sumter, Charleston, and the Beginning of the Civil War*. Harcourt, 2001.

Gallman, J. Matthew. *The North Fights the Civil War: The Home Front*. Ivan R. Dee, 1994.

Geary, James W. *We Need Men: The Union Draft in the Civil War*. Northern Illinois University Press, 1991.

Education

Nasaw, David. *Schooled to Order: A Social History of Public Schooling in the United States.* Oxford University Press, 1979.

Newcomer, Mabel. *A Century of Higher Education for American Women.* Harper and Brothers, 1959.

Pelletier, Lawrence L. *From a Reliance on the Smiles of Heaven: The Story of Allegheny College.* Newcomen Society, 1965.

Zorn, Robert L. *Triumph and Tradition of the Poland [Ohio] Schools.* Poland Schools, 1997.

Family

Degler, Carl N. *At Odds: Women and the Family in America from the Revolution to the Present.* Oxford University Press, 1980.

Gillis, John R. *A World of Their Own Making: Myth, Ritual, and the Quest for Family Values.* Basic Books, 1996.

Strasser, Susan. *Never Done: A History of American Housework.* Pantheon, 1982.

Government Regulation

Abrams, Richard, ed. *The Issue of Federal Regulation in the Progressive Era.* Rand McNally, 1963.

Feller, John Quentin. "Theodore Roosevelt, the Department of Justice, and the Trust Problem: A Study in Presidential Policy." Ph.D. dissertation, Catholic University of America, 1968.

Historiography

Davidson, James West, and Mark Hamilton Lytle. *After the Fact: The Art of Historical Detection.* Knopf, 1986.

Fischer, David Hackett. *Historians' Fallacies: Toward a Logic of Historical Thought.* Harper and Row, 1970.

Novick, Peter. *That Noble Dream: The Objectivity Question and the American Historical Profession.* Cambridge University Press, 1988.

Stannard, David E. Shrinking *History: On Freud and the Failure of Psychohistory.* Oxford University Press, 1980.

New York City

Adickes, Sandra. *To Be Young Was Very Heaven: Women in New York Before the First World War.* St. Martin's, 1997.

Burrows, Edwin G., and Mike Wallace. *Gotham: A History of New York City to 1898.* Oxford University Press, 1999.

Wetzsteon, Ross. *Republic of Dreams: Greenwich Village, the American Bohemia, 1910–1960.* Simon & Schuster, 2002.

Pennsylvania

Babcock, Charles A. *Venango County, Pennsylvania: Her Pioneers and People.* J. H. Beers, 1919.

Bates, Samuel P. *Our County and Its People: A Historical and Memorial Record of Crawford County, Pennsylvania.* W. A. Fergusson, 1899.

Clark, Mabel K. *Titusville: An Illustrated History.* Inter Collegiate Press, 1976.

Dobler, Lavinia. *Black Gold at Titusville.* Dodd, Mead, 1959.

Guide to the Historical Markers of Pennsylvania. Pennsylvania Historical and Museum Commission, 1975.

Politics

Chace, James. *1912: Wilson, Roosevelt, Taft, and Debs—the Election That Changed the Country.* Simon & Schuster, 2004.

Croly, Herbert. *Marcus Alonzo Hanna: His Life and Work.* Macmillan, 1912.

Glad, Paul W. *The Trumpet Soundeth: William Jennings Bryan and His Democracy, 1896–1912.* University of Nebraska Press, 1960.

Gould, Lewis L. *The Presidency of William McKinley.* Regents Press of Kansas, 1980.

Jeffers, H. Paul. *An Honest President: The Life and Presidencies of Grover Cleveland.* Morrow, 2000.

Mowry, George E. *Theodore Roosevelt and the Progressive Movement.* University of Wisconsin Press, 1946.

Robinson, Lloyd. *The Stolen Election: Hayes Versus Tilden, 1876.* Doubleday, 1968.

Ross, Shelley. *Fall from Grace: Sex, Scandal, and Corruption in American Politics from 1702 to the Present.* Ballantine, 1988.

Unger, Nancy C. *Fighting Bob LaFollette: The Righteous Reformer.* University of North Carolina Press, 2000.

Progressive Movement

Crunden, Robert M. *Ministers of Reform: The Progressives' Achievement in American Civilization, 1889–1920.* Basic Books, 1982.

Diner, Steven J. *A Very Different Age: Americans of the Progressive Era.* Hill and Wang, 1997.

Filler, Louis. *Appointment at Armageddon: Muckraking and Progressivism in American Life.* Greenwood, 1976.

Hofstadter, Richard. *The Age of Reform: From Bryan to FDR.* Knopf, 1974.

Railroads

Bain, David Haward. *Empire Express: Building the First Transcontinental Railroad*. Viking, 1999.

Kolko, Gabriel. *Railroads and Regulation: 1877–1916*. Princeton University Press, 1965.

Lindley, Daniel. *Ambrose Bierce Takes on the Railroad: The Journalist as Muckraker and Cynic*. Praeger, 1999.

Treese, Lorett. *Railroads of Pennsylvania: Fragments of the Past in the Keystone Landscape*. Stackpole, 2003.

Religion

Boylan, Anne M. *Sunday School: The Formation of an American Institution, 1790–1880*. Yale University Press, 1988.

Vincent, John H. *The Modern Sunday School*. Phillips and Hunt, 1887.

Romantic Relationships and Sexual Identity

Acocella, Joan. *Willa Cather and the Politics of Criticism*. University of Nebraska Press, 1999.

Faderman, Lillian. *Odd Girls and Twilight Lovers: A History of Lesbian Life in Twentieth Century America*. Columbia University Press, 1991.

Leach, William. *True Love and Perfect Union: The Feminist Reform of Sex and Society*. Basic Books, 1980.

Lystra, Karen. *Searching the Heart: Women, Men, and Romantic Love in Nineteenth-Century America*. Oxford University Press, 1989.

Suffrage

Andersen, Kristi. *After Suffrage: Women in Partisan and Electoral Politics Before the New Deal*. University of Chicago Press, 1996.

Benjamin, Anne M. *A History of the Anti-Suffrage Movement in the United States from 1895 to 1920: Women Against Equality*. Edwin Mellen, 1991.

Camhi, Jane Jerome. *Women Against Women: American Anti-Suffragism, 1880–1920*. Carlson, 1994.

Kraditor, Aileen S. *The Ideas of the Woman Suffrage Movement, 1890–1940*. Columbia University Press, 1965.

Tariffs

Pierce, Franklin. *The Tariff and the Trusts*. Macmillan, 1907.

Tarbell, Ida M. *The Tariff in Our Times*. Macmillan, 1912.

War and Peace

Alonso, Harriet Hyman. *Peace as a Women's Issue: A History of the U.S. Movement for World Peace and Women's Rights*. Syracuse University Press, 1993.

Early, Frances H. *A World Without War: How United States Feminists and Pacifists Resisted World War I*. Syracuse University Press, 1997.

Women in America

Beasley, Maurine H., and Sheila J. Gibbons. *Taking Their Place: A Documentary History of Women and Journalism*. Strata, 2003.

Bordin, Ruth. *Women and Temperance: The Quest for Power and Liberty, 1873–1900*. Temple University Press, 1981.

Elshtain, Jean Bethke. *Jane Addams and the Dream of American Democracy*. Basic Books, 2002.

Epstein, Barbara Leslie. *The Politics of Domesticity: Women, Evangelism, and Temperance in Nineteenth-Century America*. Wesleyan University Press, 1981.

Marzolf, Marion. *Up from the Footnote: A History of Women Journalists*. Hastings House, 1977.

Matthaei, Julie A. *An Economic History of Women in America: Women's Work, the Sexual Division of Labor, and the Development of Capitalism*. Schocken, 1982.

Muncy, Robyn. *Creating a Feminine Dominion in American Reform, 1890–1935*. Oxford University Press, 1991.

Tarbell, Ida M. *The Business of Being a Woman*. Macmillan, 1912.

_____. *The Ways of Woman*. Macmillan, 1915.

ACKNOWLEDGMENTS

At the Alicia Patterson Foundation, executive director Margaret (Peggy) Engel administered a generous fellowship that helped finance my travels, then provided early feedback on stories I wrote about Tarbell's life for the foundation's magazine.

The three most important people in the conception and writing of this book are easy to identify: Faith Hamlin, my brainy, ever-vigilant literary agent at Sanford J. Greenburger Associates, New York City; acquiring editor Bob Weil, who shaped the ideas and the words of the narrative, all the while living up to Faith Hamlin's description of him as one of the best book people alive; and Tom Mayer, first as Bob Weil's assistant at W. W. Norton and later as an editor, who skillfully and compassionately guided several rewrites of the manuscript.

I received occasional research help from first-rate students at the University of Missouri Journalism School, where I have taught part-time since 1978.

Talented fellow authors too numerous to name here sent encouragement.

My wife, Scherrie Goettsch; my daughter, Sonia Weinberg Thompson; and my son, Seth Weinberg, helped in so many ways, directly and indirectly. They are always the audience I most want to impress.

INDEX